Handbook of
CURRICULUM EVALUATION

INTERNATIONAL INSTITUTE FOR
EDUCATIONAL PLANNING

Handbook of
CURRICULUM
EVALUATION

Edited by ARIEH LEWY

UNESCO/Paris
Longman Inc./New York

HANDBOOK OF CURRICULUM EVALUATION

First Published 1977 by Unesco, 7 Place de Fontenoy, 75700 Paris, France and Longman Inc., 19 West 44th Street, New York, New York 10036 USA

MANUFACTURED IN THE UNITED STATES OF AMERICA

Text Design by Bob Antler

Library of Congress Cataloging in Publication Data
Main entry under title:

Handbook of curriculum evaluation.

At head of title: International Institute for Educational Planning.
Bibliography: p.
Includes indexes.
1. Curriculum evaluation. I. Lewy, Arieh, 1923-　II. International Institute for Educational Planning.
LB1570.H263 1977　　375′.001　　77-24468

Longman: ISBN 0-582-28002-8
Unesco: ISBN 92-803-1073-9

Preface

This book has been designed to meet the needs of experts working on the planning and evaluation of curriculum throughout the world. It presents both a model for curriculum evaluation and practical guidelines for the task of evaluating new instructional materials. The authors have combined some of the more important theoretical considerations in this field with the practical wisdom and the experience accumulated in a variety of curriculum centers and projects.

Special consideration has been given to the needs of developing countries, where curriculum development faces the particularly difficult and important task of revising what has in many cases been an alien and ill-suited content of education into a new curriculum that is more responsive to the needs, traditions, and aspirations of the country. In the context of this major reorientation of the substantive and qualitative aspects of education, curriculum development and evaluation assumes a particularly critical role. Unless new departures in the development of instructional materials and strategies are accompanied by a vigorous and thorough evaluation, the ultimate effectiveness of these important reforms will continue to remain in question.

Thus, this book should provide a great deal of help to the many curriculum centers and projects involved in the task of reshaping the curriculum of their countries' schools. By the same token, it should be a most valuable tool in the training of specialists who are to work in the area of curriculum planning and development and who will need both the overall perspective and the detailed skills that this book provides.

The book's preparation has been a remarkable case of international teamwork. Under the distinguished and skillful leadership of Arieh Lewy, each of the twelve authors dealt with a particular problem or issue related to curriculum evaluation. The authors came from Colombia, France, the Federal Republic of Germany, Hungary, Israel, Kenya, Malaysia, Nigeria, the United Kingdom, and the United States. In addition, an earlier version of the manuscript was circulated to a large number of curriculum centers around the world, and valuable material was received from Australia, Argentina, Benin (Dahomey), Brazil, Chile, India, Japan, New Zealand, Papua New Guinea, and Tanzania, and was incorporated into the final manuscript. The richness and breadth of the experiences give the book a very special and particularly interesting appeal.

Within the context of the work of the International Institute for Educational Planning (IIEP), the preparation and publication of this handbook represents one more indication of the increasing importance that, in planning the development of educational systems, is being attached to the planning and evaluation of the content and substance of education in addition to its more quantitative and aggregate characteristics. This concern has brought about the agreement of cooperation between the IIEP and the International Curriculum Organization (ICO). This handbook represents one of the projects envisaged under this agreement and owes a great deal to the individual and collective experience of the curriculum centers that constitute the ICO.

I am very pleased that IIEP and ICO found a responsive and generous partner for this project in the German Foundation for International Development (DSE), which has provided the organizational and financial support for several planning and editorial meetings. These meetings, in addition to producing this book, have served as particularly valuable occasions for the exchange of experiences and the generation of new ideas in the field of curriculum.

Arieh Lewy, the editor of this volume, has achieved something quite remarkable: while bringing his own intellectual insights and professional experience to bear on the conceptual framework and cohesion of the book, he succeeded at the same time in bringing out the full richness and uniqueness of each author's contribution. T. Neville Postlethwaite played a major part in the initiation and preparation of the teamwork which led to this volume.

On behalf of the institutions that have sponsored this effort, I join the editor's and the authors' hopes that this handbook will become an important and useful contribution to the crucial task of developing and improving the quality of education around the world.

Hans N. Weiler
Director, IIEP

Foreword

This book contains theoretical considerations and practical advice that may help experts in curriculum development and evaluation in their work. The book consists of three major parts. The first part contains a single chapter and presents a brief view of various models that greatly affected empirical work in curriculum evaluation. It also introduces some basic concepts and describes some facets of the evaluation approach proposed in this book. Chapter 1 in itself may provide basic knowledge about the nature of curriculum evaluation for nonevaluation specialists to familiarize themselves with this topic. Thus it may be an appropriate orientation chapter for writing teams working in curriculum centers or for administrators dealing with problems of curriculum development.

The second part of the book, Stages of Development and Evaluation, chapters 2–7, defines stages of curriculum development and proposes evaluation activities appropriate for each of these stages. The partition of curriculum development and evaluation activities into six stages reflects a widespread practice in curriculum development centers around the world. Nevertheless, one should not view these stages as rigid and unalterable. Depending on local conditions, some stages may be partitioned into further substages or, contrarily, can be skipped or combined together with those preceding or following them. Thus, for example, it may happen that educational systems are urgently required to produce new instructional materials; to save time, one may propose to skip stages described in this book. In such "crisis" situation the curriculum team has to make decisions about permissible or advisable shortcuts. Nevertheless, it should be emphasized that the book suggests a realistic pattern of development procedures that is consistently practised in many large curriculum development centers and projects.

The description of evaluation activities related to the stages of program development is novel in this book and has not been systematically treated elsewhere. Chapter 2 illustrates evaluation ideas suggested by the widely used Tyler curriculum development model. It provides examples of translating abstract concepts, such as "needs of society" or "needs of learner," into empirical terms. Chapter 3 specifies criteria for evaluating the adequacy of program objectives, contents, strategies, and instructional materials. Chapter 4 is concerned with data types that one should use during the trying-out of new instructional materials. It suggests ways for collating evaluation data stemming from different sources. Chapter 5 describes differences between the preliminary tryout of bits and pieces of new instructional materials and the field trial of a fully developed new curriculum. Chapter 6 presents a detailed list of development and evaluation activities needed for implementing new curricula in a whole system. Chapter 7 applies the concept of quality control to the process of curriculum dissemination and spells out procedures that may be used to perform this task.

These seven chapters encompass the whole range of evaluation activities in a sequential order starting from the decisions to develop a new program and ending with decisions that may postulate the recycling or rewriting of existing programs.

The third part of the book, Evaluation Instruments and Strategies, chapters 8–12, contains description of methods and strategies applied to curriculum evaluation. These chapters focus on specific features of methods and strategies that fit the needs of curriculum evaluation. In this respect they differ from chapters carrying similar titles in standard textbooks of evaluation. Three of these chapters describe problems related to generating, collecting, and analyzing data of different types. Chapter 8 deals with expert judgment as evaluation data. The need to utilize expert data within the context of curriculum evaluation has been frequently emphasized, hence the importance of this chapter. The reader can find few sources that systematically deal with this issue. Chapter 9 discusses observational techniques. Several excellent reviews about observational types of data were published in the past. This chapter is not designed to be a new review of the utilization of observational techniques within the framework of evaluation. Instead, it focuses on the identification of those observational techniques that can be applied for curriculum evaluation. Similarly chapter 10, which deals with tests and scales, focuses on special problems that emerge in using these instruments for curriculum evaluation. The chapter discusses the utilization of norm-referenced and criterion-referenced tests within the framework of curriculum evaluation.

Chapter 11 deals with a unique source of data used for the purpose of curriculum evaluation, i.e., teachers' and parents' views of, and opinions about, a new curriculum. The chapter contains practical examples of using data of this type.

Chapter 12 focuses on basic methodological and statistical issues, which the reader cannot find in the standard textbook. It contains four sections. Problems of sampling are presented in a simple and practical form to help evaluators in drawing appropriate samples for curriculum tryout. The section on experimental design treats two important methodological problems that frequently confuse evaluation experts: (1) when comparative design should or should not be used, and (2) what are the consequences of perceiving the class and not the individual student as the unit of observation. The third section of the chapter deals with ways of summarizing data. This section is built on experience accumulated in curriculum centers and describes forms of data analysis that have been successfully used in the past. The fourth section of Chapter 12 discusses problems of equating scores of different tests. This section provides some information about the major ideas of the Rasch model for test analysis. Although it is not expected that on the basis of this information the reader will be able to use such a complex statistical model, it is hoped that this brief introduction will help the reader understand the power of the model and motivate him to learn more about it.

Finally, it should be said that the book does not suggest solutions for all problems emerging in the field of curriculum evaluation. It reflects the state of the art in this field. Curriculum evaluation is an emerging field of study; many problems existing in the field need further clarification before they can be successfully treated in a handbook.

Arieh Lewy

Contents

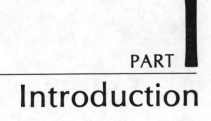

PART **1**

Introduction

1

The Nature of Curriculum Evaluation

SYSTEMATIC DEVELOPMENT AND EVALUATION OF EDUCATIONAL PROGRAM

Since the early 1950s, several large-scale curriculum development projects have been undertaken in various countries throughout the world. In developing countries the emergence of new educational systems has created a demand for a large number of major curriculum changes, whereas the impetus for new curriculum projects in the developed countries has grown out of a sense of dissatisfaction with the existing educational programs. In both cases instructional materials and methods sorely required revision so as to reflect properly the changing characteristics of students and the new knowledge, issues, and orientation of the contemporary world.

Existing educational programs were criticized not only from the point of view of their content, but also from the point of view of the mode of instruction. Although educational research had called attention to the fact that memorizing factual information contributes little to the intellectual development of the learner and does little to improve his ability to solve problems, most textbooks were still crammed mainly with factual infor-

This chapter was written by Arieh Lewy.

mation that students were required to memorize. Moreover, such textbooks also had a major influence on the nature of classroom activity.
Teachers' lectures were devoted to explaining difficult issues contained in
the textbooks, and students were asked questions in class that could be
answered simply by quoting bits of information explicitly stated in their
school books. Although contemporary views of education emphasize such
terms as "inquiry," "discovery," "problem solving," "higher mental functions," "synthesis," and "creativity," textbooks provided little or no opportunity for students to engage in activities of these types.

In response to the demand for change, funds were made available in
many countries for the purpose of financing curriculum development
projects. In a few countries (the United Kingdom and the United States,
for example) the changes were limited to a small number of curriculum
projects that typically produced one-year high school courses in selected
subjects. In a large number of countries, however, national curriculum
centers were established and assumed the responsibility of providing for
the updating of the entire curriculum for the educational system. Moreover, such national curriculum centers are charged with ensuring that the
new curricula contribute to the attainment of the educational goals of
the nation.

The Emergence of Curriculum Evaluation as a Scientific Discipline

The expansion of curriculum development activities gave impetus to
the demands for evaluating educational programs. Both the financing
agencies and the consumers wished to obtain evidence that the new programs produced satisfactory results. Information was sought concerning
the relevance of the new program to the needs of the society and the
learner, the scientific significance and validity of the new study materials,
the ability of the program to elicit certain teacher and student behaviors,
and the actual outcomes of using a given set of instructional materials. In
addition, it was necessary to answer the following questions:

Is it worthwhile to devote time to learning the materials included in
the program?
Do the educational materials reflect recent developments and contemporary ideas dominant in a given field of intellectual or scientific
behavior?
Are the study materials free from obsolete concepts and ideas?
Under the prevailing system of teaching-learning conditions can the
new program be successfully implemented?

Will the students master certain skills as a result of the program?
Will the students acquire certain desired attitudes and values?
Will the teachers accept the major tenets and objectives of the
program?
Is the new program an economic means of obtaining certain desired
goals?
What unintended or unforeseen outcomes may emerge as a result of
utilizing a given program?

In order to answer questions such as these, workers in the field of curriculum evaluation have produced systematic models of the factors involved and have suggested principles and methods for generating and summarizing the data, to be used in arriving at the necessary conclusions. The last two decades have seen the emergence of curriculum evaluation as an independent field of study in the domain of the educational sciences. Its roots are found in the more general field of educational evaluation, testing, and measurement. Because of the primary concern with the evaluation of students rather than with the evaluation of educational programs, however, a need was felt to develop a series of new concepts, principles, methods, theories, and models. These new ideas and methods are the basis for the new field of curriculum evaluation. Large universities have introduced courses in curriculum evaluation. Various professional meetings, conferences, and international training seminars have been devoted to the topic. The American Educational Research Association has published a monograph series dealing with various aspects of curriculum evaluation and journals dealing with it have been launched. At the 1974 American Educational Research Association meeting in Chicago about 150 papers devoted to this topic were presented. Such activities can be viewed as clear signs of the emergence of a new field of study. The new developments in curriculum throughout the world have posed new questions, which the growing science of curriculum evaluation is trying to answer.

Of course, such a division of labor is to some extent an oversimplification of reality. Indeed, those who deal with curriculum evaluation frequently suggest some of the types of questions that need answering; conversely, curriculum writers often present their requests and demands for the types of new evidence that they believe to be desirable and necessary within the framework of their task. Nevertheless, for both analytical and practical purposes it seems useful to distinguish between *curriculum development* and *curriculum evaluation*.

Our concern in this book is for a clear delineation of what curriculum evaluation involves and of the appropriate role of curriculum evaluation

in serving the needs of curriculum development both at the project level
as well as at the national curriculum level.

The Meaning of "Curriculum"

The word *curriculum* is used with a variety of meanings. René Ochs
writes:

> This term is often used to designate equally a programme for
> a given subject matter and for a given grade, a programme for a
> given subject matter for the entire study cycle, or the whole
> programme of different subjects for the entire cycle or even
> the whole range of cycles. Further, the term "curriculum" is
> sometimes used in a wider sense to cover the various
> educational activities through which the content is conveyed as
> well as materials used and methods employed. (Ochs 1974)

Clearly, no single method or procedure can be employed for the evaluation
of the variety of curricula subsumed under this broadly defined term.
Indeed, the task of evaluating a comprehensive educational program
comprising all the many types of learning activities may be considerably
different from the evaluation of a package of educational materials
designed for a single course in a given subject matter.

It would, therefore, seem necessary to specify the kinds of curriculum
that the contributors to this book have in mind when they discuss the
various aspects of evaluation.

The principles and ideas presented here relate to the evaluation of the
materials used in a specific course of study, i.e., textbooks and their
various accessories, instructional material kits, detailed course outlines
accompanied by a series of study materials, exercises or guidelines for
teachers on how to develop study materials, and so on. In this respect the
word curriculum is used in one specific sense, selected from the wide
variety of meanings currently attached to it; but despite this restriction of
the term, it still covers a wide range of educational programs. The term is
neutral with respect to the many controversies existing in the domain of
curriculum theory, that is, it does not take a fixed position as to the focus of
the program, the medium of instruction, the organization of the materials,
the teaching strategy, the management of classwork, or the role of the
teacher. No matter what approach one subscribes to concerning these
issues, the principles of curriculum evaluation in this book remain valid.
To stress this point we will go into further detail concerning these areas of
controversy.

The Focus of the Program

Most commonly the focus of a program is the knowledge accumulated in a particular field of study. Thus one may speak about curriculum in physics, biology, economics, literature, and so forth. This division reflects the way knowledge is generated and accumulated in our culture. But one may combine knowledge from several fields in one curriculum. Thus a science program may be developed that contains knowledge stemming from physics, chemistry, and biology; a social studies program may include contributions from political science, history, sociology, and economics. Moreover, programs may be constructed that entirely disregard the conventional distinctions between different areas of knowledge. Such programs may focus on the solution of specific problems—pollution, energy, conflict resolution, leisure-time activities—and thus make use of knowledge from various subjects related to the particular issue.

Medium of Instruction

The most widely employed medium of instruction is the printed word. But nowadays the printed word is far from being the sole medium used as instructional materials. Printed pictures, records, computers, film loops, television programs, and mechanical equipment are frequently used in contemporary schools as media of instruction. Any or all of these media may be evaluated when included in the curriculum.

In many cases curriculum development may involve the need to organize existing knowledge into systems that do not correspond to traditional subject-matter domains. Thus, for example, many developing countries make use of study material that presents the values and the traditions of the national culture. In such cases the curriculum development team itself has to gather adequate study materials and identify themes and topics that can be taught at various grade levels.

Organization of Material

Instructional material may be organized in a strictly linear fashion in the sense that the sequence of learning activities is firmly determined by the program developer. Or it may be organized in a loose way, according to which the learner or the teacher determines the sequence of activities or selects some out of a wide range of suggested activities. Or a program kit may contain an unstructured set of resource materials that the teacher uses for developing specific learning activities.

Another factor related to the organizational structure of a program is the relative importance of clearly defined behavioral objectives. In many programs one may find behavioral objectives clearly spelled out for each section of the program, while in other programs where the content is only implicitly organized around objectives, specific objectives may not be stated explicitly (Tobias and Duchastel 1974).

Teaching Strategy

A variety of teaching strategies are recommended in recent textbooks: expository presentation of the material, discovery or guided discovery learning, programmed instruction, mastery learning, and the like, or the combination of several strategies. But whatever the strategy employed, the evaluation of the program should constitute a prerequisite for its use in the schools.

Management of Classwork

A program may be designed so as to require either cooperative group work within the class or individual tasks performed by each class member. In some cases the framework of the class may be totally eliminated in the sense that the individual works on his or her own assignments in accordance with unique needs and abilities. These are legitimate variants of class management that may be subjected to evaluation in the sense in which it is used in this handbook.

The Role of the Teacher

Programs may differ with respect to the role played by the teacher in their development and implementation. Some programs are arranged so as to provide the learner with such clear guidelines that they can almost be used as self-instructional material. In other programs the teacher is expected to assume greater responsibility for explaining the materials and structuring learning activities.

Another difference that may appear concerning the role of the teacher is in the degree of teacher participation in the program development. Some programs are fully developed by a curriculum team, and the teacher is required only to use and interpret the program for the student. In such cases the teacher assumes the role of mediator between student and program, since without the help of the teacher the student cannot achieve the goals of the program. Other programs are semistructured, or even unstructured. Frequently the teacher may be required to gather additional material in order to supplement what is provided in the program itself. In this way the teacher becomes a partner or a coworker in the process of program development.

Nevertheless, it should be noted that this book does not intend to present principles and methods that should be applied to all curriculum development. As already stated, we are concerned here with curriculum programs that include some instructional materials. It is difficult to apply these methods to a syllabus that merely specifies the topics to be included in instruction. The procedures described here are suitable for the evaluation of programs that are used over and over again. In other words, focus is placed here on programs in which experience accumulated at an early stage can serve as a basis for improvement during subsequent use. This means that a short-term curriculum to be used only for a particular educational purpose would not warrant the type of curriculum evaluation described in this book. Putting this in positive terms, the topic of this book is the evaluation of curricula that contain some *recurrently* used instructional materials.

The Lack of Balance between Theory and Practice in Curriculum Evaluation

One characteristic feature of the state of affairs in the area of curriculum evaluation at present is the lack of balance between theoretical and empirical writing. Though the domain of curriculum evaluation emerged with the purpose of dealing with practical problems, reports of empirical studies in this field are extremely rare. Instead there has been a proliferation of theoretical papers. As an example, one finds that in a review summarizing the state of the art of curriculum evaluation, a 1971 issue of the *Review of Educational Research* presented a bibliography of about 100 publications, of which only some 15 were empirical studies (Baker 1969). This can hardly be considered an appropriate balance between the two types of study. One would expect that a score of theoretical papers would set the stage for, or would summarize, a large number of empirical studies.

Various models and ideas have been contributed to the practice of curriculum evaluation by many different people. Concepts such as "formative evaluation" (Scriven 1967), "adversary" (Kourilsky 1973), "responsive" (Stake 1972), "illuminative evaluation" (Parlett 1974), and the like have had their effect on empirical work in this field and have helped to enrich the repertoire of methods available to the evaluator. But the multiplicity of models has also had negative side effects. Some writers have tried to generalize on the basis of their experiences without taking into consideration the possibility of the existence of widely differing situations. As a result of this, models have come into being that lack sufficient empirical foundations (Lewy and Hausdorff 1973).

The works presented here suggest evaluation procedures that are firmly founded both in the theoretical literature and the accumulated experience of curriculum development centers around the world. An attempt has been made to identify ideas, concepts, and methods successfully adopted in these centers. It is of course possible that satisfactory solutions for all problems are not provided here. Nevertheless, taking stock of the existing knowledge may be advantageous for two reasons: (1) it provides a concise summary of knowledge available at present, and (2) it calls attention to missing links in the existing body of knowledge.

The Influence of Models on Empirical Studies

Only a few models of curriculum evaluation have been widely used. Each one focuses on some particular feature of evaluation, calls attention to some of its unique functions, and prescribes specific patterns of evaluation activities. These models do not necessarily reflect alternative approaches to evaluation; rather, they complement one another. They shift emphasis from one focus or role of evaluation to another. None of these models became monolithically dominant in the field of evaluation practice. Most of the current evaluation studies reported in the literature reflect an eclectic approach rather than subscribe to a particular model. In these terms it can be said that the variety of evaluation models has served to broaden the range of evaluation problems and has contributed to the improvement of methods and strategies used by evaluators.

Three different approaches have become dominant in the field of evaluation. These are respectively concerned with: (1) achievement of the desired outcomes, (2) assessment of merit, and (3) decision making.

A brief description of these three approaches is given here with the purpose of pointing out the contribution of each approach to evaluation practice.

Achievement of Desired Outcomes

Probably the best-known model of educational evaluation is the one proposed by Tyler (1950). Tyler describes education as a process in which three different foci should be distinguished: educational objective, learning experiences, and examination of achievements. According to his conception, evaluation means an examination of whether desired educational objectives are or are not attained.

Tyler's model is shown schematically in figure 1.1. This model has been used primarily to evaluate the achievement level of either individual students or of a group of students.

Both cognitive and affective outcomes have received attention. The evaluator working with this model is interested in the extent to which students are developing in the desired way. In the terms of the diagram

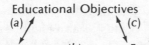

Figure 1.1. *Tyler's Model of Evaluation*

presented in figure 1.1 evaluation of this type is represented by the arrow marked with the letter (*c*).

In addition to calling attention to the need for examining goal attainment, Tyler's model also has pointed to some other relationships that play a crucial role in the educational context and that pose important tasks for evaluation. The full and systematic study of the relationship between the three foci of the educational process, as spelled out in his model, brings us closer to the overall notion of curriculum evaluation.

From Tyler's model it can be seen that the relationship between educational objectives and student achievement constitutes only a portion of the whole model. The systematic study of the other relationship described in the model is also part of curriculum evaluation. The arrow (*a*) refers to the correspondence between the objectives and the learning experiences suggested in the curriculum and realized in the actual school situation. Again, arrow (*b*) refers to the examination of the relationship between the actual learning experiences and educational outcomes.

One may add to these three evaluation foci a fourth one: determining the significance of the educational objectives and their adequacy for any specific group of learners.

Although the Tyler model deals with a variety of aspects of an educational program and describes many different activities that may be the concern of curriculum evaluation, it has nevertheless been criticized as being restrictive in that it disregards several important phenomena that must be considered before passing judgment on an educational program. Glass and Scriven have claimed that the *Tyler model does not deal with the occurrence of unplanned or unintended events* (Glass 1969, Scriven 1967). Stake has raised the criticism that the Tyler model unduly emphasizes the outcomes of the program and *does not pay attention to process variables or to the examination of the antecedent conditions* that affect the success of the program (Stake 1969).

Criticisms of this kind have led to the emergence of other models of curriculum evaluation.

The Merit of an Entity

A second approach defines evaluation as the examination of the merit of a given entity. It should be noted that this definition is general and is not restricted to the notion of curriculum evaluation. The entity to be evaluated may be a curriculum as well as any other thing.

Scriven writes: "In the abstract we may say that evaluation attempts to answer certain types of questions about certain entities." Some of the questions he poses are: "How well does this . . . perform?" and, "Is the use . . . worth what it is costing?" (Scriven 1967).

Scriven's approach added several clearly formulated questions to the inventory of problems with which evaluators concerned themselves. But his most decisive contribution to the practice of evaluation was not the formulation of specific questions but the *importance attached to the time at which these questions are posed.* Scriven emphasized that one may pose questions concerning the merits of a program during the progress of its development or, alternatively, after the process of program development has been fully completed. In the first case, evaluation results provide information to the program developers and enable them to correct flaws detected in the program. The evaluation results may contribute to the modification or formation of the program and hence the notion of *formative* evaluation.

Evaluation that takes place at the end of the development process summarizes the merits of the program, hence the notion of *summative* evaluation. Such results may serve the consumers of the program in deciding whether they should use the program at all, or under what conditions they should use it. Since evaluation results are obtained only at the stage in which program development has been completed, they do not have any formative functions. The distinction between formative and summative evaluation is probably the most significant distinction that has been made recently in the field of evaluation. Emphasis on the formative role of evaluation has called into being many evaluation strategies that have not been used before. Many of the formative evaluation strategies will be spelled out in more detail in subsequent chapters of this book.

The merit of the program is also the major concern of Stake. He writes:

> As evaluators we should make a record of all the following:
> What the author or teacher or school board intends to do, what
> is provided in the way of environment, the transactions between
> teacher and learner, the student progress, the side effects, and
> last and most important—the merit and shortcoming seen by
> persons from divergent viewpoints. (Stake 1969)

Stake points out an important feature of formative evaluation, i.e., one must take into consideration the divergent points of view of those involved in the program. This need to consider the viewpoints of various persons also appears as an important tenet in the present book.

The Decision-oriented Approach

A different aspect is emphasized in the decision-oriented definition of evaluation. The assumption underlying this definition is the belief that *evaluation is worthwhile only if its results affect future actions*. Alkin defines evaluation as follows:

> Evaluation has been defined as the process of ascertaining the
> decision areas of concern, selecting appropriate information and
> collecting and analysing information in order to report a
> summary of data useful for decision makers in selecting among
> alternatives. (Alkin 1970)

Alkin's definition points out that the evaluator helps the decision maker through a formalized process which consists of *data collection, data analysis, and preparation of summary reports. The evaluator should not act as a consultant, he is not supposed to present his personal opinion, rather he is asked to act according to scientifically approved rules*. One important feature of this definition is that the evaluator's role is not only to assist the decision maker in selecting among perceived alternatives. His role is also to call the attention of the decision maker to the existence of alternatives even if the decision maker himself does not perceive them. This conception of evaluation is strongly stressed in the evaluation activities described in this book.

The Eclectic Nature of Empirical Evaluation Studies

A close inspection of empirical studies reveals the great impact of the models described above on the design, instrumentation, type of data, and method of analysis employed in the field of curriculum evaluation, and also on the form of summary reports produced as a result of evaluation activities. For example the concepts "formative" and "summative" have become dominant in the literature on curriculum evaluation; evaluators make use of a great variety of data types and are interested in obtaining information about the merits and shortcomings of programs from various vantage points; studies are structured in such a way as to influence decision making, and so on. Nevertheless, most evaluation studies do not fully subscribe to any single theory or model. They are eclectic in nature and utilize conceptual elements from a variety of sources.

The evaluation of a program often entails not just a simple study, but a series of substudies performed at various stages of program development and implementation. Each substudy focuses on the unique problems that emerge at a particular period of program development and utilization and employs the appropriate concepts and models. An analysis of evaluation studies carried out in curriculum centers all over the world reveals that the differences among them are related to six aspects or facets in the process of curriculum production and evaluation. The following section lists these facets and explores their significance. To conclude, an attempt is made at defining curriculum evaluation in terms of these six facets.

SIX FACETS OF CURRICULUM EVALUATION

Throughout the process of curriculum development and implementation a great variety of problems, questions, and dilemmas arise. In order to cope with this multitude of problems, a need to conduct many evaluation substudies often arises. That is to say, there may be a need to carry out more than one study concerning a particular program inasmuch as a specific evaluation substudy usually serves to furnish information about one problem only.

These substudies, or small-scale studies, may differ in many respects. Indeed, one can hardly speak about the evaluation of large-scale educational programs such as the BSCS program in the United States or the Six Year YORUBA Medium Primary Project in Nigeria. Many substudies were required for these programs, each one examining different aspects and different effects of the same educational instrument. Often the general public is familiar with only a single evaluation study of a large-scale program, as in the case of the Westinghouse study of the Head Start program, but by no means does this mean that no smaller-scale evaluation studies have been made or at least that they should have been conducted.

The problems that evaluation is supposed to deal with will vary according to the stage of program development and utilization. Accordingly evaluation methods and strategies will differ also. Moreover, different persons may well be engaged in the evaluation at different stages. The differences among evaluation studies may be classified according to six issues: (1) the developmental stage of the program, (2) the entity to be evaluated, (3) criteria, (4) data type, (5) mode of data summary, and (6) role.

The Developmental Stage of the Program
The development of a curriculum project is a process that requires a relatively long time. The calendar time needed to complete a program may

Table 1.1. **Six Stages of Curriculum Development**

Stage	Roles of Development	Roles of Evaluation
Determination of General Aims	Decision about: general aims school structure	Studies on: expected changes cultural values social forces present level of achievement feasibility of programs
Planning	Writing outlines Preparing instructional material	Examining adequacy of objectives, contents, strategies Judgment of material
Tryout	Monitoring teaching in tryout classes Modifying material	Collect evidence through observation, judgment, discussion with teachers, students Student products
Field Trial	Slightly modify the program Determine optimal conditions of program use	Select sample Collect evidence about the efficiency of program under various conditions
Implementation	Links with supervisors, examination system, teacher training	Examining final form Evidence on efficiency of system links Evidence of efficiency of teacher training
Quality Control	Implement recommendation Plan "second generation" programs	Examining quality of implementation Studying reasons for changes in efficiency Suggesting remedies if needed

vary depending on the nature of the program, on the level of perfection aimed at by the development team, on the staffing and technical facilities available, and on the intensity of the work. But even under the most favorable conditions, the time required is usually expressed not in terms of days or weeks but rather in terms of months or years. In curriculum centers all over the world, the time devoted to the development of a program generally varies from two to five years.

In most curriculum projects one can clearly differentiate between various stages in the development process. The present book makes a distinction between six stages of program development and implementation. In many curriculum centers there may well be some overlap between these stages, or, for some projects, some stages may be divided into additional substages. At each stage the development team has to focus on a particular task. Accordingly, at each stage particular types of evaluation are needed to support the successful development and use of the new program.

An overall scheme of the development tasks and the corresponding evaluation roles is presented in table 1.1.

The evaluation activities needed at each stage are detailed in separate chapters of this book. Only a general review of evaluation activities at these stages is given here.

Determination of General Aims

An educational program does not operate in a vacuum. It is affected by the values, trends, and forces prevailing in the surrounding society. The overall organizational and educational patterns existing in the schools plus the nature of educational programs provided through other social agencies will influence the programs developed for specific school subjects. Therefore, before developing a program in a given subject, decisions should be made concerning such matters as the major goals of the educational system; the overall framework of the school program, i.e., the organizational structure of the school; and so forth. In some countries these kinds of decisions do not rest in the hands of the curriculum designers but are generally the business of higher governmental authorities. The curriculum centers are presented with the decisions, and their task is to develop curricula that fit these preliminary specifications.

As a result of this arrangement one rarely encounters evaluation activities concerned with decisions of this type. This does not mean, however, that there is no need for evaluation work at this stage. But such studies, if any, are not necessarily conducted by experts in educational evaluation, but rather by teams of sociologists, economists, anthropologists, psychologists, and the like, who are generally employed to uncover facts about demographic trends and occupational, economic, or value changes in society, and other information of use in making decisions about the overall aims and goals of the educational system. Frequently quite sufficient data are already available, and no special studies by either social scientists or curriculum experts are needed to obtain such information.

In general, curriculum centers assume responsibility for evaluation only at the stage following the determination of general educational goals. The role of the evaluation expert at this stage is to call the attention of the decision maker to the need for studying various aspects of social trends and to make decisions on the basis of the findings resulting from such studies.

Planning

Once the general educational goals have been determined, curriculum centers are asked to translate them into specific curricular activities. At this stage decisions are made concerning the objectives of a particular course of study, the course content, and the teaching-learning strategies to be employed, including the communication media to be used for transmitting ideas. Subsequently the curriculum team has to develop the first version of the instructional material to be used in the class. This includes writing the text, preparing demonstration materials, devising student-activity plans, and so on. The task of evaluation at this stage is manifold. There is a need to assess the scientific quality of the materials, their correspondence to recent developments in the subject domain, their accuracy, and their clarity. Judgment on these issues will be made by experts in the particular field of study.

It is also necessary to assess the likelihood that students will be able to learn the materials, master the skills, and acquire the competencies aimed at in the program. This implies examination of the existing cognitive and affective characteristics both of the teachers and the students. If the program requires some specific learning equipment, audiovisual aid, or learning strategy, one must examine the feasibility of the successful use of such features.

It may also be necessary to conduct a preliminary tryout of some of the learning experiences contained in the program. At this stage the program is still in the process of preparation, but some parts of it are already structured in such a way that they may be tried out with individuals or small groups of students.

Another aspect of the program that should be examined at this stage is the cost of implementation. Does the program use the most economic means for obtaining its objectives? Is it feasible that the schools and the students will be able to carry the expenses of implementation? Occasionally funds are available to support the development of a very expensive program, but then no funds exist for nationwide implementation. Thorough examination of various aspects of the program at this early stage can highly increase its efficiency and can reduce costly trial and error in the later stages of its existence.

Tryout and Revision

Ever since the use of formally prepared educational programs and textbooks was introduced, little regard has been given to the idea of combining or complementing professional wisdom with empirical evidence for the job of material preparation. In the past, programs and textbooks often needed the official approval of the educational authorities; however, approval was usually based on subjective judgment. Both program development and program approval were "armchair" activities and depended primarily on the talent and wisdom of the individuals who wrote the textbooks and other instructional materials.

This method was prevalent in school systems throughout centuries of educational history. The situation was tolerable, however, in the sense that the work of judges was relatively easy. School programs varied little over decades, and professionals could easily determine whether the newly proposed program or textbook properly reflected the traditional content of school learning. Also, at this time schools had a selective admissions policy; if a group of students had difficulty in using some textbook, it was not postulated that the textbook should be changed but simply assumed that a certain group of students should be removed from the school. In contemporary society, however, the school is supposed to provide education for all youngsters and not for a selected few. One must prepare educational materials that suit the needs, interests, and abilities of the whole student population. Programs have to be adjusted to the needs of the student, rather than students selected to fit program requirements. For this reason program developers must seek evidence about the adequacy of an educational program for a particular student population. This means that educational programs should be empirically tried out before they are approved for use on a large-scale basis.

Most curriculum centers established in the last few decades have adopted this approach, and it has become common practice to try out educational programs before putting them to full use in a school system. The tryout is usually done in from two to six classes. These classes are selected according to the principles of judgmental sampling so that they represent the different subgroups of the population for whom the program has been designated. Usually only those schools and classes are selected in which the teachers have agreed to cooperate with the curriculum development team and have participated in the prescribed teacher-training program. The tryout is frequently carried out as soon as some self-contained sections or chapters of the program are ready for use. Thus, during the tryout stage students may learn some portions of the new program before the full course has been completed.

During the tryout stage the curriculum team carefully observes the teaching-learning process in the classroom situation; employs a variety of formative evaluation instruments, including tests and student work sheets; and encourages both teachers and students to point out any problems or difficulties encountered in using the program. At the same time the curriculum team submits the study material to various types of experts and asks

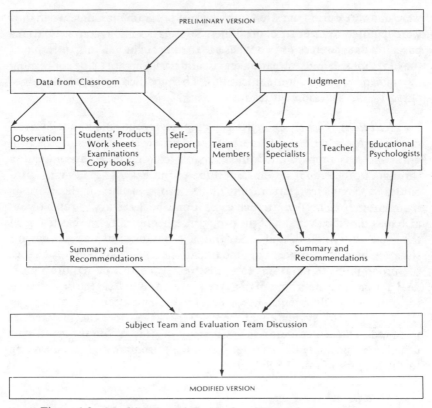

Figure 1.2. *Modification of Curriculum Material*
(adapted from Silberstein 1971)

them to pass judgment upon the material, indicating any specific modifications that need to be made. On the basis of the results of both the empirical trial run and the experts' judgments, a series of recommendations are made concerning desired alterations of the original version of the program.

A flow chart of the transition from a preliminary version to a modified version is given in figure 1.2. Two types of information source are considered. First, a variety of empirical data is collected in the classroom, which includes *records* of observed classroom events, *student products* such as working sheets, examinations, and the like, and student *self-reports* of what they experienced in class. Second, judgmental data are gathered from experts in the subject field, teachers, educational psychologists, and finally by the development team itself. At this stage, members of the development team may detect some flaws in the program of which they were unaware during the strenuous work of program planning, when they were required to meet strict deadlines. Summaries and recommendations based on data sources of two types are then brought to a joint meeting of the development and evaluation teams, and decisions are made concerning recommended program modifications. The modified version is then prepared by the development team.

Iterations. Clearly enough, if during the tryout only minor difficulties emerge, the writers may correct the deficiencies detected in the program and may prepare a modified version for widespread dissemination throughout the school system. But if the tryout has disclosed many difficulties, a complete restructuring of the program and of the learning materials may be needed. In such cases it may be necessary to run a tryout also on a modified version of the program. Theoretically one has to repeat the cycle of trying out and modifying a program until one reaches the situation in which any necessary modifications do not substantially change the program. Such iterations can be extremely costly and require a great deal of time; thus iterations of this type may unduly extend the time needed for program development. The high cost of each iteration cycle underlines the value of good evaluation at the planning stage, since this may reduce the need for further iterations. Curriculum centers for the most part usually produce only one trial version of their program and then move on to the preparation of the final draft.

Field Trial

At the tryout stage major sections of the program are taught in a small number of classes with the aim of identifying weak points in the program and of generating suggestions for its improvement. On the basis of systematic formative evaluation results, the preliminary version of the program is revised. When the revised instructional material is available for a whole course of studies, the program undergoes a field trial with a representative sample of the target population. Generally, only at the field-trial stage is it possible to observe the operation of the whole program in a situation that resembles its actual expected use in the whole system.

The field trial differs from the preliminary tryout with respect to goals, program characteristics, and evaluation design. A schematic representation of these differences is given in table 1.2.

As indicated in table 1.2, at the preliminary tryout stage the goal of evaluation activities is to detect flaws in the program and to provide suggestions for program modification, while at the field-trial stage the evaluation goal is mainly to specify how the program is to be used, i.e., to

Table 1.2. **Two Stages of Evaluation**

Issues	Preliminary Tryout	Field Trial
Program Characteristics	Provisional version	Final form
	Intervention of development team	Standard form
	Close contact with development team	Bureaucratic communication pattern
Design	Judgmental sample of 4–8 classes	Random sample
	Large number of instruments	Relatively few instruments
	Small number of respondents	Large number of respondents

identify the conditions under which the program can be successfully implemented. Questions raised at this stage are of the following types: Is the program equally suitable to the needs of both urban and rural student population? Are teachers who did not go through special training able to teach the new program? Can the program be used in schools where the average number of students per class is above thirty?

With respect to the conditions for program use, three points should be mentioned. First, at the tryout stage the program is available only in a provisional form, and frequently some portions of the program or some equipment to be used have not yet been developed. Second, the preliminary tryout is performed with a small number of classes under the direct guidance and close supervision of the development team. In the field trial, as well as in the widespread usage of the program, the development team is generally not able to maintain close contact with the teachers, and communication between the development team and teachers becomes a formal matter. Thus, there is a need to examine whether or not the program functions well in this new setting. Third, at the tryout stage the development team is able to follow closely each step of class activity; whenever some flaw is detected, they may suggest certain modification. The development team at this stage does not assume the passive role of observer, but rather intervenes with suggestions for ways of improving the program's results. Hence, the tryout stage may be characterized by intervention by the curriculum team. In contrast to this, the field trial is characterized by the employment of a more stable form of the program with only limited opportunities for the curriculum team to institute program changes.

Finally, certain points should be mentioned about the evaluation design. First, at the tryout stage 4–6 classes are usually selected on the basis of judgmental sampling, while at the field-trial stage most curriculum centers choose 30–50 classes using random sampling procedures. The actual size of the sample depends upon the size of the system and upon the variation of cultural, geographical, linguistic, and socioeconomic factors within the society. The greater the heterogeneity of a school population, the larger the sample needed for the field trial. A second difference is the variety of data collected. At the tryout stage, in relatively small numbers of classes, many types of data are collected by means of such instruments as classroom observation records, judgments, formative tests, student work sheets, and so forth. At the field-trial stage, because of the magnitude of the sample, evaluators must restrict themselves to collecting only a few types of data. Evaluators are more likely to use multiple-choice examinations and questionnaires and rely less on personal observation and impression than they do at the preliminary tryout stage. Third, at the tryout stage a relatively small number of respondents serve as the data source; at the field trial the number of respondents is relatively large.

Implementation

Implementation means the open use of a program throughout an entire school system. In centralized educational systems a program may either become compulsory for all schools of a certain type, or be among a list of authorized alternative programs from which each school chooses the most suitable for its needs. In both cases implementation entails certain changes within the system. First, teacher-training programs must be adjusted to the requirements of the new program. This implies modification in both pre-service and in-service training activities. Occasionally teachers themselves are in need of further instruction in the content area of the new program. New teaching methods, strategies, or class-management practices may also constitute the focus of a retraining course. Almost always, teachers should be trained to monitor the program, to identify flaws, and to diagnose learning difficulties.

A second implementation problem is that of obtaining the support and cooperation of the supervisory staff. Without their cooperation one can hardly expect successful implementation of the program.

A third problem is in making the appropriate changes in the national examination system, if it exists. If programs are changed but national examinations remain unaltered, teachers may not have the motivation for altering the focus of their educational work.

At this stage of development, the evaluator's role is to examine the efficiency of the changes and adjustments made. This may be done through observation of the teacher-training program, through analytical examination of both teacher programs and the examination system, and by means of the judgments and opinions of experts.

Quality Control

A program that has been successfully introduced into an educational system and has been warmly received by teachers may deteriorate over time. Deterioration, in whole or in part, may occur throughout the entire system or only in certain areas or schools. To prevent this from occurring, permanent follow-up and quality control of the program should be maintained. Quality control should be designed in such a way that it encourages those schools in which the program is adequately implemented to support other schools where the implementation has been faulty. In addition quality control may reveal when some or all portions of the program should be altered or replaced. In this way quality control may lead toward the updating of an old program or the development of new programs. This fact emphasizes the need to view curriculum development and evaluation as a cyclical activity. A program that operates very satisfactorily over a certain period of time may gradually become obsolete and will need to be substituted by a new one. Indeed, many curriculum centers that developed innovative programs several years ago are now contemplating producing "second-generation programs," which respond better to the existing needs of the system than did previous ones. The quality-control results may serve as warning signals calling attention to the need for innovative activities.

The Entity to Be Evaluated

Essentially, evaluation is concerned with the efficiency of a program as a whole. Thus the basic concern of evaluation is the success of the entire program including all its components. Quite frequently, however, evaluation may deal solely with specific components. The focus of a small-scale evaluation study may be a particular chapter of the program, a particular activity associated with its use, such as the organization of the dissemination network, or a particular type of instructional materials included in it such as the textbook, the teacher's guide, audiovisual aids, enrichment supplements, experimental equipment, or the teacher-training program. Moreover, an evaluation study may be concerned only with specific features of these components. For example, evaluation may deal with some unique aspect of the textbook such as the quality of the illustrations, the clarity of explanation, the readability of the text, the sequence of learning experiences, or the adequacy of the exercises. Some unique aspect of the program as a whole may be investigated, such as the efficiency of the type of classroom management prescribed by the program or the efficiency of a unique learning strategy employed.

As a rule, at the initial stages of the program it is more common that program components are evaluated separately; as one reaches the later stages, the entity to be evaluated is more likely to be the comprehensive unit of the program or the program as a whole.

Criteria

Evaluation is used to answer a variety of questions. Is the program a good one? Does a particular component of the program fit the needs of the students? Should one prefer strategy X to strategy Y in the presentation of a particular topic? Should objective X receive more emphasis in the program than objective Y? Do teachers improve their performance by using the teacher's guide? And so forth.

In order to answer these types of questions one needs to specify the conditions that will serve as a basis for making judgments. "Good" may mean different things to different persons. Preference may be determined on the basis of a variety of considerations. One may be concerned with the social relevance of topics dealt with in a program, with the students' interest in the material, with cognitive outcomes of the program, with teachers' acceptance of or identification with the program, or with all these issues. Each issue, event, or specific trait which provides a basis for judgment is termed here "criterion." Scriven provides a long list of criteria for items such as cognitive outcomes, motivation, perceptual, psycho-motor, and social skills, which may be used for judging the merits of a program (Scriven 1967). He points out that the evaluation of any entity should be performed according to a weighted series of criteria. This means that in assessing the goodness of a program, one should keep several criteria in mind, although different weights may be associated with each.

Frequently evaluators employ criteria related to the desired outcomes of a program. The list should be extended to include all processes associated with utilization of the program and the fit of the program to certain standards.

Outcomes

The most frequently used criteria concern program outcomes. For several decades, only this group of criteria was used in the context of educational evaluation. This explains the fact that this set of criteria has received more systematic treatment than any other.

It is common to differentiate between kinds of outcomes along several lines. First, one may differentiate between short-range and long-range outcomes. Educational evaluation has been in general concerned with short-range outcomes, which were examined immediately upon completion of a program or a short time thereafter. Long-range outcomes were seldom examined, despite the fact that their importance has been strongly emphasized (Ochs 1974). This neglect or disregard mainly results from the fact that evaluation takes place within a short span of time following the program's completion. Several widespread educational programs have been in use for a number of years, and thus the opportunity exists for examining long-range program outcomes too.

A second dimension upon which classification of outcomes is made is the intended vs. unintended outcome spectrum. Recent educational writings have emphasized the need to deal with the unintended as well as with the intended outcomes of educational programs (Scriven 1972).

Classification of outcomes is also made with regard to the type of behavior exhibited. It is common to distinguish between cognitive, affective, and psychomotor types of behavior. Elaborate taxonomies provide detailed classification schemes of all three behavioral types (Bloom 1956, Krathwohl 1964, Harrow 1972, De Landsheere 1975).

Processes
A second set of criteria used in evaluating curricula concerns the processes generated by using or learning the program. Some writers refer to these phenomena as *transactions* (Stake 1967). Such processes include *student participation in certain activities, interest in the program, student satisfaction and initiative*, and the desired pattern of communication between students and teachers. To summarize, we may ask the question: Are the planned or intended processes, classroom activities, and interactions patterns really taking place?

Fit to Standards
Evaluation should concern itself with examining the fit of the program to certain standards based on the desired program traits. Questions of the following types may be posed when employing such criteria: Does the program contain accurate and updated information? Does the program deal with crucial issues in the subject field? Are program goals relevant to problems of contemporary life? Are the instructional materials satisfactory from the point of view of aesthetic features, durability, cost, and so on? Standards may have their roots in *pedagogical principles* (appropriate provision of feedback, reinforcement, sufficient amount of repetition), *communication principles* (clarity of presentation, proper sequence, vocabulary control, multisensory cues), *curricular principles* (correspondence between objectives and planned activities), and the like.

Most curriculum centers employ a variety of standards for judging the merits of a program, but more work is needed for systematizing evaluation criteria of this type.

Data Type
Evaluation means the provision of information through formal means (Stufflebeam 1969). This implies that the evaluation is more than the passing of judgment about some entity. It entails the act of collecting and analyzing data (Alkin 1970). In the context of curriculum evaluation one encounters three major types of data: *judgment, observation, and students' products.*

Judgment
At various stages in the program's development, selected experts from different fields are asked to assess its merits and shortcomings either as a whole or with respect to its various aggregate parts. In addition, sometimes the consumers or would-be consumers of the program, such as students, parents, teachers, or community representatives, are asked to give their opinion of a program. Data of this type may be elicited in various ways through the use of unstructured or structured interviews, open-ended or multiple-choice questionnaires, or group discussions. *One specific method of judging used in the context of curriculum evaluation is a systematic content analysis* of a textbook or some other type of educational material. Experts are asked to determine the *proportions* in a particular text of content elements of various types such as factual statements, explanations, comparisons, open questions, and so forth. No matter by which technique one elicits data, the utilization of this kind of data requires systematic planning with respect to the selection of respondents, the formulation of questions, and data summary.

Process Observation
One of the most powerful ways to identify the merits and short-comings of a program is through observation of the program in operation. Several highly formal observation schemes have been developed that serve to focus the observers' attention on some specific aspects of the teaching-learning process. Despite the existence of these schemes, evaluators quite often construct their own observational schemes to fit the unique requirements for the evaluation of a particular program.

Observational studies can be useful for at least three purposes. First, they enable the *identification of some of the unintended or unplanned consequences of using a program.* Second, they can provide *valid informa-*

tion concerning the appropriate implementation of the program. Through observation one can assess whether what is going on in the class corresponds to the program's prescription. Third, through observation one may best obtain direct evidence about the mastery of certain process skills such as the ability to perform an experiment or use a microscope. Thus observations may yield a *detailed record about the student's ability to perform complex cognitive and psychomotor skills.*

Student's Products

The student's product most commonly used for evaluation purposes is the set of cognitive or affective responses to a given stimulus. Questions that adequately represent a well-defined domain of skills are useful for determining whether students have acquired competency in a given task.

A series of such questions, usually called "criterion-referenced tests," are more useful for the sake of curriculum evaluation than the so-called norm-referenced tests, which serve the purpose of comparing the relative performance level of various individuals (Glaser 1968, Alkin 1974). In addition, other types of student product may also be used for evaluation purposes. For example, students' work sheets that contain their responses to regular class assignments may serve as an important source of information. They serve primarily as a learning experience, but can also be analyzed as a source of information about student achievement. Lindwall and Cox have systematically analyzed sets of such exercises, and have referred to them as "curriculum-embedded tests" (Lindwall and Cox 1970). An industrial product such as a working tool or scientific instrument, an artistic product such as a painting, statue, poem, or short story, may also serve as evaluation data. In addition, collectively prepared products such as an exhibition, a school newspaper, a drama performance, a film or television program can also be used as evaluation data.

The Mode of Data Summary

As indicated above, in the area of curriculum evaluation a variety of instruments are used to generate data, such as expert judgments, questionnaires, observation models, tests, students' school work of different types (e.g., essay, drawings, woodwork, bookkeeping record). Summary and analysis of the data may be carried out in one of two ways: quantitatively and qualitatively. Quantitative analysis uses statistical tools for organizing data and for producing results, while qualitative methods are descriptive without using exact numbers and statistical formulas. Qualitative analysis has been frequently employed in the work of anthropologists. Recently several attempts have been made to employ qualitative data analysis in curriculum evaluation. Thus, for example, in an evaluation study of a new educational program, Smith and Carpanter (1972) summarized observational records in the following qualitative statements:

> Throughout this report we have indicated . . . that the classes were settings full of learning activities and, for the most part, enjoyable to be a part of. . . . For the children, it was like having Christmas every Friday. An immense amount of pleasure was expressed in being able to purchase . . . a large candy and a toy, or just a toy or a small candy depending on the tokens they have earned.

No matter which type of instrument serves to generate the data, the mode used for summarizing and for presenting the results may be either qualitative or quantitative. For example, judgment may be passed in the form of qualitative statements given by experts or through precoded questionnaire responses. In the first case the treatment of the data is likely to be qualitative, i.e., the evaluator will present a variety of opinions and point out areas of agreement and disagreement among the referents. In the second case analysis is likely to be quantitative, and statistical parameters will be computed. When observational methods are employed, most of the data summary will be done in a quantitative fashion, that is, according to structured classroom observation schemes. Many observational studies in education have been analyzed using a variety of statistical methods (Dunkin and Biddle 1974). There are also excellent examples of qualitative analysis of observational records (Smith and Carpanter 1972). Analysis of test responses may be carried out both quantitatively or qualitatively, the former being the most common. The type of qualitative analysis that might be done, however, would include something such as a list of commonly occurring errors made by students together with hypotheses concerning the sources of the errors. This mode of data treatment is substantially different from the conventional statistical analysis of test results.

Roles of Curriculum Evaluation
Scriven differentiates between two major roles of curriculum evaluation: the "formative" and the "summative" (Scriven 1967). While these two terms have become extensively used in the domain of curriculum evaluation, it seems advisable to indicate more the specific roles of curriculum evaluation in terms of decision-oriented activities. Upon review of the activities in a great many curriculum centers, three major roles suggest themselves: (1) selection of program elements, (2) modification of program

elements, and (3) qualification of program usage. The first two roles correspond to what Scriven called formative evaluation and the third one to summative evaluation.

Typically, each evaluation role is characteristic of a particular stage of program development. Thus, for example, "selection of program elements" is typical of the planning stage, and "modification" is typical of the tryout stage. Nevertheless, there is no one-to-one relationship between evaluation roles and developmental stages. It is possible to gain some insight about desired conditions for program use at the planning stage as well as suggesting modification of program elements at the quality-control stage.

Selection of Program Components

At the early stages of program development, questions arise as to what should be included in the program, what should be taught, what strategies should be employed, and so on. Frequently several alternatives are presented to the program developer, and he has to select the most appropriate one.

Modification of Program Elements

At the tryout stage of the program it may turn out that some element (e.g., some exercises, illustrations, or explanations) contains certain flaws. Perhaps they do not adequately help the students to reach certain desired goals, or perhaps they may be producing undesired effects. Evaluation results may call attention to such problems and may help program developers improve their program by eliminating the flaws.

Qualifying the Use of the Program

A third role of evaluation may be qualifying program usage. In other words, evaluation may aid in the specification of the optimal or minimal conditions for usage. Unlike the other two roles, which deal with issues related to the formation of the program, this third role is not related to the amendment of a program but rather focuses on the task of recommending how and under what conditions a program should be used.

Conditions may be specified for the various aspects of a program. Specifications may be given about teacher training; availability of equipment, space, time, professional prerequisites; the consent and support of the community or the broader environment; existence of a skilled supervisory or monitoring staff; and so on. For any particular school, the specification of conditions constitutes a basis for the selection or rejection of a particular program.

A WORKING DEFINITION OF CURRICULUM EVALUATION

The six facets of the curriculum evaluation process have been described above. Using these facets it is possible to describe curriculum evaluation in the form of a mapping sentence. Mapping sentences of this type have been frequently used in various fields of the behavioral sciences (Guttman 1969, Kernberg 1972). They also have been employed for the comparison of several curriculum evaluation approaches (Lewy and Shye 1974).

The overall definition presented in the mapping sentence in figure 1.3 contains a variety of evaluation activities; their totality makes up the more general concept "curriculum evaluation." This definition suggests that evaluation essentially is the provision of information for the sake of facilitating decision making at various stages of curriculum development. This information may pertain to the program as a complete entity or only to some of its components. Evaluation also implies the selection of criteria, the collection of data, and data analysis.

Evaluation in the provision of information at the
$\left\{\begin{array}{l}\textit{A: Stages}\\ \text{determination of aims}\\ \text{planning}\\ \text{tryout}\\ \text{field trial}\\ \text{implementation}\\ \text{quality control}\end{array}\right\}$
stage of program development

concerning
$\left\{\begin{array}{l}\textit{B: Entity}\\ \text{teacher's guide}\\ \text{study material}\\ \text{equipment}\\ \text{the whole package}\end{array}\right\}$
from the point of view of
$\left\{\begin{array}{l}\textit{C: Criteria}\\ \text{fit to standards}\\ \text{eliciting processes}\\ \text{yielding outcomes}\end{array}\right\}$

on basis of
$\left\{\begin{array}{l}\textit{D: Data}\\ \text{judgment}\\ \text{observation}\\ \text{examination of}\\ \quad\text{product}\end{array}\right\}$
summarized in
$\left\{\begin{array}{l}\textit{E: Mode of}\\ \quad\textit{summary}\\ \textit{qualitative}\\ \textit{quantitative}\end{array}\right\}$
mode for the

sake of making decisions about
$\left\{\begin{array}{l}\textit{F: Role}\\ \text{selecting elements of}\\ \text{modifying}\\ \text{qualifying the use of}\end{array}\right\}$
the program

Figure 1.3. *Mapping Sentence Definition of Curriculum Evaluation*

One may define a particular substudy in the process of program evaluation by selecting a single line from the six facets appearing in the mapping sentence. Thus, for example, one may conduct a small-scale study at the planning stage of a science program concerned with the safety of the equipment to be used by the students. Observational data, qualitatively analyzed, will facilitate the decision about whether or not to include that particular instrument in the program.

In a similar fashion one may define other substudies. As indicated above, the totality of all substudies concerned with a particular program constitutes its evaluation. It should be noted that certain combinations of keywords appear more often in empirical work than others. Moreover, for certain combinations it may well be difficult to find empirical examples. The validity of this definition is dependent upon the fact that all empirical activities can be described by some combination of the keywords; however, there is no requirement that all possible combinations should correspond to some empirical phenomenon.

MINIMUM EVALUATION REQUIREMENTS

It has been indicated that the evaluation of a particular educational program is not performed through a single study. At various stages of program development, alternative pathways of action may appear, or doubts may arise concerning the merits of some parts of the programs. In such cases the evaluator may be asked to define a problem area precisely to collect appropriate data and to summarize them in a way that may help decision making. Thus, each substudy concerned with the evaluation of a program focuses on a unique, well-defined problem area. Two such substudies may differ one from the other from the viewpoint of the focus of the investigation, type of data collected, and so on. A problem that may be of great interest in the process of the development of a certain program may lack significance in another curriculum project. Thus, in one project there may be a need to assess the safety hazards of using certain experimental equipment, while such an assessment may be entirely irrelevant in another program. The mapping sentence presented in the previous section summarizes the variety of evaluation studies that may be performed during the life cycle of any new program. Indeed, it is very advantageous to evaluate a single program from numerous points of view and to gather information about its merits and faults as perceived by different persons.

Nevertheless, one should be cautious not to overevaluate a program. A great variety of evaluation foci, methods, strategies, and instruments are mentioned here, not for the sake of encouraging the evaluator to utilize all of them in the context of dealing with a single program, but to provide a broad inventory from which activities most relevant to answer crucial questions may be selected. Working conditions differ widely from one curriculum center to another, and each center has to determine the extent and depth of the evaluation activities it will undertake. The availability of alternative curricula, the necessity to operate in a "crisis situation" when schools urgently need the instructional materials, the budget available for program development and evaluation, the availability of trained manpower—all these factors should be considered in planning evaluation.

Neither a theoretical basis nor accumulated experience exists for determining the minimum evaluation requirements to be met in order to certify a new program for widespread usage in an educational system. Each system should determine standards of evaluation on the basis of local circumstances. A system in which a great variety of programs are available may impose higher evaluation requirements for curriculum development than might emerging educational systems in which few programs are available.

In a "crisis situation" it may be permissible to combine two different stages of program development, but one should keep in mind that educational innovation is justified only insofar as evidence can be obtained about the beneficial aspects of innovations.

BIBLIOGRAPHY

Alkin, M. C. "Products for Improving Educational Evaluation." *Evaluation Comment* 2, no. 3 (1970): 1–15.
Alkin, M. C., et al., eds. *Problems in Criterion-Referenced Measurement.* Los Angeles: University of California, Center for Study of Evaluation, 1974.
Baker, Robert. "Curriculum Evaluation." *Review of Educational Research* 39 (1969): 339–58.
Bloom, B. S., et al., eds. *Taxonomy of Educational Objectives: Cognitive Domain.* New York: McKay, 1956.
DeLandsheere, V. and G. *Definir les objectifs de l'éducation.* Paris: Presses Universitaires de France, 1975.
Dunkin, M. J., and Biddle, B. J. *The Study of Teaching.* New York: Holt, Rinehart & Winston, 1974.
Glaser, R., and Cox, R. C. "Criterion-Referenced Testing for the Measurement of Educational Objectives." In *Instructional Process and Media Integration,* edited by R. A. Weisgerber. Chicago: Rand McNally, 1969.
Glass, G. V. "The Growth of Evaluation Methodology." Laboratory of Educational Research, University of Colorado, 1969. Mimeographed.
Guttmann, L. A. "General Non-Metric Technique for Finding the Smallest Coordinate Space for Configuration of Points." *Psychometrika* 33 (1968): 469–506.

Harrow, Anita. *A Taxonomy of the Psychomotor Domain.* New York: McKay, 1972.

Kernberg, D. F. "General Comments on Facet Theory." *Bulletin of Menninger Clinic* 36 (1972): 91-96.

Kourilsky M. "An Adversary Model for Educational Evaluation." *Evaluation Comment* 4, no. 2 (1973): 3-6.

Krathwohl, D., et al., eds. *Taxonomy of Educational Objectives: Affective Domain.* New York: McKay, 1964.

Lewy, A., and Hausdorff, H. "Emerging Models in Curriculum Evaluation." University of Pittsburgh, Department of Research in Education, Working Paper No. 23, 1973. Mimeographed.

Lewy, A., and Shye, S. "A Facet Analytic Approach to the Definition of Curriculum Evaluation." Curriculum Center, Ministry of Education, Jerusalem, 1974. Mimeographed.

Lindwall, C. M., and Cox, C. R. *The IPI Evaluation Program.* Chicago: Rand McNally, 1970.

Ochs, René. "Some Implications of the Concept Life-Long Education for Curriculum Development and Evaluation." Paper presented at the Seminar on the Evaluation of the Qualitative Aspects of Education, International Institute for Educational Planning, Paris, September 1974.

Parlett, Malcolm. "New Evaluation." *Trends in Education,* no. 34 (1974): 13-18.

Scriven, M. "The Methodology of Evaluation." In *Perspectives of Curriculum Evaluation,* edited by R. W. Tyler. Chicago: Rand McNally, 1967. Pp. 39-83.

Scriven, M. "Prose and Cons about Goal Free Evaluation." *Evaluation Comment* 3 (1972): 1-4.

Silberstein, Moshe. "Modification of Curriculum Material." Lecture delivered at Curriculum Center, Ministry of Education, Jerusalem, 1971.

Smith, L. M., and Carpanter, P. C. "General Reinforcement Package Project: Qualitative Observation and Interpretation." St. Anne, Mo: CEMREL, 1972. Mimeographed.

Stake, R. "Countenance of Educational Evaluation." *Teachers College Record* 68 (1967): 523-40.

Stake, R. "Language, Rationality and Assessment." In *Improving Educational Assessment,* edited by W. H. Beatty. Washington, D.C.: Association for Supervision and Curriculum Development, 1969. Pp. 14-40.

Stake, R. "Responsive Evaluation." Center for Instructional Research and Curriculum Evaluation, University of Illinois, 1972. Mimeographed.

Stufflebeam, D. "Evaluation as Enlightenment for Decision Making." In *Improving Educational Assessment,* edited by W. H. Beatty. Washington, D.C.: Association for Supervision and Curriculum Development, 1969. Pp. 41-73.

Tobias, S., and Duchastel, P. "Behaviourial Objectives, Sequence and Anxiety." *CAT Instructional Science* 3 (1974): 231-42.

Tyler, R. W. *Basic Principles of Curriculum and Instruction.* Chicago: University of Chicago Press, 1950.

PART II

Stages of Curriculum
Development and Evaluation

2

Determination of General Educational Aims and Specification of Major Objectives*

GENERAL AIMS EMANATING FROM THE POLICY

In any educational system, whether it be formal or nonformal, decisions must be taken on what and how children will learn in the institutionalized education in which they take part. On the basis of these decisions, learning materials—textbooks, mimeographed materials, or whatever—are produced as aids to the children's learning. Such decisions are bound by several constraints, and their originators do not act in a social vacuum. In many countries general educational aims are formally stated by governmental or legislative acts; in countries where such formal acts do not exist, they are implicit in the value system of the society and in its educational tradition. Those who determine the school program have to act in accordance with these general aims.

*The information in the section dealing with New Forms of Education was supplied by Dr. Herbert Bergmann of the German Foundation for International Development.

This chapter was written by T. Neville Postlethwaite.

The general aims of education are of political significance. They are usually stated in broad terms so that they secure the consensus of the great majority of the society. They serve as the basis for making decisions on how school life should be organized and on what should be taught in school, but in themselves they do not constitute or directly determine the practical details of school life. Examples of such political aims state that education must "allow equal opportunity for all children," "be a preparation for life," "increase the mean level of achievement," "encourage social integration," "make school life a more enjoyable and friendly experience," "develop more complex thinking in the children," "increase enrollment in elementary school," "increase the supply of high-level manpower," "educate students for easy assimilation into the labor market," and "combine academic studies with practical and professional preparation."

Various examples can be given of general educational aims enunciated by different sources within the society. In Tanzania, for example, President Julius K. Nyerere wrote a book entitled *Education for Self Reliance*, which contains many statements of general educational aims for the country. Such statements are used by Tanzanian curriculum developers as a basis for determining the overall curriculum (Nyerere 1967). Often governments will set up ad hoc committees to reconsider the role of education in the society. In Malaysia in 1951 the Barnes committee enunciated such general aims as:

    (a) a common Malayan culture should be developed;
    (b) equal opportunity for free primary education;
    (c) Malay and English should become the media of instruction. (Miller 1968:chap. 7)

Again, in 1960 in Malaysia the Education Review Committee stated such aims as:

    (a) increasing the relevance of school experiences to national identity;
    (b) [the acquisition of] good citizenship in the fullest sense of the word;
    (c) the inculcation of high standards of moral and social behavior. (*Report of the Education Review Committee* 1964)

Certain general educational aims can be found in written constitutions. Article I of the Fundamental Law of Education in the 1947 Japanese Constitution states:

Education shall aim at the full development of personality,
striving for the rearing of the people, sound in mind and body,
who shall love truth and justice, esteem individual value, respect
labor, and have a deep sense of responsibility and be imbued with
the independent spirit of builders of the peaceful state and
society.

New Zealand recently attempted to canvass opinions on education from
many people within the society (New Zealand Educational Development
Conference 1974). The following extracts indicate the process involved
and the types of goals mentioned:

Instead of recalling a limited number of people to confer, the
Government decided to seek a widespread opinion on education,
invite participation from interested New Zealanders in regional
seminars and involve overseas visitors.

To reach the community and to make the conference more
responsive to local views, the Minister invited the six universities
to plan and run seminars in their own regions. Groups were
encouraged to register with the extension department of the
nearest university so that they could receive material for study.
Two booklets, *Let's Talk Education* and *Proposals for Change*,
were sent out. About 50,000 copies of each booklet were
distributed free to all groups who, after discussion, recorded their
views, wishes, opinions, and recommendations and forwarded
them to the extension departments. 8,000 submissions from 4,000
study groups representing 60,000 persons throughout the country
arrived. Each submission was placed under one of 17 categories
derived from the booklet *Let's Talk Education*.

Opinions related to the topic *What Should Schools Teach* are
listed below.

"Teachers should beware of taking too positive a stand on
controversial issues such as sex and religion—but it would be
just as bad for students to see staff taking no stand at all."
"Few children are taught about sex at home—it lands like a hot
potato in the schools' laps."

The question of religion in the curriculum was debated at
several seminars and in a number of discussion groups. Several
groups felt strongly that the secular clause should be dropped
from the Education Act. Some quite plainly wanted Christianity

"taught" while others preferred a study of the main world religions on a comparative basis.

Another group argued for humanism as a basis for determining values. But all appeared to agree that children needed some base to work from and some standards upon which to build their own value judgements.

Many subjects which could be added to the secondary curriculum were suggested—rarely were removals wanted. Requests came for courses in child rearing, marriage, health, house buying, building, hire purchase, divorce, insurance, drugs, psychology, driver education and politics—to name a few.

"Economics as a compulsory subject at high schools is more beneficial than cutting up frogs," said a teachers' group. "Broaden the secondary curriculum to enable pupils to meet the needs of life"—another group of teachers.

The concept of "work experience" was well received and many thought that such schemes should be extended for the benefit of larger numbers of pupils. An Auckland group proposed that students from the fourth form onward work one day a week in different industries. This opinion, in varying forms, was shared by a number of groups.

Goals stated by the National Commission of the Reform of Secondary Education in the USA (1973) suggest the following aims: communication skills, computation skills, critical thinking, occupational competence, perception of nature and environment, economic understanding, responsibility for citizenship, knowledge of self, appreciation of others, adjustment to change, respect for law, clarification of values, and appreciation of achievement of man.

The statements of general aims sometimes reflect ideas toward which the society strives and sometimes present an image of the "ideal man" in a given society, although as can be seen from the above examples, more *specificity* is sometimes given.

THE TASKS OF THE CURRICULUM DEVELOPER

In most countries groups of people operate in curriculum centers, curriculum units, or curriculum projects. These people are responsible for translating the general educational goals of the system into specific curriculum objectives of what should be taught, and for the production of the materials for this learning. In many instances the personnel within these curriculum centers, units, or projects make these decisions, but final decisions on these objectives can also be reached by the curriculum developers in consultation with many other groups within the society. In some cases members of the teaching force, the inspectorate, the teacher-training personnel, public and political administration personnel, or various combinations of these groups, may be involved in curriculum decisions. This varies from country to country, but in this section we shall use the term "curriculum developers" to denote whatever group or combination of groups is making the decisions.

Curriculum developers have to make decisions concerning the organization of the educational program in school. Relying partly on the implications of the general educational aims and partly on systematic data that they generate or collect, they have to answer questions such as the following:

Which subjects should be taught in schools and what should the balance (in terms of time) among subjects be? What criteria should be used to determine this balance? How often should the balance be reviewed?

What should be the length of the school year in which these subjects should be learned? Should the length of the school year vary from one level of education to another? At what age should different subjects begin to be learned? Should social studies be an integrated subject or should history, geography, and civic education be taught separately; or should social studies be integrated for certain levels of education and separate for others? The same question can be asked about science (earth sciences, biology, chemistry, physics) and mother tongue (grammar, essay writing, reading comprehension, literature).

There are many sources of learning apart from the school: the home, the mass media, the employment situation, the church, youth movements, the military, and so on. Which educational objectives are best learned in school and which in other settings? In other words, those responsible for determining what should be learned must always question the role of the school in the total learning process.

Individuals within a society differ, but certain areas of learning are common to all children. Are there differences in the needs of rural and urban children? Should learning be different for these two groups of children (bearing in mind the apparently inevitable flow of children from rural to urban life)? If different, how different should it be? Indeed, should the objectives be different for boys than for girls?

Every nation has some tradition of schooling. What is normally taught in the schools? Is what is not taught in the schools taught somewhere else? Are there areas of learning not taught anywhere that should be introduced into the school?

What are the mechanisms used in each country to review these problems regularly? What criteria are used? Many problems are highly relevant to the work of curriculum developers, but the decisions are often taken by senior civil servants and politicians without any discussion with curriculum developers. The curriculum developers should continuously review these problems and make their views known.

The subject matter itself evolves, i.e., changes occur in content and concepts. Since the dynamics of the economic, social, and political forces within this society are changing, it is necessary for educational practices and sets of curriculum objectives to be reassessed at regular intervals. Educational aims or curricular objectives that are appropriate or relevant in year X may be outdated and redundant in year X-plus-four. Hence the cyclic nature of the reassessment of aims, practices, and objectives is a critical matter at different levels in the school system. The amount of resources available within a society also varies; as a result, the amount of effort and resources that can be put into this cyclic reassessment differs. Nevertheless, in most countries of the world where such reassessment is made, it takes place every four to seven years.

MAJOR EDUCATIONAL OBJECTIVES

Thus far we have dealt with educational aims, which were defined as political decisions that provide orientation for educational planning. Before the curriculum writer can define specific educational objectives and prepare learning materials, however, it is necessary to determine the Major Educational Objectives (MEOs) that will be covered in the domain of each area of studies. Since school learning is mostly structured according to subject-matter areas, the MEOs will typically be stated separately for each subject-matter area. This is a convenient practice but not a necessary one. If learning is not organized according to subject-matter areas, then the MEOs will be adjusted to that organization. Thus, for example, one may organize MEOs according to problem areas, performance projects, and so forth.

As an illustration, the MEOs in history in one system were formulated in the following six points:

1. The pupil acquires knowledge (information) of terms, concepts, facts, events, symbols, ideas, conventions, problems, trends, per-

sonalities, chronology and generalizations, etc., related to the study of history.
2. The pupil develops understanding of terms, facts, principles, events, trends, etc., related to the study of history.
3. The pupil develops critical and creative thinking.
4. The pupil develops practical skills helpful in the study and understanding of historical phenomena.
5. The pupil develops interests in the study of history.
6. The pupil develops healthy social attitudes.

In another school system the MEOs of history were defined as follows:

Cognitive:
The knowledge of important historic events
The acquisition of competencies needed for independently studying history
The acquisition of basic concepts to describe historical phenomena and to explain them
The perception of historic phenomena in the context of values and ways of life of the past
The development of historical thinking (analytic, imaginative, synthetic)

Values:
The judgment of historical events according to universal moral criteria
The development of sympathy and tolerance toward the way of life of other nations
The development of identification with the State and the People

The MEOs of a course in home economics for girls were defined as follows:

The student should know materials which are in use in the household.
The student should understand the principles of consumption (consumer behavior) and should apply these principles in her habits of buying products.
The student should enjoy working in her home.
The student should develop awareness of the implications of running the household for the health of the whole family.
The student should cherish aesthetic aspects related to keeping her house.

Table 2.1. **Science Education General Aims**

Content	Knowledge and Comprehension	Processes of Scientific Inquiry	Application of Scientific Knowledge and Methods	Manual Skills	Attitudes and Interest
Biology					
Physics					
Chemistry					
Earth and Space Sciences					
Miscellaneous					

Another way to present the MEOs in a given field is to present a two-dimensional chart, as in table 2.1.

If we take the Biology row of table 2.1 we can see that there are five general aims: knowledge and comprehension of biological facts and principles, the process of scientific inquiry in biology, the application of scientific knowledge and methods in biology, manual skills in biology, and attitudes and interest in biology. These are general aims. It has yet to be determined what specifically (i.e., the specific curriculum objectives) will be taught under the first general aim: knowledge and comprehension of biological facts and principles. This will be dealt with in chapter 3, although, as will be seen below, evaluation studies undertaken to establish general aims quite often yield information on specific objectives.

IMPORTANT CONCEPTS

Several basic concepts either permeate or appear at various places in the procedures for the identification and specification of general educational aims and consequently major educational objectives.

The Concept of Critical Changes in Society

As mentioned, changes take place constantly in a society. It is necessary to identify the most important changes and undertake studies of them in order to see what their implications are for new or modified educational objectives of what should be learned in institutionalized schooling. Each society, or rather each group of curriculum developers, must determine where the most critical changes in society are occurring. Are they in the economic domain, the social domain, the health domain, or where?

Manpower Employment Patterns at a Particular Point in Time

It is clear that manpower employment patterns change. The typical manpower employment agencies are agriculture, the civil service, different sectors of industry, different sectors of commerce, or further schooling institutions. If during a five-year period there is a switch of some 10 to 20 percent of the population of school leavers going into industrial sector X rather than Y, or if there is a significant switch from agriculture to industry, obviously the types of knowledge, skills, and values that will be required of these people will change. To be an effective citizen in the society will continue to require certain knowledge, skills, and values that are more or less common; but the particular knowledge, skills, and values for particular types of work employment will be somewhat different. Thus it is necessary to study what the employment patterns are at different points in time and to assess the types of knowledge, skills, and values required by the different "receiving agencies" for those people leaving institutionalized schooling at different points in the school structure.

Two major problems beset this kind of approach. The first is that to take manpower employment patterns in the society as they exist at present is to take a static view of the needs of employers. The second is that to attempt to forecast the manpower employment pattern for five years hence is very difficult; in fact, experience has shown that it is impossible to do this accurately. Many persons point out that this is a very limited and utilitarian approach. The response to this criticism is that this is only one of many inputs to the determination of the curriculum (and has to be weighed against the other inputs), but that without such information one would have no idea of the exigencies in terms of knowledge, skills, and values of the economic role of individuals within the society.

Most school systems have two or three major points of exit for the students. Nonformal educational institutions offer courses of study that last for anywhere from two weeks to twelve months, after which the students exit. In each case it is possible to identify the sectors of employment to which such students go. These sectors of employment we have named "receiving agencies." These can be different types of industry, commerce, agriculture, administration, civil service, and so on. In some cases, it is recognized that students who leave school may take one to two years before they find regular full-time employment. It is necessary to discover the employment pattern of such people and at the same time to discover in exactly what activities they engaged during this waiting period. As soon as these activities are identified, it is possible to sample the activities and assess the types of knowledge, skills, and values required for them.

Thus, once all the various sectors of industry, agriculture, commerce, and the like have been identified, it is possible to take a random sample of these receiving agencies and identify the persons responsible for the on-the-job training of young people (or sometimes old people) entering those enterprises. Given the existing curriculum of the last two or three years of schooling to which those children have been exposed, it is possible to draw up a check list of knowledge, skills, and values expressed in some operational way. It is then possible to request the receiving agencies to rate each line in the check list on various aspects. One aspect might be the extent to which each objective is required by the receiving agency for their new-comers now (i.e., in year X); another rating might be the extent to which they think they will require this objective in year X-plus-five. Another aspect might be the rating of the extent to which they get the competence in the objective now. Yet another type of rating might be the extent to which people in the receiving agencies think that every citizen of their country should possess a particular type of knowledge, skill, or value in order to cope with life in their society. This last rating can of course be extended outside the employment area, and various subsections of the society can be queried concerning their opinions in these matters.

Table 2.2 is a simplified example of how the questionnaire might look for such a study. The first column's "subject-matter theme" is a list of all the relevant subject-matter parts in the curriculum of the school leavers in question. This list will be supplied by the curriculum developers. In the

Table 2.2. **Questionnaire to Employers**

Subject-matter theme	Need for theme in work	Knowledge of students in theme
A.		
B.		
C.		
etc.		

second column the employer records his perceived need for that theme in the work the school leaver will pursue. He may be asked to mark his responses using a scale such as:

5 = to a very high degree
4 = to a high degree
3 = in some but very important connections
2 = in some but not very important connections
1 = not at all or very little

In the third column the employer records his opinion about the knowledge students coming to his firm have in that theme. For this rating another scale may be developed, such as:

5 = very satisfactory
4 = satisfactory
3 = not fully satisfactory
2 = unsatisfactory
1 = extremely unsatisfactory

The evaluation procedures involve survey sampling, questionnaire and scale construction, and data analysis. In particular, the data analysis should include the establishment of the degree of consensus among the various receiving agencies on how desirable it is for all learners to master their particular objective. A good example of this kind of survey was that undertaken by Urban Dahllöf in Sweden (Dahllöf 1963).*

In many cases a curriculum or educational research center may not have the necessary resources to undertake such large-scale work. Where few resources are available, it is still possible to undertake pertinent evaluation. For example, one exercise might be of the type where villagers in a particular area are asked to give their opinions on what knowledge, skills, and values are considered of particular importance for young people either going to the village school or to the community education center. Empirically the evaluation will consist of assessing or counting the responses and assessing the amount of concordance among those villagers asked to give an opinion. In this case the evaluator may attend a meeting of the village

*Dahllöf sampled the various receiving agencies in Swedish society (including the faculties of the various universities) for pupils leaving the Swedish *gymnasium*. The ratings used were very similar to those given above. Using coefficient of concordance, he established the commonality among receiving agencies for particular sets of knowledge, skills, and values. This information was then used for a revision of the curriculum of the three-year *gymnasium*.

council and do some quick head-counting or, alternatively, may interview a sample of the village council.

New Behavior Requirements in Health, Welfare, and Political and Social Activities

All countries are experiencing an evolution in the social and cultural patterns of behavior. Changes should be identified, and the curriculum should ensure that young people acquire the generalized competencies to cope with everyday living in their society. There is a transition from traditional to scientific medicine; there are new attitudes toward hygiene. In some cases specific diseases may have been eradicated or new diseases may have appeared. Here specific action can be taken in the curriculum, but usually it is the generalized competencies that need to be updated. New welfare regulations for medical care, unemployment benefits, and the like are introduced; clearly all citizens must be able to cope with the various ways of obtaining their rights.

New voting patterns may be introduced for certain types of elections. Or old customs (e.g., the wearing of veils in certain countries) may begin to disappear and yet be retained by a few citizens. In order to cope with these changes or to have higher tolerance of certain conflicting values within the society, such phenomena must be taught and explained in the school so that children about to leave school will be aware of, and be able to cope with, the "evolving technology" of everyday life.

Glaring anachronisms of curriculum, particularly in newly independent countries, are manifold: British history or French geography is taught, instead of that of the country itself; biology is taught with examples of flora and fauna from Europe rather than from the new country. These are examples of a curriculum that is irrelevant to the social needs of the learners. Clearly, the developers of the curriculum must amend these anachronisms and replace them by a curriculum relevant to the country in which the children are being educated.

In Malaysia, where Bahasa Malay is being introduced as the common language of the country, the Reading Materials Development Project of the Curriculum Development Unit has been changing the stories used in the English books from stories about England to stories about Thailand, Burma, and the Philippines, where the expected language of communication with Malaysians is English.

In the case of new health and social phenomena, the evaluators' main task is to help identify and specify the "target populations" who should be requested to give their ideas of new phenomena and collect the opinions of such persons as to what should be introduced into the curriculum. In most cases this will consist of drawing judgment samples from the various target populations. It should perhaps be mentioned that these target populations could be, for example, politicians, trade-union officials or members, administrators in a particular section of the welfare administration, groups of parents, and/or teachers, and so forth. Once the target populations are defined, it becomes a technical matter to draw either a judgment or, in some cases, a probability sample.

It is necessary to collect information from the identified target populations. This information gathering will take many forms and will vary from situation to situation. In some cases it may be structured or unstructured interviewing, in others it may take the form of open-ended or even closed questionnaires (where the necessary pilot work has been undertaken to ensure that the closed questionnaires are fully comprehensive). In still other cases it may involve various types of rating scales or attitude scales.

Changes in the Perceptions of Students Regarding Their Learning Needs

It is desirable to check on what the learners themselves feel about the curriculum they receive, and in particular about the curriculum they do not receive, e.g., what types of things would they like to learn that they are not learning now. Many secondary school students are said to want information on such topics as population growth, pollution of the environment, contemporary politics, and the like, which they are not currently receiving. How true is this and how relevant is it for decisions concerning what should be in the curriculum? What evidence can be collected from the learners themselves about which parts of their curriculum they perceive to be irrelevant, and what they think is missing? General and educational aims often have to be inferred from such evidence.

In Australia, Anderson has recently undertaken a survey to discover possible reasons for students' dissatisfaction with school (Anderson and Beswick 1973, Anderson 1975). Part of this inquiry was also concerned with educational objectives and revealed that students saw certain aspects of the curriculum as irrelevant to their needs; on the other hand, they felt that such issues as environment pollution, population growth, and current frictions in international politics, which were not dealt with in school, should have been.

It is interesting to note that for contemporary teen-agers in Australia, Anderson discovered that not only was the curriculum considered in certain parts irrelevant, but also that it was the general authoritarian regime of certain schools that was causing the students to "rebel," since the regime of the school contrasted drastically with the more permissive attitude of the larger society. This is an example of a large-scale probability survey, requiring the full techniques of probability sampling, careful instrument construction, and data analysis. The amount of detailed information that will result from such an inquiry for curriculum developers will very much depend on the type of specific questions asked.

Choppin (1974) examined the achievement and attitudes of students in particular branches of science according to whether they were undergoing a Nuffield science program* in that branch or not. He was able to show that certain programs developed favorable attitudes to the subject, whereas others did not. Such information on current school programs is of importance in determining lacunae in the programs.

It is, however, more typical for curriculum centers to gain their information about student needs from fairly unstructured interviews with selected groups of students (judgment samples).

New Developments in Subject-matter Content

In natural sciences, social sciences, and languages in particular there appear new findings, new topics, new structures, new words. How are these identified and how is consensus arrived at about those parts that should be included in a revised or new curriculum?

In most curriculum centers it is typical to form groups of university professors (in the subject area), teacher-training personnel, and teachers themselves. Informal discussions are conducted to identify the new developments that are considered important to be introduced in either the primary or secondary school curriculum. In most cases absolute consensus can be obtained through such informal discussions; when this occurs there is no need for further study. In some cases, however, there is considerable disagreement on the desirability of introducing a particular new development into the school curriculum. Here the evaluator can identify the amount of disagreement and, if necessary, undertake an inquiry whereby larger groups of professors, teacher-training personnel, and teachers are sampled for their opinions. The resultant evidence is useful for the developers to make up their own minds on the introduction of such educational objectives into the curriculum.

---

*A series of textbooks and instructional materials of different types produced in England and supported by the Nuffield Foundation. Some of these programs are briefly described in footnotes throughout the book.

From each type of studies mentioned above, the information gathered will clearly depend on the questions asked. If the questions deal with general aims, the information will be on general aims; if with the Major Educational Objectives, so on these. In fact, information is usually forthcoming on both. Employers will indicate large areas in the curriculum that they need or do not need, but often they will be specific. For example, they might well indicate that the comprehension of the concept of base in mathematics is important as a subarea of the understanding of mathematical principles.

It is important to emphasize that evaluation helps to provide the information on which decisions will be based concerning the specification of objectives. Studies can be undertaken on the requirements of various receiving agencies regarding the types and amounts of knowledge, skills, and values they require, and to quantify the amount of concordance among the various receiving agencies. Nevertheless, there must always be a final decision on how each cell in a matrix (such as that given in table 2.1) is weighted, i.e., the importance to be given to a particular educational or curriculum objective. This decision depends on the value systems of the persons taking the decision. Evaluation evidence never makes this decision, it only provides information as a basis for helping the curriculum developers make the decision.

"Relevance" and "Balance"

The major reason for examining the critical changes in society is to ensure that the needs of the society will be met in terms of what young people (or old people) entering a particular section of the society must know in order to cope with their home and work lives. Assuming that most, if not all, the major requirements of society are identified, and assuming that the resultant specifications of objectives reflect these needs, then it should ensue that the curriculum taught in the schools is relevant to the needs of the persons entering the society at various points. *Relevance* means that the curriculum corresponds to an existing need in the society. *Balance* means that the curriculum developers have weighted the importance they have given to each need; usually this implies that consideration is given to all needs without undue emphasis on any one need. The reason for stressing this is that a tendency prevails in certain countries for some ad hoc curriculum experts to suggest that the curriculum should be revised to become more balanced by putting in such subjects as domestic science, commercial subjects, or technical subjects. Once the various critical changes have been examined, such statements would not be necessary.

Indeed, there is strong evidence that the advice of curriculum experts should rather be to suggest that the systematic examination of forces should be undertaken so as to arrive at tables of specifications rather than global suggestions about the introduction of such subjects as domestic science.

The Language of Instruction

Many children in developing countries are instructed in their first, second, or third language. For example, in certain parts of Nigeria a child will first learn his vernacular language, then a main Nigerian language (e.g., Hauser, Yoruba, or Ibo), but the language of instruction in elementary school is English.

There is evidence that children will learn more and quicker in their first or second language than in English *(IFE Six-Year Primary Project—Progress Report* 1974). Moreover, a foreign language is in many cases ill adapted to express nuances existing in the local language. There is an increasing demand in certain countries for a definite language policy in the schools, and changes are occurring.

In other countries decisions have already been taken to have one national language, e.g., Kiswahili in Tanzania and Bahasa Indonesian in Indonesia. A foreign language is introduced some years later, say in grade 4 or 5.

It is important either to have specific policies on the language of instruction or that the curriculum developer has information on what the current practices are before he begins developing his curriculum. If he does not have this, then either his program may soon be redundant or the level of language complexity he uses may be inappropriate.

Changes in policy about the language of instruction are of great importance to the curriculum in certain countries.

New Forms of Education

In several developing countries that have recently emerged from colonial rule there is a movement either for a new social order or for a different type of education. In Tanzania, for example, the concept of self-reliance was introduced. In the United Republic of Cameroon (and other African countries) there is a movement toward closer links between the school and the community. Many countries wish to revive certain cultural traditions (which some colonial regimes suppressed) and inculcate these into the schoolchildren of today. There is also a tendency to make school less "bookish" and to gear education more toward work. This often embodies such concepts as "education for development," "rural education," "education and work," and "lifelong education." In these cases, an effort is being made to depart from the traditional concept of school as it exists in most countries.

Where such new concepts are introduced, there is usually no evidence on how feasible they are or on the problems that can occur for the curriculum developer in the development and implementation of the new curricula he must produce. For example, if schools and pupils are to be "self-reliant," how does the curriculum developer ascertain what activities and behaviors the pupils and schools should undertake to become "self-reliant"? Schools may accomplish this through high production of a routine nature, i.e., the children may cease to inquire into the whys and wherefores of the phenomena with which they are dealing and, in many ways, may choose to learn. How much time should be spent on, say, farm production and how much on learning the 3Rs? How general or specific should the teaching skills be? Specific skills may become unusable in five to ten years' time; but if general skills are taught, how does the curriculum developer determine what these should be?

Where close links are desired between schools and communities, what joint activities should occur? What resources can the community put at the disposal of their school? What sorts of projects (agricultural, industrial, etc.) exist in which pupils can participate as part of their learning experience? Are new roles implied in this for the teacher? To what extent should the teacher be a working member of the community, how much "pastoral" work should he undertake, and what leadership roles (e.g., in teaching or village leadership) can he assume?

There is very little evidence for the curriculum developer to make decisions on issues such as these. Evaluation, therefore, plays an important role at the planning stage. One example of how this might be tackled comes from the United Republic of Cameroon (African Regional Advanced Seminar for Systematic Curriculum Development and Evaluation 1975). A survey was conducted to discover the existing links between sampled schools and their communities in order to assess the extent to which these schools and communities could work together and in which fields of activity. Information was systematically collected on parental attitudes toward school, the involvement of parents in teaching in school, the participation of the school in community work, and the transfer effect of modes of farming from the school farm to the village farms. Local farms were visited, and a catalog of the types of handicraft and agricultural skills was compiled. In general terms parents supplied information on the types of behavior they perceived as desirable for young adults to become respected and accepted members of their communities. Summaries of such data provide a description of the existing state of affairs such that the curriculum developer has empirical evidence for the whole country to help him begin to understand the need for certain types of learning, the contexts in which it will take place, and the extent to which certain actions are possible.

New reforms can often be hindered by the existing local administrative machinery. Attempts can be made by the evaluator to assess to what extent the proposed reforms can be undertaken with the existing administrative machinery and/or the changes that should be undertaken in that machinery. Such attempts require that the evaluator has a good working knowledge of the bureaucratic routines in education in the country, and his work usually takes the form of semistructured interviews and observation. It is important that the policy and decision makers are aware of the forthcoming tasks they will have to perform in order for a new strategy to be implemented.

Where it has been ordained that new subject areas or new elements should be introduced into the curriculum (e.g., local culture, environmental studies including locally oriented agriculture and crafts), the curriculum developer must have some basis for determining the major educational objectives in these domains. Too often the typical experts—the anthropologist from the university, the agricultural extension officer, and so on—will pronounce themselves unable to be of help. In this case it often falls to the evaluator to conduct studies to provide basic information on the content area. Again, the United Republic of Cameroon collected information on local customs and lore, types of farming in different environments, division of labor, and the like. This information allowed basic decisions to be made on major curriculum objectives. In some cases the decisions are self-evident, but in others the curriculum developer must check with the national political authorities on which aspects of culture it is thought should be introduced into the school curriculum and which not.

The above paragraphs have referred to new forms of education in some developing countries. In many developed countries new forms of education are also being introduced. These include the "open school," the comprehensive school, individualized instruction, mastery learning, and the forging of stronger links between home and school. Many of these are matters of educational or social policy, some being national directives and others being started by ad hoc groups. In some cases systematic research is undertaken (Kim 1974) to obtain the necessary information on the implications for educational objectives.

It should perhaps be emphasized that such departures from traditional schooling as have been mentioned require research that is typically more costly than the low-cost techniques for estimating consensus. Visits to schools and communities are essential.

"Minimum Learning Requirements" for Curriculum Construction

A great deal is spoken and written about "basic education," or "minimum learning requirements." This concept is meant to denote the knowledge, skills, and values that all persons at a particular stage in human development, or at a particular grade level, should learn in order to be able to play their roles adequately in society. Attempts have been made to define what this is, but clearly basic education will vary from age group to age group within a society and from society to society, for the reasons given earlier in this chapter.

As will be seen from types of evaluation studies in the area of manpower employment patterns, it is possible to estimate the percentage of an age group or a grade group for whom it is considered desirable to master a particular educational objective. In some cases 100 percent of all learners probably should master the objective. More likely, the percentages could vary between 20 and 90 percent. In certain school systems the minimum learning requirements could vary from one type of school to another, and in all school systems it will vary from age group to age group. Where compulsory education exists, say for four or six years, it is possible for all subject areas within the compulsory years to be examined and to determine those cells that contain minimum learning requirements for the whole population. The educational system then must ensure that all children master these objectives.

CONSTRAINTS IN CURRICULUM DEVELOPMENT

From what has been said so far, it can be seen that a variety of evidence can be collected from different groups of persons in the society concerning what they think is needed in terms of knowledge, skills, and values for learners exiting the system at different points in time. The various demands of the "critical changes" must be balanced against each other by the curriculum developers who will make the final decision on the educational objectives. Nevertheless, the evidence produced by the evaluators from their studies of the various changes will be tempered by various constraints operating in society. Studies of such constraints by research workers/evaluators can be of great help. Let us examine the nature of some of these constraints.

Political Constraints

Political constraints might include the following issues. In some countries the ministry of education will form either ad hoc groups of educators or national commissions of educators to decide on the broad educational objectives to be followed in the curriculum. These objectives are handed down to a curriculum center whose job it is to operationalize them into "specifications of objectives." In the operationalization of the objectives the curriculum center will still need to undertake some studies of the critical changes in society, as mentioned above. At the same time, they must ensure that these are within the overall stated objectives as handed down from the ministry. Where the curriculum center has less latitude is, typically, in the area of civic education or political education in certain countries. In the operationalization of some of the objectives the evaluator at the curriculum center may well wish to poll major groups in the society for their interpretation of some of the global educational objectives. Again, this will include the identification of the target populations, the sampling of them, systematic data collection, and the ensuing analyses. An example of such a study is given below.

The general educational aims of the Israeli system denote several value areas among them: liberty, equality, tolerance, mutual help, and love for others.

To translate these objectives into operational terms a two-stage study was conducted. In the first stage a series of interviews were made with a group of 23 prominent scholars and leaders in fields of philosophy, sociology, psychology, history, education, political science, economics, and law, and with leaders of political parties. Each of them gave interpretations of the meaning of each general aim. On the basis of these statements educational objectives were formulated. In the second stage of the study a questionnaire containing 120 objectives was sent to 222 persons who represented teachers, educational administrators, experts in various fields, and parents. The respondents indicated (on a 1–3 scale) the importance they attached to each objective.

On the basis of these responses, 5 categories of objectives were identified:

1. High acceptance level—high consensus
2. High acceptance level—moderate consensus
3. Moderate acceptance level—moderate consensus
4. Low acceptance level—high consensus
5. Low acceptance level—low consensus

The highest priority in writing curriculum materials was given to objectives in the first category (Eden 1975).

Sociocultural Constraints

Examples of sociocultural constraints operating against the introduction of change of social behavior in various cultures are numerous. To enumerate but a few: the traditional religious values such as the concept of fatalism, or the concept of the salvation of the human being through meditation, or a resistance to technological development, sexual values (e.g., high resistance to family planning), values concerning the sacred nature of animals (e.g., whereby they will not be killed except for sacrificial purposes). Other values would include respect for and nonquestioning of the opinions of elder people within the society and respect for long traditions, e.g., never boiling water except for ill and weak people, not eating particular fruits (despite their high vitamin value), and so on. Some of these might fall under the heading of anthropological constraints, but for the time being they have been placed under cultural constraints.

How do these values constrain the introduction of new objectives of education? Many values are held unquestioningly, but from time to time certain values are queried, and a debate ensues in the society. The society must decide on the introduction of new educational objectives; the job of the evaluator is to estimate the degree of concordance or discordance concerning a particular value that is currently being questioned in the society. Such evidence (e.g., 70 percent in favor of changing the value, 10 percent don't know, 20 percent in favor of retaining the value) is useful to curriculum developers when making decisions on the advisability of introducing a new educational objective. Such estimates give the amount of likely resistance in the society to the introduction of an objective.

However, the whole area of the acquisition and change of value systems is one where relatively little research has been done and where practically no research is being done on the ways in which values change as a result of the manifest and latent curriculum in institutionalized education. Clearly much more work is necessary in this area. At present the role of evaluation is limited to that of assessing the amount of agreement or disagreement on the introduction of an objective from the various subsections of society.

Psychological and Pedagogical Constraints

Another set of constraints might be termed psychological and pedagogical constraints. The studies of what might loosely be called "cognitive style" can be very useful in helping to operationalize specific objectives. In

Isfahan, Iran, studies were undertaken of the mathematical processes practiced by Isfahani farmers in terms of four basic arithmetical skills. These studies showed that the type of cognitive process in these skills was very different from what the curriculum developers were considering identifying to be taught. Thus, the actual specific behaviors for, say, addition, were given differential weights on the basis of the study. These weights were different from those that had been anticipated by the curriculum developers (Bazany 1972).

Another example from Isfahan is also of interest. It was noted that the size of a cattle herd was considered very important by farmers, despite the fact that the production of a large herd in terms of milk or beef might be very small. A small herd that produced more beef or milk was not considered as important as a large herd. Hence there was a conceptual discrepancy between quantity and quality. This in turn influenced the weighting of the curriculum in herd production as to the specific objectives. The existence of this psychological phenomenon was discovered from a psychological study. Here we see the utility of certain limited psychological studies on the target population for which the objectives are being developed.

Havighurst (1973) has shown how individuals play different roles at different stages of life—preschool, primary school, adolescence, middle age, and retirement (each of which can be further subdivided). Havighurst's examples are for the North American society, but some might be easily generalized to other advanced industrialized societies. Sociologists in each society need to undertake studies of the various roles at various ages so that the need for playing the roles can be identified and related to the curriculum at any point of formal or nonformal schooling. Each role has certain implications for the knowledge, skills, and values required for an individual to play that role adequately. Rarely are the knowledge, skill, and value implications for a role spelled out. There is a gap between what the sociologist can offer and what tangibly the curriculum developer can use. It is to be hoped that in the near future sociologists and curriculum developers will work together more closely in this field and that mechanisms can be established for the production of information of immediate utility to the curriculum developed.

In certain societies the structure of education is laid down, e.g., comprehensive schooling or multipartite schooling. A multipartite system assumes that there should be a differential curriculum for the different groups of students in different schools. One of the evaluation tasks is to identify the amount of overlapping in terms of objectives among the different school types. This has implications for the restructuring of the school system, but it is also useful in terms of the amount of common curriculum and that part of curriculum which is different.

Large-scale educational surveys of the IEA (Postlethwaite 1974) and the National Assessment for Educational Progress (Womer 1970) show the relationship between variation among social backgrounds of students, variation in their learning conditions, variation in their exposure to media, and so on, and the variation in either cognitive achievement or in attitudes of the same students. Some results indicate that certain outcomes of education are more influenced by variations among homes than variations among schools, whereas for certain other outcomes (mostly attitudinal) the variations in exposure to media and learning conditions in schools are more important than the variations in home background. Many details of what sort of outcomes are affected by what sorts of antecedent factors can be seen in the IEA publications. These sorts of findings have great implications for curriculum development in terms of relating the learning that goes on in school to the learning that goes on outside school, so as not to duplicate work and at the same time to maximize the efficiency of what transpires within the school itself. In Hungary (Báthory and Kádár-Fülöp 1974), it was discovered that the school curriculum was unnecessarily repeating certain aspects of science knowledge that had been learned outside the school. The evidence on what was learned outside school fed straight into the curriculum center, which was then able to modify some of the programs in the light of this.

Different types of analyses of survey data are able to indicate the necessary amount of time required in school learning to achieve "competence" in certain cognitive outcomes. However, the level of competence achieved depends not only on the amount of time the subject has been studied but also on the motivation and interest of the students at different points during their school career and on the competence of the teachers. There are "tradeoffs" between these various input and process variables, and these tradeoffs have implications for the structuring of the curriculum as to what is taught, when, for how long, and under what conditions.

Carroll (1975) has shown that on average, it takes students 6.5 years of regular school study to become "competent" in reading comprehension in French. However, if the teachers are of a certain quality, this can be reduced by 6–9 months and, again, if the students have a certain level of motivation, this can be reduced by another half year. These types of studies have implications for differentiated curriculum planning according to the learning conditions of different groups of students.

These are but a few of the constraints in need of study, both by curriculum evaluators and other social science research workers in the society.

CONCLUSIONS

In order to determine the general aims of a system of education and consequently specify the major objectives of areas of study (both formal and nonformal), we must examine systematically the evidence available from many sources. Each child has an economic role and a social role to play in the society. Studies of the major types of employment into which students go; the social roles they will have to play; new knowledge required by all citizens in the areas of health, welfare, and politics; and new developments in particular branches of human endeavor are critical in the production of information for use by curriculum developers in arriving at an overall plan for the curriculum This is true both in time allocation for major areas of study and time allocation for subareas of each major area for all students and for different subgroups of students within the society.

The final decisions concerning the inclusion or exclusion of areas of study are made by curriculum developers in conjunction with major groups of educators, senior educational administrators, and other groups of persons representing the society. Evaluation studies are important at this stage to provide empirical evidence on the views of students, parents, employers, and other interested parties.

REFERENCES

"African Regional Advanced Seminar for Systematic Curriculum and Evaluation." Paris: IIEP, 1975. Mimeographed.

Anderson, D. S., and Beswick, D. G. "Secondary School Students Survey." In *Secondary Education for Canberra*. Canberra: Commonwealth of Australia, 1973. Pp. 126–79.

Anderson, D. S. "Education for Adolescents in Australia." *International Review of Education* 21 (1975): 177–93.

Báthory, Z., and Kádár-Fülöp, J. "Some Conclusions for Curriculum Development Based on Hungarian IEA Data." *Comparative Education Review* 18, no. 2 (June 1974): 228–36.

Bazany, M. "Evaluating an Experimental Functional Literacy Project—The Isfahan Experience in Planning Out-of-school Education for Development." Paris: IIEP, 1972. Mimeographed.

Carroll, J. B. *The Teaching of French as a Foreign Language in Eight Countries*. Stockholm and New York: Almqvist & Wiksell and Wiley, 1975.

Choppin, B. H. "The Introduction of New Science Curricula in England and Wales." *Comparative Education Review* 18, no. 2 (June 1974): 196–206.

Dahllöf, U. S. *Kraven på Gymnasiet.* Stockholm: Iduns Tryckeriaktiebolag Esselte AB, 1963. With summary in English, "Demands on the Gymnasium," pp. 257–65.

Eden, S. "The Translation of General Aims into Functional Objectives: A Needs Assessment Study. *Studies of Educational Evaluation* 1 (1975): 5–12.

Havighurst, R. *Developmental Tasks and Education.* 3rd ed. New York: McKay, 1973.

"The Ife Six Year Primary Project—Progress Report." Ife: University of Ife Institute of Education, 1974. Mimeographed.

Kim, Hogwan, "Development of Mastery Learning in Korea." Paris: IIEP, 1974. Mimeographed.

Miller, T. G. W. *Education in South East Asia.* Sydney: Ian Novak, 1968.

National Commission of the Reform of Secondary Education in the USA. New York: McGraw-Hill, 1973.

New Zealand Educational Development Conference. *Talkback: Report of Public Discussions.* Wellington: Governmental Printing Office, 1974.

Nyerere, Julius K. *Education for Self Reliance.* Dar-es-Salaam: Information Services Division, Ministry of Information and Tourism, 1967.

Postlethwaite, T. N., ed. "What Do Children Know?" *Comparative Education Review* 18, no. 2 (June 1974): 157–63.

Report of the Education Review Committee 1960 (the Abdul Rahman Education Report). Kuala Lumpur: Government Printer, 1964.

Womer, F. B. *What Is National Assessment?* Ann Arbor, Mich.: National Assessment of Educational Progress, 1970.

3

Evaluation at the Planning Stage

CURRICULUM DEVELOPMENT ACTIVITIES

Among the activities that are normally carried out at the planning stage of curriculum development are the following:

1. Identification and formulation of instructional objectives
2. Specification of the scope and sequence of the content of instruction
3. Selection of teaching-learning strategies
4. Development of instructional materials

These activities do not imply that all curriculum development efforts need to be done in the same sequence. For example, some curricular efforts are primarily concerned with devising instructional strategies while keeping intact the original instructional objectives and curriculum content; others may be concerned with the development of learning materials only. The above four activities are not intended to represent a recommended model. As it is generally accepted that there are many ways of going about developing a curriculum, there are also many ways to conduct evaluation

62   *This chapter was written by Chew Tow Yow.*

for *improving course development*. What follows is an attempt to delineate the possible subphases in the curriculum development process at the planning stage and to suggest some possible ways to seek and obtain data for the improvement of course development.

ROLE OF EVALUATION

Curriculum development plans and materials generally undergo a series of revisions until the curriculum developers feel that the specified instructional objectives, content of instruction, teaching-learning strategies, and materials planned would meet the general objectives of the program. The *purpose of evaluation* at the planning stage of curriculum development is therefore to provide some form of assurance that these activities will in fact lead to the achievement of agreed-upon educational goals. Obviously, only at the tryout stage can we have empirical evidence about the effectiveness of a program. Nevertheless, at the planning stage we need to know how well we have selected, conceptualized, and formulated the activities so that we can detect and eliminate flaws and make up for inadequacies in planning and development, thus saving subsequent investment of human and financial resources in the trying-out of poorly planned materials and activities.

EVALUATION OF INSTRUCTIONAL OBJECTIVES

Once the general goals of a particular curriculum program have been identified, the task of the curriculum developers is to formulate specific instructional objectives for individual units or subunits of the program.

The aim in evaluating the derived list of instructional objectives is to get some sort of agreement from others outside the curriculum team that the instructional objectives are:

1. Related to the objectives of the program and likely to contribute cumulatively to the attainment of the program objectives
2. Clearly stated
3. Appropriate for, and attainable by, the pupils at the particular level of education and stage of mental development
4. Important enough to encourage further learning by the pupils in the next level of the course or in related subject areas

The best "test" of the assumptions underlying the formulation of the instructional objectives would be to evaluate pupil achievement and other related pupil behavior after the total curriculum program has been tried out in schools. But since this is not possible at the planning stage of curriculum development, when the program is still very much on the drawing board or, at best, developed in draft or prototype versions, the alternative would be to seek and analyze relevant opinions and judgment from experts.

The task before the curriculum developers and evaluators is to identify experts to evaluate the instructional objectives that have been formulated. The selection of experts and the number of experts to be invited in each category depend on how wide a representation of views is sought. Presented in table 3.1 is a suggestion regarding the possible types of experts one may wish to consult in terms of the four criteria mentioned earlier. Neither the list of criteria nor that of experts is intended to be prescriptive, and it is not exhaustive.

The actual techniques for obtaining and analyzing opinions and ratings are discussed in detail in chapter 2. Basically, what is desirable at this stage is to obtain a general agreement or disagreement, from among the select group of respondents, on the list of instructional objectives

Table 3.1. **Criteria and Possible Evaluators for Instructional Objectives**

Criteria Experts	Related to Aims	Stated Clearly	Appropriate and Attainable	Important for Further Learning
Curriculum specialist	X	X	X	X
Educational psychologist		X	X	X
Educational sociologist	X	X		X
Subject expert	X	X	X	X
Educational administrator	X	X		
Curriculum evaluation specialist	X	X	X	X
Teachers	X	X	X	X
Potential employer (particularly for vocational subject areas), etc.	X	X		X

Table 3.2. **"Agreed" Responses**

Criteria Objective	Criteria and Percentage of "Agreed" Responses			
	Related to Aims	Stated Clearly	Appropriate and Attainable	Important for Further Learning
Objective 1				
Objective 2				
Objective 3, etc.				

according to a set of criteria. This information will assist in decision making on whether to retain, reject, or modify the instructional objectives. Open-ended responses in terms of suggestions for the restatement of the planned instructional objectives may also be solicited. Table 3.2 is a useful device to present the "status" of responses for further decision making.

A major concern in curriculum development today is the rapid rate at which knowledge is expanding. No curriculum can hope to teach more than a mere fraction of what is known in a given field of study. The need is to develop in schoolchildren the ability to learn further. Thus curriculum programs, in addition to achieving specific course objectives in specific subject-matter areas, must pay adequate attention to the types and modes of learning experienced by pupils.

For example, using the categories of learning suggested by Gagné, one could reexamine the instructional objectives to see which categories of learning would need to be strengthened and promoted through the content of instruction and teaching-learning strategies. Gagné suggests the following categories of learning: chaining (S-R learning), verbal association, multiple discrimination, concept learning, principle learning, and problem solving (Gagné 1970). Thus, if a particular curriculum program calls for the development of scientific concepts, say, in chemistry, then it is necessary to evaluate whether the instructional objectives have adequately emphasized such "learnings." An analysis can be conducted with the aid of a panel of educational psychologists and curriculum specialists, using the matrix in table 3.3.

Such a simple device has the advantage of assisting the evaluation panel in seeing whether adequate attention has been paid to the categories of learning envisaged for the program; in other words, whether a satisfactory balance between different types of objectives has been established.

Closely related to the categories of learning required for instructional objectives are the intellectual processes and cognitive skills expected of

Table 3.3. **Matrix for Identifying Categories of Learning in**
Instructional Objectives

Types of Learning	Chaining	Verbal Asso- ciation	Multiple Discrim- ination	Concept Learning	Principle Learning	Problem Solving
Objective 1		X	X			
Objective 2			X			
Objective 3			X	X		
Objective 4				X	X	
Objective 5						X

pupils. In the process of instruction, pupils are normally expected to exercise a range of intellectual abilities—from naming, identifying, and stating rules to describing, demonstrating, and applying rules. The *Taxonomy of Educational Objectives* provides a useful classification of the cognitive processes implied in instructional objectives (Bloom 1956). In using a classification of cognitive processes as a criterion for evaluating instructional objectives, it is possible to ensure that the desired balance of cognitive skills is maintained in a course program. For example, in a social studies course that eventually requires children to apply rules regarding the demand and supply of food for a particular society, it may be necessary first for pupils to be able to identify, order, and distinguish between different types and quantities of food consumed, before they can describe the nature of food demand in a society and formulate rules and principles about the demand and supply of food.

Obviously not all instructional objectives can be analyzed and thus evaluated according to criteria of cognitive intellectual processes. The so-called traditional instructional objectives, such as "Pupils should understand the relationship between the demand and supply of food for community X," would not lend themselves readily to such an analysis. Curriculum evaluators and developers would have to decide whether this additional criterion would be useful for the evaluation of instructional objectives.

EVALUATION OF THE SCOPE AND SEQUENCE OF THE CONTENT OF INSTRUCTION

Most curriculum programs are subject-based in that they derive their substantive content from one or several established disciplines. Some programs may select highly specific content from specific disciplines, e.g., mathematics for elementary schools, using criteria for selection such that the content should provide for pupils' further learning of the subject at a higher level. Others may select content from more than one discipline as well as other sources of information in order to achieve certain program objectives.

Similarly, there is no standard procedure for the presentation of the content of instruction. Some programs prepare only a table of content to be taught, the syllabus, while other programs may prepare elaborate scope and sequence charts of course content.

Curriculum developers, who are also subject specialists, are normally responsible for identifying and organizing course content. In some instances, committees of experts and teachers are given the task. The selection of course content is based on their understanding of the requirements of the instructional objectives and on their understanding of the subject matter. The purpose of course-content evaluation at the planning stage is to seek a wide representation of views as to the relevance and potential effectiveness in achieving the course objectives.

Criteria

The following are possible criteria for the evaluation of course content.

Relevance to Instructional Objectives

Curriculum developers are well aware that the selection of course content for school pupils is not based on the notion that content is a watered-down version of the subject matter. Rather, the criteria of selection is that the content is related to, and effective in, the achievement of the instructional objectives. The problem faced by curriculum developers is more likely to be what to leave out in content selection rather than what to put in. Judicious selection and efficient organization of content are crucial if it is to be meaningful and effective for instructional purposes. In attempting to validate the relevance of content to objectives, the opinions of the following people could be sought: curriculum specialists, educators, subject specialists, educational psychologists, and prospective employers in the case of vocational subjects.

Up-to-dateness of Content

The content selected at the planning stage should be validated by competent authorities from the point of view of its current status. Subjects such as science, civics, and economics undergo rapid changes in respect of their content and need frequent updating. Other subjects, such as music and art, have elements that are permanent in nature, although innovations do take place in these subjects as well. The purpose of evaluation, then, is to seek some form of assurance that the content selected is in keeping with the latest accepted thinking in the subject field concerned. Judgment could be obtained from experts who are active in the particular field of studies.

Relevance to the Child and His Environment

Evaluation should be concerned with verifying whether the content is related to the *stage of mental development* of the pupils in question. It is unrealistic to specify content calling for a high degree of abstraction of ideas when pupils are not developmentally ready for such cognitive processes. For example, teaching about government to elementary school pupils would be unsound if pupils have to conceptualize the complicated infrastructure of the government machinery. A great deal of research in the field of child development has provided generally accepted findings, validating the selection of content in terms of child developmental needs.

Relevance to pupils' experience and environment is another important criterion used for the evaluation of the content of instruction. For example, one may use different flora to teach a principle in botany, but it is psychologically preferable to select flora from the pupil's immediate environment. Thus content that provides for the pupil's interaction with his or her immediate environment is more likely to lead to better achievement of course objectives.

Another psychological concern in the evaluation of content of instruction is *how it has been sequenced for learning by pupils*. Content topics can be sequenced in a number of ways, the common ways being: from the easy to the difficult, from the part to the whole, from the known to the unknown. Whatever organizing principle one chooses in order to sequence content, the main concern should be that the topics in the content be sequenced to maximize learning by pupils. To the extent that idiosyncratic human behavior is a familiar phenomenon, it is difficult not to have reservations regarding any form of rigid sequencing of instructional content and thus of pupil behavior. It is important that the sequencing of content and the implied learning tasks be carefully evaluated at the planning stage so as not to develop a scope and sequence of content that is inherently incongruent with the readiness and experiences of pupils. The views of educational psychologists and experienced teachers can be sought at this stage and their recommendations incorporated into the content organization, if any.

Content Balance

Content balance may be viewed in the following context:

1. Balance between various subdivisions of the subject matter. For example, in a course on national history, seek experts' views on whether the different aspects of national history such as social life, economic activities, have been adequately treated in the course content. In history there has been a tendency to overemphasize one aspect over another, e.g., political over social history, depending on the availability of historical documents.

2. Balance in the content in terms of pupil activities envisaged. The objectives of a course may require that pupils acquire competency in several areas of knowledge, certain attitudes, and skills. In the identification of instruction of content, it is generally easier to identify the knowledge component than the content that will ensure the development of desirable attitudes. For example, in curriculum areas such as music, drawing, and fine arts, besides the knowledge component, nonverbal as well as the so-called nonscholastic activities should be given due place. Even in the predominantly verbal areas of studies such as social studies and science, nonverbal and manual activities should be given appropriate weight. It is therefore important for evaluation to ensure the provision of a balance in the content between pupils' learning activities and learning outcomes.

Organizational Structure of the Content

In content evaluation, one should take care that in the process of selection and organization of content, *emphasis has not been put on specific bits of knowledge that are not interrelated vertically and horizontally.* One should also ensure that due attention has been paid to those aspects that constitute *the structure of the subject*, such as key concepts of the curriculum area, tools and methods of inquiry specific to the subject. In other words, evaluation should validate whether the content has been selected and organized in such a way as to provide the tools of inquiry, basic starting points, practice grounds for acquiring the methods and tools of learning, bearing in mind that no course content can provide for all the desired learning and that much knowledge is likely to become obsolete in the lifetime of the individual.

The organizational structure of the content is also related to the *total educational environment of the pupils.* In this context, course content must have vital links with educative experiences in other areas of studies as well as with pupils' learning experiences in the home and community. Views of curriculum developers in other related areas of studies, teachers, and educators need to confirm, modify, or revise the selection of course content.

Evaluation Design

Having identified some of the more important areas of concern for the evaluation of the content of instruction, the next task is to decide on the most practical means of obtaining responses from those best placed to help. As a starting point for discussions among curriculum evaluators toward the formulation of appropriate evaluation designs, an attempt is made in table 3.4 to outline a schema for this aspect of curriculum evaluation.

It is obvious from table 3.4 that subject-matter specialists and educational psychologists are expected to play key roles in the evaluation exercise. One questionnaire can be developed for all categories of respondents, bearing in mind that the questionnaire should not be too demanding in terms of format and length. *If time is a constraint and if representativeness of views is not too critical a factor, evaluation by panels of experts in face-to-face meeting sessions would be more desirable.*

EVALUATION OF TEACHING-LEARNING STRATEGIES

In the two preceding sections we were concerned with the *wherefore* and *what* of a curriculum program. This section is concerned with the *how* of the program, i.e. the plan to bring about interactions between pupils and the content of instruction by means of a series of teaching-learning strategies and sets of instructional materials. (Issues concerning the evaluation of instructional materials are discussed in the following section.)

Teaching-learning strategies imply more than just the techniques of teaching to be adopted by teachers. The term "teaching-learning strategies" is defined here as being the means to bring about changes in pupil behavior through the use of some structured processes involving the use of instructional materials. Thus, for example, a teaching-learning strategy may include, inter alia, self-instructional programmed educational material, the splitting-up of the class into small working groups, or the systematic provision of corrective learning material for those who failed a diagnostic or formative test. Within the context of curriculum development, a teaching-learning strategy includes:

Table 3.4. **Outline of an Evaluation Design for the Evaluation of Content of Instruction**

Criteria	Category of Respondent	Possible Evaluation Instrument	Responses Sought
Relevance to objectives	Curriculum specialists Subject-matter specialists Experienced teachers	Questionnaire, with structured responses	Yes/No responses
Up-to-dateness	Subject-matter specialists	Questionnaire, with content topics itemized	Yes/No + free responses and corrections
Relevance to the child and his environment	Educational psychologists Teacher-educators Experienced teachers	Analysis proforma, with ratings on relevance	Ratings on relevance; comments on weak areas, alternative suggestions
Content balance	Subject-matter specialists Educational psychologists Curriculum specialists Experienced teachers	Questionnaire: setting out areas of knowledge, attitudes, and skill components and related pupil activities	Yes/No responses; with allowances for comments and suggestions
Organizational structure of content	As in section above	As in section above	As in section above

1. Principles for structuring teacher activities and corresponding pupils' activities
2. Instructional materials for use by teachers and/or pupils, e.g., textbooks, work sheets, self-instructional materials, actual environmental phenomena

In some curriculum development projects it may not be necessary to make any explicit suggestion regarding the kinds of strategies to be used because teachers are given a free hand to adopt whatever strategies they consider effective. This is particularly true when teachers are well-trained and experienced, and no new or innovative teaching procedures are called for in the implementation of the new or revised program.

Curriculum programs that aim at introducing new teaching-learning strategies require careful planning both at the tryout and implementation stages. New teaching techniques, which are unfamiliar to practicing teachers, require teachers to acquire a new set of professional skills and, in some instances, the redesigning of physical structures and facilities. For example, teaching-learning strategies in science often require teachers and pupils to spend much time in science laboratories and to use a variety of equipment. In all cases one should examine the possibility of adapting existing facilities to the requirements of the new program. It is very easy for enthusiastic curriculum developers to climb on the bandwagon of new educational approaches without giving due consideration to their implementability in the existing school framework.

The planning of a set of teaching-learning strategies for a curriculum program is normally done by a team. They study and review strategies that have been found effective in similar situations by teachers or educational innovators. Such a team may develop entirely new strategies that have not been tested before in actual classroom situations. It is necessary that such innovative programs be tried out before they are recommended to teachers.

The Integrated Primary Curriculum Project of the Malaysian Curriculum Development Centre is an example. The project is concerned with the development of a three-year integrated curriculum beginning with grade 1. Before attempting to organize a curriculum content that would remove rigid subject demarcations, the project proceeds to experiment with a small group of teachers in six elementary schools, to find ways to integrate the teaching of languages and social studies using the existing content of instruction. Following the classroom experimentation involving curriculum developers and classroom teachers, decisions will be made regarding the organization of content and the teaching-learning strategies to be recommended for use in the new curricular program.

There appears to be no standard procedure by which a curriculum team identifies, devises, or adopts and eventually recommends a set of teaching-learning strategies. The problem before the curriculum evaluators is when, where, and how to evaluate the planned strategies. Obviously, decision making based on views about a set of strategies planned on paper is unlikely to be very reliable as to the economy and efficiency of such strategies in achieving the course objectives. Some suggestions on evaluation procedures are made later in this section.

Evaluation Criteria

The following set of criteria may be adopted for the evaluation of a teaching-learning strategy:

Effectiveness and Economy

Effectiveness and economy in achieving the planned learning outcomes. The real test of the effectiveness of a strategy is obviously possible only when it has been used in an actual teaching-learning situation. At the planning stage, one can seek experts' and practitioners' judgments of the relative effectiveness of strategies. Research and experimental findings are also useful in helping curriculum developers and evaluators to make some form of judgment regarding the effectiveness of a strategy. Related to the effectiveness of a strategy is economy—economy in terms of time taken to carry out a learning process and the resources needed to back up the learning process. For example, in a chemistry program one may feel that the discovery approach to learning is an effective learning process, but one has to be realistic in terms of the time, laboratory space, and equipment available for pupils to find their way to discovering a chemistry principle. In terms of the range of instructional materials required for pupil learning, evaluation can provide additional opinions on what is desirable and adequate.

Research and experimental findings as well as teachers' own experiences have indicated that a teaching-learning strategy that has a high degree of active pupil participation in learning is more likely to be effective. Thus a strategy may be analyzed in terms of teacher and pupil behavior. Some strategies are dominated by teacher behavior—the teacher-directed or teacher-centered approach—others may emphasize pupil self-direction in learning. In the evaluation of teaching-learning strategies, it would be desirable to analyze and subsequently judge which strategy would be appropriate for what pupil learning outcomes and what emphasis should be given to the roles of teachers and pupils in the learning process.

Feasibility in Classroom

In evaluating the feasibility of a strategy in an actual school situation, one needs to analyze the demands of the strategy in terms of the constraints existing in schools. Time available for the new course within the total school curriculum; physical facilities such as classrooms, laboratories, workshops, and equipment are points to be considered. Teaching-learning strategies in social studies, for example, suggest a combination of classroom activities and pupil participation in community activities that may be unrealistic if time and the relationship existing between school and community do not permit such an approach. Evaluation should be able to identify the constraints and suggest applicable strategies. If time and physical facilities are identified as major constraints for the discovery approach to learning, evaluation may be able to suggest substituting a higher degree of guided discovery learning or a combination of discovery and reception learning.

Teacher Competence

When new and innovative approaches to teaching are planned for in a curriculum program, evaluation of teacher perception and readiness (attitude and professional competences) to adopt and carry out the strategies is crucial to the success of the program. A realistic assessment of the requirement of the planned teaching-learning strategies in terms of what the teachers perceive as their capabilities to carry out the strategies is important and should be carried out at the planning stage. Teacher retraining programs should be an integral part of the curriculum development process at the planning stage. Therefore, preliminary evaluation of actual teacher competence is required in order to plan them.

Evaluation Procedures

Curriculum evaluators together with curriculum developers may conduct in-house analysis and discussions of the planned strategies and also conduct tryouts of the innovative strategies in experimental laboratories using procedures such as micro-teaching or simulation techniques of other types. One disadvantage of in-house analysis and simulation is that the teaching-learning situation is somewhat artificial.

Limited experimentation of the planned strategy in the actual classroom situation at the planning stage and in the presence of curriculum evaluators would supply additional data on its applicability and practicability as well as its effectiveness. For such experimentation or limited tryout to be meaningful, curriculum evaluators would have to keep precise records of each phase of the strategy as it is being enacted. Evaluation instruments, such as pupil achievement tests for the subunit under tryout, pupil interest inventory, schedules for classroom observations, and teacher perception questionnaires, would be useful. Unless the "bugs" are identified and removed early at the planning stage and the strategies revised accordingly, there is a likelihood that the program might eventually prove too difficult for implementation; such a program may later require major revisions following tryout or pilot trials.

Table 3.5. **Possible Procedures for the Evaluation of Teaching-learning Strategies**

Procedure / Criteria	In-house Analysis	Experts' Panel	Simulation at Center	Limited Tryout in Schools
Effectiveness and economy	X	X	X	X
Feasibility	X	X	X	X
Teacher competence	X	X		

It must be pointed out here that the tryout suggested above is different in design and scope from the tryout of the completed program discussed in the following chapter. The purpose of the suggested tryout is to obtain additional data for the improvement of planning. In fact, too many tryout activities of this type at the planning stage may seriously slow down program development activities. Tryout of teaching-learning strategies in actual classrooms at the planning stage is desirable only if in-house simulation data and judgments by competent evaluators are considered inadequate to make decisions on the effectiveness, suitability, and practicability of the planned strategies. Usually, data collected from consultations with experienced teachers and competent evaluators would provide adequate support for including innovative teaching-learning strategies in the first draft of a program. The choices open to curriculum evaluators in designing evaluation procedures are summarized in table 3.5.

EVALUATION OF INSTRUCTIONAL MATERIALS

Instructional materials prepared at the planning stage of curriculum development come in many forms and media. Textbooks, workbooks, self-instructional materials, supplementary readers, ETV programs, slides and filmstrips, prerecorded tapes, and kits are but a few of these. Depending on the course objectives, course content, teaching-learning strategies, as well as the competent personnel for materials production and the financial resources available, each curriculum project would determine what materials are to be planned and developed, and in what form.

Assuming that some forms of instructional materials have been developed, evaluation at the planning stage should be concerned with gathering data that would identify a given set of instructional materials as "good" or "bad," "effective" or "ineffective," in pupil learning. Time and resources must not subsequently be spent on materials that are unlikely to have any real educational value. The constraint of materials evaluation at the planning stage is similar to that of teaching-learning strategy evaluation, which means that valid evidence about its adequacy can be obtained only later, at the tryout stage.

Evaluation Criteria

Materials evaluation at the planning stage should be concerned with both the pedagogical and practical characteristics of the materials being developed, viz.:

A. *Instructional Characteristics*
   1. Contents related to instructional objectives
   2. Contents valid and reliable
   3. Contents logically organized
   4. Contents psychologically relevant—conformity to the principles of learning and developmental stages of pupils, interesting, and self-motivating
   5. Accuracy and suitability of language used, and suitable and appropriate illustrations
   6. Appropriately sequenced learning tasks
   7. Reinforcing to pupils, allowing for immediate feedback and appropriate practice
   8. Ensuring the development of understanding and critical thinking
   9. Providing preferably multisensory-stimulation approach
   10. Transfer value
B. *Practical Characteristics*
   1. Cost range—to allow dissemination of the program throughout the total system
   2. Flexibility to adapt the programs to a variety of teaching-learning conditions
   3. Durability
   4. Easiness to use—appropriate size of unit for manipulative materials, no excessive demands on the motor coordination of young children

5. Attractiveness—proper use of color proportions, quality of finish
6. Adequate guide/instructions to teachers for maximizing use of the materials
7. Easy replacement of parts that are lost, torn, broken, or soiled by use

The above lists of criteria are not exhaustive nor in any order of importance. Some criteria can be further refined or subdivided into sub-criteria, depending on the actual type and form of materials produced. As an example, below are sections of a questionnaire used in India to collect teachers' opinions about instructional material (Rastogi 1970).

Questionnaire for the Teachers for Evaluation of
Textbooks in Mother Tongue
A. Academic Aspects
Selection and gradation of the content:
1. Ideational content
Are the themes included in the book in conformity with the instructional objectives of this grade?   Yes/No
Do you think there is sufficient variety of themes in the book?   Yes/No
Does it present characters and situations with whom the child can identify himself?   Yes/No
Does it satisfy the needs and interests of the children?   Yes/No
Does it suit the general intellectual level of the children of the class?   Yes/No
Does it possess the variety of concepts?   Yes/No
Are the concepts and values given in the book in conformity with national goals?   Yes/No
Have these values been presented through the experiences of the children?   Yes/No
Does it complement or supplement the topics covered in the textbooks of other subjects?   Yes/No
Is there unnecessary duplication of content of other subjects in the language textbooks?   Yes/No
Is the time adequate for the completion of the textbook?   Yes/No
2. Linguistic content

Is the vocabulary in conformity with the instructional objectives?   Yes/No

Is the vocabulary controlled? (in classes 1, 2)   Yes/No

Do you feel that the vocabulary used is rich enough to fulfill different instructional objectives?   Yes/No

3. Presentation of content
   a. Exercises
      Are there some exercises that help in diagnosing the weaknesses of the children?   Yes/No

      Are the activities suggested in the book practicable?   Yes/No

      Are the activities suitable to the children of this age group?   Yes/No

      Does the child feel involved in solving the exercises?   Yes/No

      Are the questions suitable to the mental maturity level of this age group?   Yes/No

   b. Illustrations
      Do they contribute to the development of aesthetic sense in the child?   Yes/No

      Do the illustrations attract the children?   Yes/No

      Do the illustrations assist the recognition of concepts and thus motivate the children?   Yes/No

   c. Physical aspects
      Is the type size suitable to the children?   Yes/No

      Is the layout of the book appropriate for the children?   Yes/No

      Is the design of the book attractive?   Yes/No

      Is the binding of the book durable?   Yes/No

Who Should Evaluate?

There are many persons from whom we can seek views and advice. *Subject-matter experts* from within the curriculum development institution, the teaching profession, and, possibly, institutions of higher learning can be approached to comment and advise on the authenticity, accuracy and up-to-dateness of the content. Their views on the logical structure of the content and its organization would also be helpful.

Views of *curriculum specialists* are desirable for evaluating the relatedness of the materials to instructional objectives, the appropriateness of the organization of the materials, their adaptability to a variety of teaching-learning situations, the grading and articulation of the contents of instruction.

Experienced teachers, who are the potential users of the materials, are in many instances the best judges of their appropriateness for the target population, their adaptability to various teaching-learning situations, the time required to master the materials, and pupil interest in them.

Judgment needs to be sought from *educational psychologists* on whether the materials are congruent with the developmental characteristics of pupils, conform with principles of learning, contain appropriately sequenced learning tasks, are reinforcing the learners, and allow for transfer of learning.

Materials production experts, a category in which we may include educational media technologists; graphic artists; printers; production engineers in wood, metal, plastic, and so on. Their views on the practical characteristics of the instructional materials—e.g., cost range, durability, reproducibility, attractiveness—are important aspects of evaluation.

Very often in evaluation the opinion of the *prospective user of the programs* is not considered. Questions related to interest in or to the easy manipulation of the materials are best answered when the new materials are exposed to the pupils concerned. Involvement of pupils at the planning stage of materials development is a worthwhile consideration. The value of pupils' reactions to the instructional materials cannot be overemphasized at this stage.

Evaluation Procedures

In the evaluation of instructional materials, more detailed and specific data are expected to be collected than in the evaluation of instructional objectives and content of instruction, mainly because instructional materials are, by their very nature, specific and elaborated forms of overall curriculum objectives. Consequently one has to be careful in structuring evaluation procedures. An effort should be made not to impose on the respondents an unduly heavy burden. For example, one should avoid long questionnaires. Thus a neat, type-set, easy-to-read and easy-to-look-at instrument that can be quickly sized up by the respondent is more likely to be completed and returned. Similarly, provision should be made to ensure sufficient time for the evaluators to examine the material thoroughly.

Evaluation procedures that can be adopted generally fall into the following categories:

Panel Evaluation

Evaluation panel meetings and discussions can be either by a specific category of experts, e.g., subject specialists or teachers, or by a mixed panel of experts. A mixed panel is sometimes preferable as it would be possible to evaluate all aspects of the materials simultaneously. The panel meeting of experts, as an evaluation procedure, has the advantage of making it possible to decide on the spot the nature and extent of revisions that have to be made to the materials. The problem is one of getting the relevant experts together at the same time and of ensuring that the evaluation is not done superficially.

Evaluation by Mail

Evaluation procedures using check lists, questionnaires, and analysis proforma through the mail have the advantage of reaching a large group of respondents; if desired, one may design an evaluation instrument to seek a fair representation of views. The problem is in designing an instrument and a procedure that will have a high rate of returns and that will be easily collated and analyzed.

Users' Reactions

One may be tempted to argue here that the evaluation of the actual usage of instructional materials is best left till the tryout stage of curriculum development. On the other hand, it would be foolish to go ahead with designing elaborate teaching kits without having some preliminary test of the educational value and feasibility of sample kits in actual learning situations before further commitment is made to package similar kits for other units of the program. While it may be difficult to submit each bit of a new program to empirical tryout at the early stage of planning, the curriculum team may identify some more or less representative parts of the total program that can be tried out before the whole draft of a particular unit has been produced.

Task Analysis

This procedure involves the detailed analysis of the hierarchical structure of a task to be taught by the unit. The task may be a routine arithmetical operation, the comprehension of a concept, the application of a principle for solving a particular problem. Task analysis specifies the sequence of particular activities, operations, and the like needed to perform a given task. An example of task analysis is presented in figure 3.1 (Levin 1971).

The task analysis of instructional material enables us to see whether all the requirements for dealing with a certain task are properly presented and sequenced in the unit. Examples of task analysis carried out on program plans are presented by Gagné (1970). Yoloye carried out task analysis of instructional material for the purpose of verifying the adequacy of its hierarchical structure (Yoloye 1971).

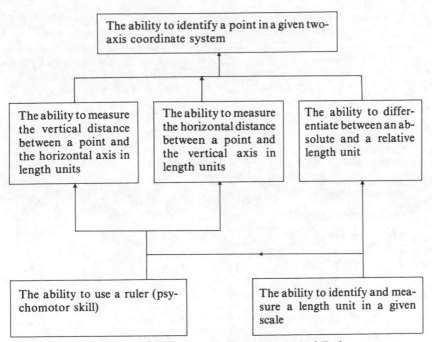

Figure 3.1. *Hierarchical Structure of a Mathematical Task*

To facilitate curriculum evaluators' initiation to discussions on the design of evaluation procedures, table 3.6 (page 82) summarizes the possible areas of evaluation concern by category of "evaluators."

EPILOGUE

Ideally, curriculum planning should be a cooperative venture among educators, curriculum specialists, educational psychologists and sociologists, subject-matter experts, experienced teachers, and even pupils. In reality, certain types of experts often do not participate in the development of the program.

Curriculum plans and materials undergo a series of revisions before they are "passed" for use in schools. Evaluation activities at these stages may be hindered by the demand of administrative bodies to hasten development activities. Thus curriculum developers may find it difficult to pause and evaluate their efforts because they are under considerable pressure to proceed with the job in order to get the program off the ground.

Table 3.6. **Possible Areas of Evaluation Concern by Category of "Evaluators"**

Criteria \ Evaluators	Subject-matter Experts	Curriculum Specialists	Experienced Teachers	Educational Psychologists	Material Production Experts	Pupils
Instructional Characteristics						
Contents related to objectives	X	X	X	X		
Contents' validity and reliability	X					
Logical organization	X	X				
Psychologically relevant		X	X	X		
Accuracy and suitability of language		X	X	X		X
Hierarchical structure and sequence of learning tasks		X	X	X		
Reinforcing to pupils		X	X	X		X
Understanding and critical thinking	X	X	X	X		X
Multisensory approach		X	X	X		X
Transfer value	X	X	X	X		
Practical Characteristics						
Cost range					X	
Adaptability	X	X	X			
Durability		X			X	X
Easy to use		X			X	X
Attractiveness		X			X	X
Adequate guides	X	X				
Replaceability		X			X	

On the other hand, the planning stage is a crucial one in the curriculum development process. Unless the planning has been done well, the waste of time and of human and financial resources at a later stage can be considerable. Evaluation at the planning stage does not unduly prolong the time needed for program development, and some additional time devoted to evaluation at this stage may considerably reduce the time needed to accomplish various tasks at later stages of the program's life cycle.

This chapter has attempted to address itself to the tasks of evaluating four activities in curriculum planning. For each activity, an attempt has been made to initiate discussions among curriculum developers and evaluators in the why, what, and how of evaluation for that activity. No attempt has been made to discuss in detail the instrumentation of evaluation since this aspect is dealt with in other chapters.

This chapter is not complete in the sense that other legitimate activities at the planning stage, such as planning for the implementation of the program, planning for the packaging and dissemination of the program, and planning teacher retraining, have not been dealt with. This chapter can be considered to have achieved its objectives if curriculum developers and evaluators are convinced that evaluation at the planning stage is both important and feasible, and if they are motivated to formulate their own evaluation plans and procedures along the lines of these and other legitimate activities in curriculum planning.

REFERENCES

Bloom, B. S. *Taxonomy of Educational Objectives: Cognitive Domain.* New York: McKay, 1956.

Chew Tow Yow. *Integrated Primary Curriculum Project.* Kuala Lumpur: Curriculum Development Centre, Ministry of Education, 1973.

Gagné, Robert. *The Conditions of Learning.* 2nd ed. New York: Holt, Rinehart & Winston, 1970.

Levin, Tamar. "Development and Validation of a Learning Hierarchy for a Mathematical Task." Master's thesis, Tel-Aviv University, 1971.

Rastogi, K. G. et al. *Preparation and Evaluation of Textbooks in Mother Tongue.* New Delhi: National Council of Educational Research and Training, 1970.

Yoloye, E. A. "Evaluation for Innovation." Educational Development Center, Newton, Mass., 1971. Mimeographed.

4

Tryout and Revision of Educational Materials and Methods

The tryout and revision stage should occur when a curriculum center or project has produced some curriculum materials, instructional methods, instructional tryout equipment, or learning materials that are ready for trying out in a small number of classes or schools. It is assumed that a curriculum team has previously developed a curriculum or instructional plan (which has gone through some feedback, evaluation, or other procedures) that the curriculum group regards as workable. Having adopted this plan, members of the curriculum team have prepared some materials, methods, equipment, and so forth that it now believes are appropriate to the plan but that need a tryout under actual school conditions before being accepted or revised.

Although the curriculum teams have put their best effort into the preparation of the materials, they are not entirely certain that they are appropriate for a given group of students or are they entirely confident that they will produce the kinds of changes in students called for by the objectives specified in the curriculum plan. They may also be uncertain that teachers can actually use the materials in the ways they believe they

This chapter was written by Benjamin S. Bloom.

should be used for instructional purposes. In short, they have produced curriculum materials and/or instructional methods that are ready for formative evaluation. That is, they are ready for evaluation feedback, which will help them revise the materials where they are in need of modification and which will inform them of that portion of the materials or procedures that works well and should be retained with little or no revision other than minor editing or putting into a form for later large-scale use and evaluation in a representative sample of the target population.

"Formative evaluation," as we use the term, refers to the gathering of evidence during the processes of forming or developing parts of the curriculum. Here the task of evaluation is to determine what kinds of evidence can be used by members of the curriculum team to determine the adequacy of the materials in general as well as the kinds of evidence that can be used to determine in some detail what needs to be revised as well as why and where the revision is needed. Merely to know that the materials or methods need to be revised is of little value to members of the curriculum team. They need to know precisely what needs to be revised and why the revision is necessary—otherwise they may change what works well and fail to change or modify what works less well.

Ideally, the curriculum team includes at least one member who has some training and competence in evaluation. This curriculum worker should be clearly aware of the overall curriculum plan (and the learning objectives), should be a cooperating member of the team in that he knows the ways the team has been working, and should identify with the curriculum team. He should be as interested in having the materials work well as are the other members of the curriculum group. The main point is that he is a sympathetic coworker in the group rather than an adversary who is out to prove that the work to date is not good. He is sympathetic in that he is attempting to secure evidence that will help other members of the group produce excellent materials for use by the appropriate teachers and students.

TYPES OF EVIDENCE

As we view the types of evidence being used at this stage of the curriculum development process in curriculum centers throughout the world, we find them to be of three major types. One type of evidence involves *judgmental data* in that experts, teachers, supervisors, as well as students (who have made use of the curriculum materials and methods) provide opinions, judgments, and reactions to the curriculum materials. This type of evidence is gathered by ratings, questionnaires, interviews, and forms as well as by answering questions or other more open responses by the appropriate persons who react to the materials or methods under conditions that make the best use of each type of specialist. The primary problem in gathering this type of evidence is to determine the appropriate specialist for each type of response or judgment.

One advantage of judgmental data is that it can be gathered with a minimum of difficulty and time. If it is gathered well and analyzed properly it can reveal strengths of the materials as well as weaknesses in sufficient detail to permit the curriculum developers to use the evidence quickly. A major source of difficulty is that some specialists may have particular biases and attitudinal sets toward new approaches that may be more negative than may be desirable. For this reason, some curriculum centers insist on additional types of evidence, which may confirm or deny the evidence gathered on judgmental and opinion data.

A second type of evidence involves *observational data* in that trained or untrained observers systematically observe teaching-learning situations in the classroom or elsewhere and report their observations. This type of evidence is obtained by recording direct observations in a free manner, by structured observations making use of particular teacher-student-material interactions, by rating or questionnaire forms, and even by judgments about opportunities to develop particular kinds of concepts, skills, abilities, interests, attitudes, and the like in particular learning situations.

Observational data of this kind are relatively costly to obtain in that they require one or more observers to secure reliable and relatively consistent observations over some time period. Nevertheless, an important advantage of observational data is that, under appropriate conditions, they permit the teaching-learning process to go on without serious disturbance while the data are being collected.

Observational data may constitute a vital set of data to be related to the judgmental data to support or oppose each other, to add a different dimension to the judgmental data, as well as to find solutions to some of the problems that emerge from both types of data. That is, the concurrent validity of the two types of evidence as well as the supplementary or additive qualities of the two types of evidence may be determined by various ways of relating the combined evidence.

A third type of evidence more nearly approaches the central problems of curriculum development: What kinds of student learning take place when the curriculum materials and methods are used properly? Here the key evidence has to do with student learning that takes place in relation to curriculum. While this may be determined by observations of students, by interviews of students, and by student reports, in most curriculum centers it involves the use of *structured or semistructured test questions, scales, oral examinations,* or other procedures of determining what students can do, as well as how they feel in relation to particular kinds of learning relevant to the curriculum. This requires that particular instruments or procedures be constructed that are appropriate to the kinds of learning intended by the curriculum materials and that evidence be gathered on student responses to these instruments and procedures.

One advantage of this type of evidence is that it is the most direct evidence of the effectiveness of the curriculum materials and methods. Therefore, it can serve to support or deny the evidence already collected. Although it is sometimes difficult to secure this evidence, it is essentially the strongest evidence a curriculum center can obtain about its products and procedures. This, however, entails problems of how the evidence can be procured so as to provide information of value to the curriculum development for determining what works well in the classroom and what is in need of further modification.

While evidence on positive aspects of student learning is strong evidence when it can be secured, evidence on negative aspects of student learning rarely by itself indicates *why* it works poorly. That is, the evidence can indicate what is learned well or what is learned poorly, but usually this evidence does not indicate, by itself, why this is so or exactly what needs to be done to improve it. For supporting evidence on why it behaves as it does or what needs to be done to change it, curriculum teams typically must turn to the *judgmental evidence* and/or *observational evidence.* Thus, under most conditions of curriculum development, tryout and revisions of curriculum material and methods must depend on the linkages between the three kinds of evidence—*judgmental, observational,* and *student learning.* The next three sections of this chapter discuss and illustrate the problems, procedures, sampling methods, and data analysis techniques for utilizing each type of evidence at the *tryout and revision stage of the curriculum development process.* Each method is further discussed and illustrated in detail in chapters 8, 9, and 10.

Preliminary judgment of curriculum material is usually done at the stage of program planning. Typically such judgment relates the curriculum plan to particular curriculum materials produced by the team. Such judgments usually determine which objectives and specifications of the plan are embodied in the curriculum materials. In addition, experts may be asked to predict how effective they believe the materials will be under school conditions.

At the tryout stage, expert judgments are largely to determine the experience the experts have had with the materials under school conditions. Thus, the major focus at the tryout stage is in obtaining judgments from teachers, supervisors, and students who have participated in the teaching-learning situation with the new learning materials. If judgments of new materials by subject-matter experts have not been conducted at the planning stage, it is still possible to collect and use such judgments at the tryout stage. This may be especially useful at the tryout stage because more of the materials have been developed and because these judgments help to explain why some material works well while other material is less effective in actual classroom use.

Judgmental Evidence

Judgmental evidence may vary from detailed judgments by well-qualified and trained specialists to simpler reactions, observations, and opinions from students as well as parents and citizens. In each case the person making the judgment does so with regard to curriculum materials, equipment, procedures, or some other product of a curriculum team. This may include textbooks; workbooks; concrete curriculum materials; procedures and such audiovisual material as films, radio, and sound recordings; or TV materials. It may also include programmed instructional materials, learning games, as well as student interactions of many kinds. What we are saying here is that instructional materials, instructional processes, as well as learning processes, when put into some form for educational purposes, can be subjected to judgmental processes.

The judgments are intended to provide specific help to the curriculum team in identifying aspects of the curriculum materials and procedures that are likely to be effective as well as those that are in need of modification. Members of the curriculum team should find these judgments, reactions, suggestions, and opinions of great value (especially when they are related to other kinds of evidence) in supporting the work that has already been done, in indicating *what* needs to be modified, as well as *why* and *how* the modification can improve the curriculum materials and procedures.

A major problem in the use of judgmental evidence is the determination of the kind of expertise or specialization needed and the kinds of questions or problems for which each type of expert or specialist can provide useful judgments, observations, and reactions or suggestions. Thus, a Nobel Prize winner in physics may be an expert on the nature and structure of the subject of physics, but he may have little competence in making judgments about what a sixteen-year-old student can learn about physics. Similarly, a teacher of science at the secondary level may have much experience with the capabilities of students at this level in one type of school but may have little expertise to offer on the capabilities for learning science of students in other schools or regions of the country.

There are no clear rules for identifying experts or specialists or for determining the exact problems or questions on which they can express sound judgments. In general, the broader the experience and training, the greater the range of problems on which they can offer useful judgments and opinions. Many curriculum centers attempt to identify the experts by some nomination procedure, with some subsequent attempt to arrive at a consensus about which persons to select finally for a given type of curriculum problem judgment. In most nations it is possible to secure the interest and efforts of almost any person nominated for a particular judgment role in curriculum development. This is so because of the widespread recognition of the importance of education and the fundamental role of curriculum in determining the quality of education in a specific country. If the amount of time or work required to make the judgments is a limited one, most persons invited to participate in the process are likely to play their proper role in it.

With regard to the proper questions or problems on which judgments can be made by each *kind* of expert, there are no clear rules. The following paragraphs suggest some kinds of questions or problems on which judgments can be made by particular kinds of experts. Here we are thinking about groups or classes of experts. In fact, a particular person may be an expert in many areas; such a person could, in principle, respond to problems in a number of areas.

Experts in a Particular Subject or Area

Curriculum teams generally are composed of persons who are expert in a particular part of the curriculum—whether that part be regarded as a *subject field* (science, mathematics, language, etc.), a particular *level of education* (primary, secondary, etc.), or a particular *broad field* (industrial arts, physical development, adolescent development, etc.) within the curriculum. Members of the curriculum team may be regarded as experts for judgmental evidence, especially when the materials to be judged have been produced by other members of the team.

In addition to members of the curriculum team, there are other experts in the subject or field for which the curriculum material and methods are being produced. These may be university scholars in the field, faculty members in the teacher-training institutions, or specialists in industry and the community who have special training and experience in the field.

While practices in the centers differ, a relatively small number of subject-field experts are likely to be needed for particular judgments—something between five and ten appropriate experts may be sufficient.

Some of the types of judgments or questions to which such a group might respond are the following:

A.　From the viewpoint of the subject field or curriculum area, how accurate or correct are the particular curriculum materials?

Are there any errors in the materials from the viewpoint of the field?

How sound is the subject matter with regard to current views of the subject or field?

What suggestions can be made for correcting these errors or inadequacies?

B.　How are the parts of the curriculum materials related to one another?

Do they provide for a sound relation to one another and does the sequence of the parts of the materials appear to be appropriate from the viewpoint of the subject as well as from the viewpoint of the learners?

Are there any proposals for improving the internal relations among the elements and parts of the curriculum material and procedures?

Chapter 8 offers some of the forms, questionnaires, rating sheets, and other instruments for securing expert opinion and judgments. In addition to such instruments, some curriculum centers make use of interviews with experts and record the main points made by the experts. Some centers also gain much of this type of evidence in meetings with groups of experts where individuals may make specific points, but, in addition, the group attempts to arrive at some conclusions about the major points, suggestions, or reactions they have to offer the curriculum team about the curriculum material and the relations between the curriculum materials and the curriculum plan.

Teachers and Supervisors of a Particular Subject or Area

Although we regard teachers and supervisors as experts, they may serve two functions at this stage of the curriculum development. If the teachers and supervisors are regarded as *subject experts,* they would function as do other experts with regard to the kinds of judgments considered at the *planning stage* as well as the tryout stage as described in the previous section. However, if they are regarded as experts in the *teaching* of the subject, they might respond to the kinds of questions emphasized in this section.

Teachers and supervisors may be asked to respond to the questions listed here as experts on the teaching of these materials without actually using the materials with their students. On the other hand, if they actually try to use the curriculum materials under the teaching-learning conditions suggested by the curriculum team, their judgments and suggestions about the materials are of special value to the curriculum team for making particular revisions.

For this stage of the curriculum process, the number of teachers and supervisors responding to the materials alone may vary from as few as 5 or 10 to a very large number such as 50 or 100. It would be desirable to include a representative sample of teachers and if educational conditions vary greatly from place to place, from urban to rural, or for different kinds of schools, a few from each special condition may be necessary. If the curriculum center desires large numbers of teachers and supervisors to get acquainted with the materials, this might be viewed as the proper time to do this. Nevertheless, it should be borne in mind that the curriculum team is seeking judgments primarily to serve for revision purposes (rather than to persuade teachers of the value of the materials), and they should secure those judgments they regard as necessary for this purpose.

Every teacher who participates in the tryout stage of using the materials in the classroom should provide judgmental data on his or her experience with the materials. These judgments should be of great value in revealing strengths and weaknesses in the curriculum materials. Such evidence should also be analyzed for its value in suggesting some of the problems and concerns for the implementation stage and especially for the in-service training of teachers who are expected to use the finally developed curriculum program.

Some of the types of judgments or questions to which teachers and supervisors might respond are the following:

C. Are the materials feasible and practical for use by teachers in the schools?
    Do the teachers need special retraining in order to understand the materials and to teach this part of the curriculum in the way it needs to be taught?
    Are the costs of the materials likely to be too great?
    Are there any suggestions for making it more easily used, less costly, and more practical for teachers and students in the school?

D. Are the explanations and illustrations clear?
Can they be improved for both teachers and students?
What detailed parts are in need of improvement in these respects and what suggestions can be made for making the materials more easy to understand?

E. Are the materials at about the right level of difficulty for the students?
What detailed points were too difficult or too easy?
Which groups of students found it especially difficult and why and where was this true?
Which groups of students found it too easy and what accounted for this?
How might the materials be modified to make them more appropriate in difficulty for the students the teacher usually teaches?

F. Are students likely to find these materials interesting?
Which detailed parts are likely to be most interesting and which parts are likely to be least interesting?
Which groups of students are likely to find these materials of greatest interest and which students are likely to find it lacking interest?
(The same types of questions could be rephrased to make them more appropriate where the teachers have actually *taught* these materials to groups of students.)

G. What special teaching problems are teachers likely to have with these materials?
What special features of the materials account for these teaching problems and what suggestions can be made for solving these teaching problems by teacher training or by changes in the curriculum materials?
How much teaching time is likely to be necessary for these materials?
What changes could be made to reduce the amount of time required?
(Here again the questions could be altered for teachers who have actually used the curriculum materials with their students.)

H. How relevant are these materials to the students' interests, needs, and aspirations?
Are they more relevant for some students than for others and why is this so?
What changes could be made in the materials to make them more relevant for particular groups of students the teacher usually has in class?

I. What overall judgments, views, and suggestions does the teacher have about these materials?

What changes should be made?

J. Are there any judgments about desirable and undesirable changes likely to take place in students other than those specified in the curriculum plan?

Do the materials and the ways in which they are likely to be used change the role of students and teachers, change student attitudes toward the subject, and make demands on students and teachers that may make for new problems and conditions that were not originally foreseen?

In addition to some of the types of forms and techniques found in chapter 11, some curriculum centers find it useful to interview teachers who have used the curriculum materials and to record the problems and suggestions they offer. Other centers ask the teachers to keep a log or a daily diary of these problems, judgments, and suggestions. Sometimes group discussions with teachers at regular intervals are found to be most satisfactory. But in all cases the evaluation process should get as detailed judgments and suggestions as possible on each part of the new curriculum materials or procedures.

Student Opinions, Observations, and Reactions

While we do not necessarily view students as experts on curriculum materials, the students who have tried to learn from the new materials and procedures are very good observers of their own problems and reactions.

Systematic questionnaires, rating sheets, and interviews with small random samples of students are likely to provide very useful evidence to the curriculum team. Especially is this true if the student is asked questions about *his* own interactions with the learning materials and the teaching procedures.

Some types of evidence that might be gathered are suggested in the following questions. (*Note:* The letters in parentheses indicate that these questions were also used in a different way with teachers in the previous section.)

(D) Were the explanations and illustrations clear to you?

Where were they least clear and where were they most clear?

(E) Did you find the materials too easy or too difficult for you?

Why was this true and which parts of the materials were too easy or too difficult?

(F) Did you find the materials interesting?

Which parts of the materials were most interesting or least interesting?

Why was this true for you?

(H) How do these materials relate to the kinds of things you would like to learn?

How do they relate to your further educational plans and aspirations?

What kinds of materials would you prefer to this set of curriculum materials?

Results of the Different Types of Judgments

What the curriculum team needs for the revision of curriculum materials and methods is some way of bringing all the judgments and observations together in relation to each part of the curriculum materials. If the evaluator can find some way of putting into tabular form the judgments, reactions, and observations of the evidence from experts, teachers and supervisors, and students, the curriculum team can quickly note those parts or details that appear to be satisfactory from the point of view of each group as well as the parts or details where there were many negative judgments and suggestions for changes. These kinds of judgments, the source of the judgments, and the suggestions for modification can then be considered as a basis for making the necessary revisions.

When the revisions have been made, it might be desirable to check much the same types of questions with a small sample of each type of expert or student. Where the major negative judgments were about a particular part of the materials or a particular type of problem or question it may be possible to ask the selected experts only about those aspects of the curriculum materials that were changed and only about those questions that were relevant to the change. Some centers make use of a new group of experts and observers and repeat the original process of securing judgmental data to determine whether the new group have more positive views than the previous group. Other centers may use a small group of the original panel of experts to determine whether their original judgments and suggestions about changes were adequately met.

Classroom Observation

When new curriculum methods and materials are utilized in actual teaching-learning situations, much can be gained by observing the interactions between *teachers-students* and *materials, problems, procedures, and so on.* For some of the observations one or more persons may be trained to make the observations that will be of greatest value and relevance for the new curriculum methods and materials.

The training of observers will depend on the complexity of the observations needed, on the sampling procedures that will yield the data in a systematic and reliable form, and the degree of objectivity needed in the observations.

It is assumed that the new materials and methods are being tried out with teachers who have been given the necessary background and training to use them in the ways intended by the curriculum team. It is also assumed that the classes of students are the ones for which the curriculum materials are intended.

The observers may participate in preparing the instruments and procedures they will actually use in their classroom observations. In any case, they should be thoroughly familiar with these instrument and procedures and should engage in one or more pilot studies and then be given additional training and help on using the procedures *before* they participate in gathering usable data in the target classes or classroom situations. We will comment further on the requirements for observational data in relation to some of the types of major questions for which observational data are needed in curriculum evaluation.

1. *Appropriate conditions of instruction and student response* (E, G). A new set of curriculum materials and instructional procedures are unlikely to work well in the classroom if the conditions of instruction and student response are inappropriate. With the new materials and procedures, the curriculum team has usually defined the particular conditions of instruction and student activity that they believe to be necessary. These conditions may be specified in a teacher's guide or they may have been made explicit in the in-service training provided by the curriculum team for the teachers who are to participate in the tryout of the materials.

In the tryout classes it is necessary to secure observations to determine how the curriculum materials and procedures were actually used and the extent to which the uses correspond to the criteria or specifications that the curriculum team regards as necessary. These observations are especially important as a basis for explaining the evidence on student learning (which will be considered later in this chapter). That is, if the materials and procedures are tried out in four to six classes, can the differences in the results in these classes be explained by the differing extent to which teachers and students used the materials in the appropriate ways?

The appropriate conditions may be specified in some detail, and these specifications are then translated into the specific things to observe in the classroom. These may include some of the following: the kinds of explanations given by teachers; the kinds of questions teachers are to raise; the roles students are expected to assume; the kinds of answers and questions students are expected to make; the types of materials, equipment, and observations that teachers and students are expected to use and the ways in which this is to be done; the ways in which students are to be grouped within the class; the types of interactions (including questions and answers) between student-teacher-materials desired; and so forth. Each of these and other conditions must be specified in enough detail so that the observations will be clearly related to the conditions that the curriculum team regards as necessary for the tryouts to be appropriate for an effective use of the curriculum materials and procedures.

These observations may then be made in a sample of the classroom sessions for each of the tryout classes involved. The consistency of the results over several sessions may be used to determine the number of classroom periods that constitutes a sufficient sample of observations for each teacher and class group. By "consistency" we are referring to the extent to which repeated observations yield similar results. For example, if the observation of three sessions of a class yield certain findings, does a fourth or fifth session yield much that is new or different? There are statistical methods (see the concept of reliability in chapter 10) that may be used to determine this. However, the experience of observers may be a better guide—what did they find in the fourth or fifth session that was not already found in the first three sessions? Such subjective reports may be used as a guide to the number of classroom periods generally found to be sufficient for the purpose.

The results of the observations may then be summarized in terms of the extent to which each of the criteria has been met. The same results may be analyzed by one or more judges and a rating scheme used to judge the extent to which each criterion has been met. In addition, particular details may be referred to later in explaining why or where the results on student learning were very good or very poor.

The observer (s) may also note changes in student attitudes, relations, and roles that may suggest unforeseen consequences of the new curriculum materials and instructional methods. Are students developing a great distaste for the subject? Are their affective and cognitive changes not specified in the curriculum plan and objectives?

Where it is regarded as necessary, recordings of the classroom interactions may be made by sound recordings, film records, or TV cameras. It should be pointed out, however, that these records must then be analyzed to determine the extent to which each criterion has been met in the classroom for which such recordings have been made.

It is also possible that the observers may find it unnecessary to record all the observations, where it is evident that all that is needed are brief summaries of the procedures used in a classroom and a series of systematic ratings or judgments by the observer on the criteria set by the curriculum team.

2. *Degree of student attention and involvement* (F). Another kind of observational data that a curriculum team may find useful is the degree to which the new materials and procedures (when used appropriately in the classroom) enlist good attention and involvement from the students. Some excellent data on this may be obtained by observing a sample of students in the classroom to determine the amount of time they appear to be actively attending to the learning activities in the class. This may be done by observing each student at a number of times during a given class to see (and record) whether he is attending or not, or the degree of his attention each time he is observed. This may be viewed as a measure of his *overt* involvement in the classroom activities.

Somewhat more complex is the degree of his active thinking about what is going on in the learning activities of the class. Here it has been found to be feasible to make a sound recording of the class session and then, within a day or two, to play this back to students and ask them to tell (or write) what they were thinking about at different points during the *original* classroom session represented by the recording. This method of stimulated recall (Bloom 1954) has been used to determine the amount of relevant thinking (covert attention) as well as to study the kinds of thinking students do with a new set of curriculum or instructional procedures.

These studies of overt and covert involvement of students may be translated into data about a sample of students (perhaps 10 to 15 students in each class) to determine the percent of time they were actively involved in the learning activities, the points in the new materials when the students were high or low in their involvement, and the characteristics of students that made for high, average, or low involvement. It should be noted that various studies (Bloom 1954, Anderson 1973) find a high degree of relationship between student achievement on a formative or summative measure and their degree of involvement in classroom activities. Also, it is found that materials that students like, find interesting, or is at the proper degree of difficulty secures higher involvement than curriculum materials that are too difficult, too easy, are disliked by students, or that they find to be uninteresting.

Thus measures of involvement (overt and covert attention) may be related to teachers, students, and expert opinion as well as to measures of student learning.

It is also possible to get crude measures of involvement (both overt and covert) by asking students in interviews or questionnaires to describe their attention and types of thinking in the original class in which they participated. These may provide useful measures about the students' own reports of their attention, but it is not likely that these will be as objective and accurate as those made by observers.

The measures of student involvement (perhaps judged as *high, average,* or *low*) should be related to each part of the curriculum materials and/or point in the instructional process. Where possible, these indicators should be related to the teachers' judgments and experts' judgments about the material, to determine where the different kinds of evidence and judgments confirm one another and where they differ. The curriculum team should take these into consideration as they attempt to determine the changes needed in curriculum materials.

3. *Problems posed for teacher training* (C). The observations in a classroom may be as systematic as those described in *A* and *B* of this section, or they may be confined to an observer's judgments and impressions about the difficulties encountered by teachers and students in using the new curriculum materials and procedures.

Either type of evidence may be used to secure observational data or judgments about how well the new materials are used in actual classrooms, the problems that teachers and students have in using the new materials, and the kinds of orientation students need for the new curriculum Finally, these observations, judgments, and inferences may provide valuable leads to determining what kinds of in-service (or pre-service) training teachers will need if they are to use the new materials properly. It may be that this information (and the expert and teacher judgments reported earlier) can suggest modifications in the curriculum to reduce the training period or suggest ways in which the training of teachers may be vastly improved. This is especially needed before the new curriculum can be implemented in the many classrooms and schools for which it is intended.

While we have suggested some ways in which observational data have been or can be used in curriculum evaluation, much more detail and suggestions for observational methods are found in chapter 9.

Student Learning

As pointed out at the beginning of this chapter, the most critical evidence on a new curriculum is the extent to which it leads to appropriate kinds of learning by the students. The learning may be cognitive or affective and may also include particular social and psychomotor skills and other kinds of learning.

When a new unit of curriculum materials or procedures has been developed, it is possible for one or more independent judges who are familiar with the materials to determine what kinds of learning are likely to be expected from this new curriculum unit. The detailed new terms, facts, rules and concepts, applications and inferences students are expected to develop from the new unit may be listed (see Bloom et al. 1971: chap. 6 for detailed procedures). It has been found that two independent judges— after a brief training period—can agree about 90 percent of the time on the kinds of learning expected of the new material. If the judges are asked to determine the hierarchical and sequential relationship among the detailed learnings, they can do this with about 85 percent agreement.

These detailed analyses of a new curriculum unit can furnish the test specifications for a formative cognitive test on the new unit. This set of specifications also yields an analysis of the learning expectations for a unit that may be compared with the original set of objectives for the unit in the curriculum plan or with the curriculum team's intended objectives for the unit. This comparison of independent specifications is useful for making the curriculum team aware of different views about the same curriculum materials and may alert them to some of the problems they may attempt to take care of when they revise the first draft of the new curriculum unit.

The same analysis provides the specifications for the construction of a *criterion-referenced* formative test over the same unit. In the formative test, the test makers attempt to construct a brief test (under 30 minutes in length) that will include the important terms, facts, rules and concepts, applications and inferences that students should be able to know or make if they have learned the new curriculum unit well (Bloom et al. 1971). (The construction of such criterion-referenced tests is also described in chapter 10.)

It is anticipated that each tryout class of students would take the formative test at the end of each unit of learning in the new curriculum. While centers differ, results on about six carefully selected classes are likely to be sufficient for the first tryout stage. Where a more extensive tryout is warranted, one might expect the analysis of the data to be limited to about a dozen carefully selected classes. It should be remembered that the tryout stage is useful for making detailed revisions in the curriculum materials. Too few classes may provide insufficient or unreliable data for this purpose. On the other hand, to make the tryout too extensive in terms of number of classes may be so costly in terms of amount of data processing and time required to collect and analyze data as to delay the revision procedures unduly. A small number of carefully selected classes with well-trained teachers is the ideal tryout condition for student-learning evidence.

After students have had a chance to learn the new curriculum unit, the results of their performance over the formative test may be analyzed to determine what they have learned well or poorly. This analysis may be done for each tryout class and for each subgroup of students in the tryout classes.

The analyses may show the scores made on the tests, the variation and central tendency, the performance on each item in the test, the kinds of errors made by the students, and the relation of the hierarchy and sequence in the unit to the errors and difficulty level of each test item or pattern of test items. These kinds of data may be used by the curriculum team to determine where particular changes are needed and where the new materials and procedures are working well. If major changes are made, the revised curriculum materials may be tried again with students and teachers to determine whether the changes in the materials have led to more effective learning than was the case before the revision.

It is of course important that the curriculum team attempt to relate the formative test results to the judgments of the teachers and the expert group as well as to the classroom observational records.

In addition to the cognitive and psychomotor tests where appropriate, it is important that the interests, attitudes, and other affective characteristics that students are expected to develop be evaluated at the tryout stages. Some of these may develop more slowly than the cognitive and psychomotor objectives and so may be sampled less frequently in the tryout period.

Finally, it is important that the curriculum center and the curriculum team set clear standards in advance, not only as to the learning objectives and criteria on which the new curriculum units will be judged, but also the level at which these objectives and criteria might be expected to be performed.

Thus, for the formative tests it may be decided that a curriculum unit is satisfactory if the tryout group of students gets at least 70 percent correct on each unit. If much less than this is found, then the unit should be revised where the results indicate this is necessary.

One might expect that if students find this interesting—perhaps 60 percent of students have a positive view of the materials and find them an interesting subject—this is satisfactory. Here again, changes may be made if the student results are below this level.

Table 4.1. Curriculum Criteria and Types of Evidence Needed

Issues Being Considered	Judgmental Evidence				Observations in the Classroom	Student Learning
	Subject Experts	Other Specialists	Teachers and Supervisors	Students		
A. Accuracy and soundness of materials	X	X				
B. Internal structure and sequence	X	X	X			Criterion-referenced formative tests
C. Feasibility, cost and practicality	X	X	X		Problems posed for teacher training	
D. Clarity and meaningfulness	X	X	X	X		What has been learned well? Overall effectiveness
E. Level of difficulty	X	X	X	X	Student responses	
F. Interest value for students	X	X	X	X	Student attention and involvement	Interest and attitude questionnaires and scales
G. Special teaching problems	X	X	X		Conditions of instruction	What needs to be revised?
H. Relevance to students' needs and aspirations	X	X	X	X		
I. Overall reactions to materials	X	X	X			
J. Unintended learning and effects	X	X	X		General and specific comments by observers	

So each of the criteria we have proposed throughout this chapter may be put into a standard and the new unit be judged in terms of its success in meeting these standards and criteria. It may take some research and experimentation by a curriculum center before it can establish both the *criteria* and the *standards* for judging each new curriculum unit and program devised by the curriculum center.

Finally, it is important that the curriculum team attempt to relate the formative test results to the judgments of the teachers, students, and expert group as well as to the classroom observational records. Table 4.1 summarizes the different criteria as well as the different kinds of evidence. However, each curriculum center and, in fact, each curriculum team must find ways of studying its own curriculum material on the basis of each type of evidence and then determine where changes are needed and where the materials are effective in meeting the different criteria.

DATA ANALYSES

Most of the judgmental evidence has to do with the curriculum materials. For some judgments the evidence has to do with the entire unit, and the data must be summarized to show the source of the evidence as well as the criteria to which they refer. In many cases, the specific judgments and comments may be retained in their original form for use by the curriculum team. In other cases, simple counts of favorable and unfavorable views may be what is needed.

Where the judgments have to do with particular details of the materials, frequency counts of appropriate criteria may be summarized for each subpart of the curriculum materials. Where the number of experts and judgments used is relatively small, here again the original judgments and observations may be provided for the curriculum team.

Much of the observations may be summarized for each class at each session and the results shown for the particular curriculum unit. Others of the student responses, attention, and involvement may be relevant to particular parts of the curriculum unit. Here, the analysis may show the special problems and responses to each detailed part of the unit so that the curriculum team may be guided in making the detailed changes needed— where this is clearly indicated by the evidence.

The student-learning changes as indicated by the criterion-referenced formative tests may be analyzed for each class separately as well as summarized for all the tryout classes. Item analysis of the results for each class may be provided so that the curriculum team may note which ideas and processes are too difficult and which ones are learned well. It is to be hoped that the curriculum team would attempt to determine whether particular changes in the material or methods used would reduce the number of items that are too difficult.

Where there are distinct subgroups of students in terms of scholastic ability, level of prerequisite learning, school attitudes, and the like, the test scores (and item analyses) may be analyzed to show the different levels of student learning and learning difficulties of each subgroup.

Further details about data-analysis procedures relevant to this chapter can be found in chapter 12.

REFERENCES

Anderson, L. W. "Time and School Learning." Ph.D. dissertation, University of Chicago, 1973.

Bloom, B. S. "Thought Processes of Students in Discussion Classes." In *Accent on Teaching,* edited by S. French. New York: Harper & Brothers, 1954. Pp. 23–48.

Bloom, B. S.; Hastings, J. T.; Madaus, G.; et al. *Handbook on Formative and Summative Evaluation of Student Learning.* New York: McGraw-Hill, 1971.

5

The Field-trial Stage
of Curriculum Evaluation

THE NEED FOR A LARGE-SCALE TRYOUT

Curriculum writers often resemble prophets: they have faith that their endeavor will be a success. But school practice has frequently proved that faith and conviction are not enough to ensure success. It is essential, therefore, to check empirically the instructional material, suggested teaching methods, learning activities, and learning equipment before they are used widely in the schools. In other words, before the large-scale implementation of a new curriculum, one has to make certain that the beautiful ideas really do work effectively in promoting learning.

The previous chapter described the preliminary tryout of a new program in a few classes and provided detailed suggestions concerning the data to be collected, methods of data analysis, and the use of the data in checking and improving the program. On the basis of such preliminary tryout the curriculum team is able to identify the major flaws in the program and to produce an improved version of it. But in most curriculum development centers the first revised version of the program is not immediately implemented across the whole educational system. A field-trial

104   *This chapter was written by Zoltán Báthory.*

stage or a large-scale tryout generally follows before the program is considered ready for widespread use in the system.

The second tryout, which will be referred to as the "field-trial stage in curriculum evaluation," is needed in order to deal with problems that remained undetected and thus unresolved in the small preliminary tryout. The utilization of a new educational program throughout an educational system may raise problems that do not appear at the preliminary tryout stage. It is necessary to extend the tryout to a wide-scale field trial, where conditions are more like those in the widespread use of the program than those at the preliminary tryout. Such a field trial is especially necessary to determine the conditions under which the program will work well and those where it may be less than satisfactory for teachers and students in particular schools and classes.

The field trial differs from the preliminary tryout in several respects, such as methods used for evaluation, data collected, design of the study and purpose of the evaluation, nature of the instructional material, mass-production cost, communication patterns with teachers, and intervention of writers in the program tryout.

EVALUATION METHODS

Evaluation methods at this stage differ in many respects from those utilized in previous stages. The most important of these are the sample, the data, and the design.

The Sample

As far as the sample is concerned, differences appear between the field trial and the preliminary tryout both from the point of view of the size and from that of the selection procedure. From the point of view of size, generally only 4–6 classes are involved in the preliminary tryout, while for the field trial the sample size may require as many as 30–60 classes or schools. As for selection procedures, the preliminary tryout is usually drawn on a judgmental basis, whereas at the field trial attempts are usually made to draw a stratified or random sample of classes and teachers. In order to ensure the representativeness of the sample it is frequently advisable to draw stratified random samples. For this purpose it is necessary to possess reliable information about major sources of variance in achievement prevailing in the educational system.

In Hungary, for example, a survey revealed the existence of striking rural-urban achievement differences. Table 5.1 presents some of the results

Table 5.1. **Urban/Rural Differences (in stanine score)**
in Grade 4 in Hungary

General Achievement Test Scores

Pupils' Learning in:	N	Mean	S.D.
Graded capital schools	240	6.17	1.74
Graded town schools	464	5.59	1.87
Graded village schools	783	4.93	1.99
Ungraded farm schools	122	4.34	1.95

obtained in reading comprehension in town and village schools (Báthory 1973).

The IEA study* revealed large differences in achievement between students of various geographical regions in Italy. Any stratified sample has to consider the major sources of variance and to construct the sampling plan in such a way as to minimize the within-stratum variance.

A special problem related to sampling may appear if in a certain educational system a new program is to be implemented gradually. For example, in Hungary a new mathematics program is to be introduced gradually across the whole system; in the first stage of program implementation each year an additional 7 percent of all schools are supposed to introduce the new program. Under such circumstances schools joining the new program at any time are not likely to be a representative sample of the total target population. The results of each new sample of schools cannot therefore be generalized to the entire target population unless evidence is available about the representativeness of the sample. For practical reasons it may be decided that at first only a certain type of school (e.g., schools with unusually well qualified teachers) should join the new program. Such an arrangement imposes considerable restrictions on the generalizability of any results.

The Data

At the field-trial stage data should be collected about student, teacher, and school variables. Concerning students, one is interested in obtaining data about a variety of cognitive and affective entry behaviors and outcomes. Since a relatively large number of students participate in the field trial, it is advisable to concentrate on the collection of types of data that are

---

*IEA, the International Association for the Evaluation of Educational Achievement, has its international center at the Institute for the Study of International Problems in Education, University of Stockholm. Over the last twenty years this association has conducted comparative studies of educational achievement in twenty-one countries.

most valid and that can be summarized quickly. Multiple-choice evaluation procedures may play a greater role at this stage than at previous stages of program development. Whereas at the preliminary tryout stage a great variety of types of data were collected and analyzed (e.g., work sheets, observations, judgmental data, open-ended examinations, performance tests, classroom observation schemes), at the stage of the field trial one may have to be content with a more limited set of data concerning the students' performance.

Nevertheless, one can use some of the instruments developed at earlier stages of program development. For example, multiple-choice items utilized at the formative evaluation stage can be used again for the field trial, but usually only a subset of items used previously will appear in the instruments utilized at this stage. To summarize, there is a decrease in the variety of types of data collected, but at the same time there is an increase in the number of respondents to any particular question.

One way to increase the amount of information collected at this stage is to subdivide items and to present different subsets of the items to various subgroups of the sample. Thus it is possible to split a 60-item test or questionnaire into three subsets, each one containing 20 items, and to distribute the three subsets randomly among the students in each class. In this way it is possible to obtain information about 60 items from each class without imposing an undue burden on the individual student.

Thus far we have dealt with data describing individual student variables. Another type of data which should be collected at this stage relates to teacher behavior and school variables, and deals with the conditions of program usage.

At previous stages of program development classroom observation reports provided information about differences in teacher behavior or in school conditions. At the field trial, when a relatively large number of classes and schools use the new program, it is necessary to develop appropriate methods for obtaining information about between-school variation concerning program utilization. Thus one may be interested in examining the teacher's attitude toward the program, his working habits in the class, the physical conditions of the school building, and other facilities such as the library. Examples of instruments used to report teachers' working habits are presented in figures 5.1 and 5.2. The examination of such questionnaires enables us to determine which program elements were frequently used and which were discarded in school practice. In other words, data from such questionnaires tell the curriculum team which of the intended program procedures and classroom processes actually took place.

Which of the following instructional materials have you used in your course? (Mark your answer by X.)

Material	Not at all	To some extent	Very intensively
Working sheets			
Supplementary readers			
Cassettes			
Tapes			
Programmed texts			
Film loops			

Are there any additional instructional resources you would like to use in your course?   No _____   Yes, specify _____

Which of the following learning activities took place in the class during the lessons? (Mark your answer.)

Activity	Not at all	To some extent	Often
Teacher's lecturing			
Student's lecturing			
Group discussion			
Individual work on reading assignment			
Small group work			
Field trip			
Laboratory experiences			
Free reading			
Simulation games			

Source: Modified version of instruments in E. J. Anastasio, "Evaluation of the PLATO System" (Princeton, N.J.: Educational Testing Service, 1972). Mimeographed.

Figure 5.1. *Teacher's Report Sheet*

They also enable the evaluators to categorize the classes or schools according to the degree of program implementation. One may determine which schools carried out the directions of the program and which neglected the

If you introduce a new topic, do you start with:	Not at all	Seldom	Some-times	Often	Always
Presenting many examples which may lead to the com-prehension of the new material					
Analyzing problems from daily life which are closely related to the new topic					
Presenting some problem which can be solved during the lesson					
Presenting some solution of a problem and then dis-cussing how this solution has been obtained					
Presenting the new topic and then discussing its prac-tical applications					

Source: W. Edelstein, *Questionnaire for Arithmetic* (Berlin: Max Planck Institute, n.d.).

Figure 5.2. *Report Sheet on Teaching Arithmetic: Introduction of a New Topic in Arithmetic*

guidelines provided and failed to implement the program properly. Finally, a summary of data of this type may serve to determine the teaching-learning conditions that best achieve the desired program outcomes.

Design

The most common design at both tryout stages is the "one-shot case study," which is classified by Campbell and Stanley (1963) as a pre-experimental design (see chapter 12 for a fuller description). This means that at the end of the course measurements are taken in order to determine whether the program objectives were attained or not. Thus the aim of the end-of-course measurement is not the comparison of the program group with students in groups that have not used the program, but rather the examination of outcomes in the light of prescribed criteria. Frequently the "one group pretest-posttest" design is also used. Such a design enables the evaluators to determine the degree of change occurring in certain student behavior variables from the beginning of the course to the end. Such a design has some advantages over the one-shot design, since it can be used to determine the extent to which the end-of-course achievement results are attributable to different degrees of participation in the course.

In addition to these designs one frequently encounters comparisons with control groups either in a randomly selected experimental setting or in a nonrandomly assigned quasi-experimental setting. Much has been written about the difficulty of making meaningful comparisons between achievement levels of students in the experimental or innovative program and those of students in the old or traditional programs. In general, different programs have different aims; therefore it is very difficult, if not impossible, to construct measurement instruments that are equally valid for different programs. Indeed, Walker and Schaffarzik (1974) report that in most cases where the superiority of experimental-program-group students has been demonstrated, the measurement instruments had content bias in favor of the experimental program. Nevertheless, if due attention is given to avoiding content bias in the measurement instruments, such comparisons may give valid proof of the merits of a given program. Tests free of content bias can usually be constructed in the domain of basic skills such as reading, arithmetic, foreign language, or for measuring the "ability to apply"; but only rarely can they be constructed for the measurement of knowledge or the retention of specific curriculum content.

While one may encounter difficulties in comparing meaningfully the outcomes of entirely different programs, it is very important to compare outcomes of the same program used under different conditions. Thus one may compare outcomes of the same program in classes where teachers received special program-oriented in-service training versus classes where such training was not given, or of classes that devoted different amounts of time to conducting laboratory experiments, and so forth. It may be of great interest to compare outcomes of classes where instructions and guidelines given by the program writers were meticulously carried out versus classes where teachers disregarded them. For such comparisons, the arguments of content bias do not apply, and the results may possess high validity.

THE INSTRUCTIONAL MATERIALS

The instructional materials used in the field trial differ in many respects from those used in the preliminary tryout. First, as a consequence of formative evaluation results, several elements of the instructional materials have been modified and flaws removed. Second, the technical quality of the materials has been improved.

To hasten the process of tryout and also to save expense, the instructional materials are usually prepared in relatively crude form at the preliminary tryout stage. Illustrations, pictures, and photos are often bound in a separate booklet or file and are not collated with the written text of lessons and exercises. The fact that only four to six classes may participate in the preliminary tryout makes the commercial publication of the materials unprofitable. In contrast, at the field-trial stage, the instructional materials needed for a whole course are produced and printed in a better form and assembled into a complete kit. It frequently happens also that several sections of the content to be taught were not included in the preliminary trial version of the program and are included in the field-trial stage for the first time.

In these respects the revised instructional materials produced at the end of the preliminary tryout may be different from those that have already been tried out. This underlines the necessity of the field-trial stage, where in fact the revised instructional materials are put to careful use and evaluation for the first time.

MASS PRODUCTION

The field trial of curriculum may raise problems related to the mass production and long-distance transport of instructional materials. At the preliminary tryout stage when only a handful of classes use the new program, most of the equipment is hand-produced. At the field-trial stage it is necessary to examine issues related to the mass production of the instructional materials. In a physics program of electricity, for example, authors reported that they had developed a set of experimental equipment that functioned very well at the preliminary tryout. The equipment was hand-produced, and the producers obtained a satisfactory level of precision. When attempts were made to mass-produce the same equipment, however, it turned out that within the framework of price limitations the industrial companies could not provide the level of precision in the equipment that was required for carrying out the planned experiments in class. Consequently there was a need to plan different learning activities that could be carried out with lower-precision-level instruments.

COST OF INSTRUMENTS AND EQUIPMENT

Expenses may limit the introduction of new curricula. It is well known that the famous Nuffield science projects, any new mathematics course, or a foreign-language program using a language laboratory put such a burden on the educational budget that some countries—especially developing countries—cannot envisage their implementation even though the educational gain appears to be very promising. It must be noted that responsible curriculum teams do attempt to decrease the expenditure side of their projects. However strong the social demand to improve education, curriculum workers cannot proceed without careful consideration of the cost-benefit implications.

It is relatively simple to calculate the cost of instruments and equipment. One takes account of the expenses of design, production, services, and distribution, and the number of schools, classes, and pupils respectively. But how can one assess the educational benefits? How much investment is justified in order to obtain any particular educational objective? Certainly no economist can provide a full answer to such a question, but surely some sound estimate of the educational value of proposed innovations should be made. It is also necessary to examine to what extent different levels of investment affect the quality of instruction and learning. This consideration provides one more reason why the field-trial stage is needed.

The cost-benefit aspect of curriculum implementation raises special problems in the case of the adaptation of foreign programs. For example, to transplant a Nuffield physics program to a developing country would necessitate the creation of facilities for the production of program materials, the provision of appropriate maintenance services and of an effective system of distribution, and so on—not to mention the consequences of the different social and cultural backgrounds and quite dissimilar educational traditions and customs. Any shortage in instruments may discourage teachers from using the program, may lower parents' confidence, and consequently may occasion a decline in learning outcomes. Blind alleys in implementation can be avoided if the curriculum team pays due attention to these many problems even as late as the field-trial stage.

COMMUNICATION PATTERN

At the preliminary tryout the program writers maintain close and personal contact with the teachers using the program. The selection of teachers is done in a way that attempts to secure cooperation between writers and teachers. Usually the teachers who participate in the preliminary tryout are the ones who have a strong interest in the new program. These teachers are willing to make a special effort to ensure the program's success. They willingly participate in some pretraining sessions and in-service training programs where the curriculum writers personally convey their ideas about program goals, the significance of different learning activities, and so on. Frequently the communication is bilateral: teachers of the tryout classes are given many opportunities to express their ideas about the new program and may thus even become partners in the development activity. In contrast to the close and personal contact that exists during the preliminary tryout, the relationship between writers and teachers at the field trial becomes more formal and bureaucratic.

Communication between program writers and teachers is mainly written, i.e., the teachers' guide, which frequently does not communicate adequately the basic ideas and intentions of the program. The field trial is therefore designed to test the efficiency of communication patterns that will be used during the full-scale implementation of the program. It should be noted, however, that at the field trial as well as at the full-scale implementation stage the communication pattern between teachers and writers does not have to be limited to the utilization of written instructions. The program writers may train a special group of teachers who will visit schools and establish personal contact with other teachers. Television or videotape programs may provide excellent explanations and demonstrations of how best to use the program. Thus a variety of communication patterns can be used at this stage, but because of the larger scale of implementation, the writers themselves cannot keep personal contact with all the teachers. One of the roles of evaluation is to examine the efficiency of communication patterns utilized in order to guide teachers in the efficient use of the program and to suggest ways of improving these patterns.

INTERVENTION VERSUS NONINTERVENTION

The preliminary tryout of new curriculum material is performed under circumstances that enable the "experimenters" to modify the treatment during the process of its application. In this respect the preliminary tryout of a program is different from the typical scientific experiment where the treatment is fully specified and meticulously replicated several times. The program tryout constitutes a stage of the program development and is not regarded as the basis for an impartial and objective verdict about the final merits and shortcomings of the program. In the preliminary tryout the program writers are eager to ensure their program's success; whenever they detect any insufficiency in the program, they attempt to correct it at once. Thus, during the preliminary tryout neither the writers nor the evaluators act as observers; on the contrary, they intervene whenever necessary for the improvement of the program. The limited scale of the preliminary tryout on one hand, and the provisional nature of the instructional material on the other, may require such intervention.

In contrast to this active role assumed by the program developers at the preliminary tryout, later on, at the field-trial stage, it is less likely that there will be any such intervention. There are several reasons for this. First, the program writers do not maintain personal contact with the teachers in the tryout classes and therefore little intervention is possible. Second, once the instructional material has been subjected to the process of formative evaluation, it is printed in a standard form for extensive classroom use, the modification of which is consequently more expensive and complicated than the modification of the preliminary version. Finally, it is more likely that the revised version of the program will produce satisfactory results without any intervention than the first draft of the program was able to do.

THE PURPOSE OF EVALUATION

At the small-scale tryout the main purpose of the evaluation is the improvement of the instructional material. At this point, an attempt is made to identify weaknesses and to suggest program modification on the basis of formative evaluation results. To some extent the field-trial evaluation may also serve this purpose, since it may be that during the field trial some shortcomings will still be detected and modification of the program will be required accordingly. In general, however, if formative evaluation was conscientiously carried out at the tryout stage, the large-scale evaluation result will substantiate the former finding and will further determine the adequacy of the revisions in the program material.

The major purpose of the large-scale field tryout is to identify the necessary conditions for the successful implementation of the new curriculum program. These conditions may involve the student or teacher characteristics, classroom organization, the availability of certain equipment, the presence of certain learning activities in the class, and so on. *Student characteristics* that may be related to program success are, among others: general intellectual ability, previous achievement, interest, and motivation. *Teacher characteristics* related to adequate program implementation may be: the basic training, the seniority of the teacher, familiarity with the new program, special program-oriented training, attitudes toward the program, and so forth. *Classroom organization* variables of interest include: the amount of group and individual work and their nature, and the freedom given to students to initiate learning activities. Another set of variables is the *availability* of physical space, teaching aids, demonstration materials, library and equipment for carrying out experiments. Finally, *activities* taking place in the class, such as group discussion, field trips, independent reading, cooperative work, problem solving, and inductive or deductive reasoning, may all affect the success of the program. At the large-scale field tryout it is possible to examine the variables or clusters of variables that are highly associated with the attainment of the desired outcomes.

Another function of the large-scale tryout is to provide baseline data concerning the expected outcomes of utilizing the new program. Basic standards established at this stage may serve as a criterion for the quality control of the program implementation. This issue is dealt with in chapter 7.

COMBINING FIELD TRIAL WITH ANOTHER STAGE OF CURRICULUM DEVELOPMENT

Running a field trial after the preliminary tryout of the new material prolongs the process of development. Nevertheless, the payoff justifies such a delay: it may contribute to the further improvement of the educational material and may also result in suggestions concerning the improved implementation of the program.

On the other hand, one can perform many of the evaluation activities suggested in this chapter simultaneously with the preliminary tryout or with the beginning phase of program implementation. This is in fact very likely to be the case if the curriculum team works in a crisis situation where it is necessary to produce a new program in a relatively short time. Under such circumstances it may be possible to select a sample of 30–60 classes where the new program will be tried out. From this large sample one may select a small subsample of 4–6 classes, where a more thorough evaluation will be performed following the tryout procedures described in chapter 4. Thus intensive and extensive follow-up can be performed simultaneously.

Another possible shortcut may be a field trial carried out simultaneously with the initial steps of program implementation. This means that after the preliminary tryout of the material and after its first revision, the program can be released for use throughout the system, but at the same time an evaluation study will be carried out on a representative sample of the whole population. In this case, if evaluation results indicate the existence of serious weak points, it will be necessary to revise the program again. Such a revision may be rather expensive since it could result in discarding the textbooks already produced and disseminated for the new program. Thus, while combining the field trial with some other stage of development may hasten the completion of program development, it also entails the danger of producing an unsatisfactory program, the utilization of which may create frustration. The cost of discarding educational materials already circulated in the system may also increase the expense of development activities. Shortcuts do not always imply a saving.

REFERENCES

Anastasio, E. J. "Evaluation of the PLATO System." Princeton, N.J.: Educational Testing Service, 1972. Mimeographed.

Báthory, Zoltán. *Urban-rural Differences in Learning* (in Hungarian). In *Science and Permanent Improvement of Education,* edited by A. Kiss. Budapest: Akadémiai Kiadó, 1973.

Campbell, D. T., and Stanley, J. C. "Experimental and Quasi-experimental Designs for Research Teaching." In *Handbook of Research on Teaching,* edited by N. L. Gage. Chicago: Rand McNally, 1963. Pp. 171–276.

Edelstein, Wolfgang. *Questionnaire for Arithmetic.* Berlin: Max Planck Institute, n.d.

Italian IEA Report. Pamphlet of paper presented at the IEA Conference, Deutsches Institut für Internationale Pädagogische Forschung, Frankfurt, 1972.

Walker, D. F., and Schaffarazik, J. "Comparing Curricula," *Review of Educational Research* 44 (1974): 83–111.

6

Evaluation at the Stage of Large-scale Implementation

PROBLEMS OF EVALUATION

Special problems face a curriculum development team when they are preparing for widespread use of the material. This stage is reached when final versions are produced and are ready for dissemination to the target population of classes. The new problems stem from stepping beyond the relatively small number of teachers and classes involved in earlier development and tryout work to introducing ideas and materials to teachers and classes to whom the program is completely fresh. One of the basic problems is to enable teachers to use the material with understanding and confidence. Rarely can written matter for pupils or teachers adequately convey the spirit and intentions of the developers; to distribute materials without introductory or supporting courses would be to run a severe risk of having new materials used in unsatisfactory ways. Indeed it can be justifiably said that the work of curriculum development is only partly done when final teaching materials have been produced; the other part of the work, unfortunately frequently neglected up to now, is to take adequate steps for adjusting the system to the demands of the innovation.

This chapter was written by Wynne Harlen. **117**

The present chapter deals with evaluation in the part of curriculum development that concerns materials and ideas being put into practice on a large scale. This stage will generally begin when published materials are available, though preparation and planning for this stage should have begun earlier. The end of this stage is less easy to define; it can be said to be complete when initial teacher training and in-service institutions are preparing teachers for using the new curricula on a regular rather than an experimental basis, and when the necessary supporting elements in the system, such as equipment supply and external examinations, are fully operational.

The question of who carries out the evaluation during this part of the process will have different answers in different situations. In curriculum centers where the original team of developers are permanent members of staff implementation may be carried out by the team, or under their direction, and the evaluation carried out by those responsible for evaluation at earlier stages. This continuity provides the best situation because a considerable amount of information required at this stage comes from what went on at earlier stages in the development. But a development team often breaks up or goes on to developing other materials once the books and teaching aids have been sent to the publisher. Implementation may then be left in the hands of a skeleton team, or become the general responsibility of the curriculum center or sponsoring agency. It is essential that, whoever is responsible, the full range of evaluation activities at the stage of implementation is not neglected. Fortunately, some of these activities do not demand highly specialized skills and can be carried out by people who do not consider themselves specialists in evaluation. On the other hand, some aspects require advice about such things as adequate sample size, appropriate ways of collecting and summarizing data; wherever possible, someone experienced in evaluation should be connected with the work.

As at other stages, the essential role of evaluation in large-scale implementation is in ensuring a systematic approach to gathering necessary data and informing those involved in decision making. Three main aspects of this role are discussed in the following sections of this chapter. Carrying them out does not involve additional evaluation activities in all cases since some require only a drawing together of results of evaluation studies at earlier points of the project development. The first aspect is to ascertain the intentions and effects of the program and to document the conditions that favor effective use of the material. The second is to describe the existing situation, the methods and operations of the schools or wider systems so as to inform planners about what it is they are trying to change. From these two follows the identification of areas where support, instruction, or materials may be needed in addition to those provided by the program, and the provision of this information for making decisions about in-service courses. This third step also involves evaluation of the in-service courses to provide feedback for improving them.

Checking the Program in Its Final Form

At this stage in its development the program will have been revised at least once and probably several times and may be in various respects different from what was initially planned. So it is appropriate to check through it applying criteria that concern issues particularly important for implementation. Many models for analysis of curriculum material (Weiss et al. 1972, Armstrong 1973, Eraut 1974) consist mainly of questionnaires or check lists. For example, the Descriptive Curriculum Questionnaire (Weiss et al. 1972), which is designed for use with already developed curriculum material as well as for bringing together information about a curriculum being developed, is a 20-page document in which the major headings and subheadings are the following:

A. Subject-matter field
B. Student characteristics necessary to begin program as specified:
   1. General prerequisites
   2. Specific prerequisites
C. Teacher characteristics necessary to begin the curriculum program as specified:
   1. Specific prerequisites
   2. Teacher preferences as a prerequisite
D. Basic assumptions of the program as specified (views about how learning and teaching should take place)
E. Objectives of the program as specified (statement and basis of general and specific objectives)
F. Conditions of the program as specified (location and arrangement of classes)
G. Activities of the program as specified (full description)
H. Materials of the program as specified (books, work sheets, A-V aids, laboratory equipment,etc.)
I. Organization:
   1. Time requirements for the program as specified
   2. Order in which conditions, activities, and materials are to be presented.
J. Methods of implementation of the curriculum as specified:

        1. Suggested methods for teaching the curriculum
        2. General role of the teacher
   K. Evaluation of the program

Such a check list reveals missing elements as well as describing the included features of the program. In our present context, however, the concern is not merely with descriptions of the content but with guiding action in preparing teachers. Although the materials may not be able to be changed, they can be supported and presented in a way which takes account of their content and the form in which it has been expressed. The kind of checking required is therefore not a description of learning materials and activities as much as an examination of whether there are clear and consistent indications of the purpose and application of the activities, of the learning processes and of the support required to put the program into action. The evaluation role is to reveal gaps and inconsistencies that may be a problem at the stage of large-scale use of the product. While evaluation is not for the purpose of making decisions about remedies for possible shortcomings, it should result in the developers or those responsible for implementation becoming aware of deficiencies and being able to take appropriate action. Among the issues with which the evaluation for this purpose should be concerned are:

1. The objectives of the program and the relative emphasis given to different kinds of objectives. Is there greater emphasis on goals relating to the social context, to personal education of the child, to the subject matter? Are goals expressed with sufficient clarity to be unambiguously identified? Is there agreement upon criteria of achievement to be applied?
2. Whether the objectives are expressed so as to be understood by teachers. Is interpretation in operational terms satisfactory? Are teachers provided with behavioral statements or descriptive ones?
3. The teacher's role in the program. To what extent is adaptation encouraged, demanded, or discouraged? Are the materials basically a resource for the teacher or virtually a teacher-substitute?
4. The intended classroom practices and interactions between teacher, pupil, and materials. Are there conditions in which these would be expected to vary? Are they adequately conveyed to teachers?
5. The indications as to any essential support required from the system outside the classroom. Should head teachers take part in in-service courses? Are examination boards preparing suitable papers? Are necessary equipment and resources available in large quantities?

6. The criteria of effectiveness that can be applied to the program in action. What are the qualities in various aspects of a classroom in which the materials are used that would signify effective use? How much emphasis is placed upon processes or outcomes as criteria?

In many cases these things have been constantly reviewed throughout the early stages of development of the program, and many of them will be down in writing. This may make the evaluation task at this stage easier but does not remove the need for it. Changes may have taken place, there may be inconsistency in the written materials on these matters, different groups may hold different views. It will be important to reveal changes and find out whether the development team is aware of them or whether they "just happened." Early intentions may not have been fulfilled or inconsistencies have passed unnoticed, especially if projects suffer from changing team membership or have a large proportion of part-time team members.

Sources of data for providing the information listed above will vary somewhat for each item and, of course, according to the circumstances of a particular project. A suggested list of sources may help, especially in suggesting alternatives in cases where some of the more obvious sources are not available. It will not be necessary for the evaluator to examine all of these, but there should be an awareness of their potential value.

The Written Materials of the Program

Explicit statements of objectives, roles, and processes will not always be found; but positions and values with regard to them are implicit in the kinds of learning activities included and in the directions given for initiating and carrying out activities.

For example, the evaluator of the Three Phase Primary Science project of Papua New Guinea* identified from the teachers' handbook for the program the overall aims: "1. To allow the children to gain a knowledge and understanding of the world about them in as interesting a way as possible through activity and enquiry. 2. To develop this attitude of enquiry." He also confirmed by quoting other parts of the handbook that the emphasis was entirely on the personal development of the children. Intended processes and types of interaction were also revealed by such statements as, "If the children ask questions your success is great," and teachers were encouraged to use the children's vernacular if it would help to stimulate questions and discussion (Wilson 1972).

*A course developed for children aged 6 to 12, each phase of the work covering two years of the primary school. Begun in 1968, supported by Unesco, it consists of a series of activities and experiments in science and was first introduced into schools and evaluated 1970–72.

Internal Team Documents

Particularly at the early stages of a project, team members tend to clarify their ideas on paper. Perusal of these writings can reveal changes that have been occurring in various aspects of the program. To take relevant parts from these documents and ask questions such as, "Why was this statement made?" "Does it still validly reflect a feature of the program? If not, what is the position in this matter now?" helps considerably to understand statements written later.

A difference between internal and external documents was recorded by the commentator on the Integrated Studies Project, Keele, England.* The director, deputy director, and commentator held very different views on fundamental issues, such as what was meant by "integration," and on aspects such as the division of labor within the team and the relationship with publishers. "The documents issued by the project gave a clear and consistent definition. Behind the scenes there was a continuing debate. . . ." (Shipman 1974). Perusal of the original proposal for this project also showed that its purpose was conceived as being to explore "means and meaning of integration in the humanities"; any materials produced by the team were to serve only as examples, the main products coming in the form of local initiatives. But in the event the energies of the team were almost entirely taken up in materials production and "across the three years of the project this original proposal was to become increasingly remote from the actual work that was done" (Shipman 1974).

Since access to internal documents would not automatically be granted to an outside evaluator, this is a source of information that has to be justified. The purpose is not to show that there were changes between intentions and actions, but rather to clarify the true positions of the team with regard to important issues and to make sure that public statements are not oversimplified. The cooperation and active help of the project director in making use of this source of information is obviously essential.

Discussions with Team Members

This is probably the most prolific source and can provide information of almost all kinds needed to describe the program as intended in action. Nevertheless, it is possible that the team, even at an advanced stage of the project, will err on the side of describing an ideal picture, so this information should be considered alongside that from other sources, particularly the data from early trials. Also it is likely that, if no written account of objectives or of the teacher's role is to be found, the team will be unwilling to indulge in basic thinking, which they have managed without

*Based at Keele University, Keele, England, 1967–72. Sponsored by the Schools Council. Produced teaching units in the humanities for secondary pupils aged 11 to 15.

for so long. In such an event the person responsible for the evaluation at this stage may need, as well as patience and tact, to prepare a draft for the team to react to, and to change it as often as necessary until a consensus is reached. This was the approach adopted by the evaluation committee of the African Primary Science Programme (APSP).* "The committee drafted a statement of goals as they understood them and presented it to participants in the Programme for critical comment. On the basis of the reactions to this initial draft, we produced a few pages which all participants seemed to agree stated what they were trying to do" (Duckworth 1970).

Data from Early Trials

Any records of classroom observations made during trials of early drafts of materials can help to provide a realistic description of interactions and aspects of the teacher's role. Anecdotal or case-study records are useful in filling in details around statements of intended roles or classroom transactions. Examination of the items in any tests that have been given to pupils will reveal operational forms of the objectives, and the balance of items referring to different objectives may be some indication of their relative importance. Much of this evidence is only suggestive, however, and should be verified from other sources, particularly discussion with team members.

Formative evaluation trials may be particularly valuable in identifying not so much isolated features of the program but collections of conditions, events, and practices that tend to coincide when the program is operating as intended. The Science 5/13 (Great Britain) project** collected a great deal of information during its formative evaluation. Data were collected about the physical and social environment of the class and school, the classroom interactions, the teachers' opinions and comments, and the effects of the work on the teachers; instruments included tests for pupils, questionnaires for teachers, and report forms for class observers. Associations between these large numbers of items (variables) was sought using a form of cluster analysis. The groups representing the opposite poles of the main dimension were found to be easily identified as describing

---

*Begun in 1965, supported by USAID, this project has developed a number of units on science topics for ages 5 to 12. Operates through a network of locally controlled centers in several African countries. Its center is the Education Development Center, Newton, Mass. 02160.
**Based at Bristol University, Bristol, England, 1967–75, this project is sponsored by the Schools Council, the Nuffield Foundation, and the Scottish Education Department. Materials are units for teachers which enable them to carry out pupil-centered discovery work with children aged 5 to 13. No pupil books or kits of materials since teachers produce their own program of work to suit their pupils' interests.

"successful" and "unsuccessful" use of the material in relation to the values of the project. In the "successful" cluster, the items included: an increase in pupils' score on an attitude scale, informal arrangement of tables and desks, children working individually or in groups at their own tasks, an integrated timetable, children working on science activities at different times and able to initiate their own investigations, the teacher having a sound grasp of the meaning of the objectives, and the teacher warmly approving the project's ideas. Equally useful were the items clustering at the opposite pole, including: the teacher rarely using discovery methods in teaching; the children all working on the same activities; the teacher not regarding the objectives as important; the children working as a whole class, their work largely directed by the teacher; and a regular arrangement of furniture in the classroom.

From this analysis it was possible to gain a fairly complete picture of the situation in which the project material was used effectively, and of the reverse. The information was used in revising the material, and the high proportion of items relating to organizational matters that were beyond the reach of the project's units was passed on to those preparing teachers and schools for using the materials (Harlen 1975).

Discussion with Teachers

Teachers involved in formative trials may have received courses of varying formality to prepare them for taking part, and will also have tried to put the ideas and materials into practice. This experience of both theory and practice means that the picture they can provide of the program will be the most realistic of all. If these teachers had frequent contact with and visits from the project team, their understanding of the program will be better than if this was not the case; in either event there is a possibility that their grasp of the project's intentions was not complete, and their views may reflect a target for further in-service courses rather than the position to be aimed for. Again it will be essential to check evidence from this source with that from other sources.

An example of how teachers can misinterpret a program's approach is provided by the Integrated Science project in Malaysia.* Some teachers understood the "guided" or "structured" discovery learning being advocated as permission for "laissez-faire" class management. They apparently assumed there was no more need to "tell" the students anything—"let them discover for themselves"—no need to check whether experimental results

*This is an adaptation of the Scottish Integrated Science syllabus, carried out with government support 1969–74. Materials include teachers' manuals and pupils' worksheets for ages 11 to 14. Located at the Ministry of Education, Federal House, Kuala Lumpur, Malaysia.

were "correct," no need to check through written work, no need to discuss what was going on. Not unexpectedly, the teachers were unnerved by what they thought the project was suggesting, and the project took care to avoid giving this impression in further materials of courses (Malaysia 1975).

Comparison with Other Programs

When several separately produced programs exist in the same subject area and age range, there will be some commonalities and some differences between them. Examination of these is very helpful in highlighting the special features of the program. Yoloye, for example, compared APSP with other approaches to primary science—with the Nuffield and Science 5/13 projects in England and three American programs, ESS, SCIS, and *Science—a Process Approach* (AAAS).* He compared APSP with these five contemporary programs using two main factors as a basis for the comparison: the relative emphasis given to the child, the society, and the discipline; and the degree of structure in the organization of the curriculum (Yoloye 1971). As a result, APSP was seen to have most in common with Science 5/13 and ESS, two projects that are also semistructured and child-centered. Further investigation of similarities and differences among these three programs could lead to finer identification of the unique character-istics of any one of them.

Each of these sources provides information of several different kinds, and no one source is sufficient for all the information required. Each source provides only partial or somewhat unreliable evidence, but the combination of information from several sources improves the reliability. The sources considered most useful for the different kinds of evidence are indicated in table 6.1.

This table attempts to indicate which sources are of more or of less importance; the "key" sources are distinguished from others that are relevant but perhaps less fruitful. There is no entry in cells where the source

*ESS (Elementary School Science Project) was supported by the Nuffield Science Founda-tion, 1959–66. It produced teaching units for pupils aged 7 to 13 aimed at acquainting children with scientific concepts, facts, and ideas. Emphasis was on experimentation by the child and the contribution of science to understanding, rather than its technological application.

SCIS (Science Curriculum Improvement Study) was also supported by the Nuffield Science Foundation, 1962–74. It produced a program for elementary school children aged 5 to 12 aimed at the development of scientific literacy. Units deal with basic concepts of biological and physical science and include teacher and student manuals and tests.

AAAS (American Association for the Advancement of Science) was supported by government funds, 1963–74. It produced materials to give pupils aged 5 to 12 a stepwise development of skills used in scientific investigation. Mostly written by scientists and teach-ers, it produced *Science—A Process Approach,* together with kits of teaching materials. Based at 1515 Massachusetts Avenue, Washington, D. C. 20005.

Table 6.1. Sources of Information for Checking a Program in Its Final Form

Source of Information \ Information Required	(1) The objectives	(2) Conveying objectives to teachers	(3) The teacher's role	(4) Classroom practices and interactions	(5) Support needed from the system	(6) Criteria of effectiveness
Written materials	X X		X X	X X	X	X
Internal team documents	X X		X	X		X
Discussions with team members	X X	X	X X	X X	X	X X
Formative evaluation data	X	X	X	X X	X X	X X
Discussions with trial teachers		X X	X	X	X X	
Comparison with other programs	X	X	X		X	X

does not contribute very much to a particular kind of information, though this does not mean that it is always irrelevant. Not all suggested sources are available, therefore the evaluation should gather information from among those that are available and are suggested as useful. If the key sources are not present, it is even more important to use as many of the other sources as possible.

Thus the table indicates that the study of materials is likely to be particularly fruitful in providing information about the objectives, the teacher's role, and classroom practices. It may also say something about the supporting system and criteria for judging effectiveness. The study of internal documents contributes most to clarifying the objectives but may also be relevant to teachers' roles, classroom processes, and identifying effectiveness criteria. The number of entries and the large number of Xs against "Discussions with team members" indicate that this is a very important source of information and should not be neglected. Data from formative evaluation, where available, are also high in their contribution generally and especially for the description of processes, needed support from the wider system, and indications of criteria applied in judging effectiveness. "Discussions with trial teachers" is seen to contribute particularly to learning how to express objectives in a way that is understandable to them; since this is the only key source related to this matter, it is evidently important to include it whenever possible. Teachers can also give information about the kinds of help they needed, the constraints they experienced, and changes in the school or community that would facilitate their work. Finally, "Comparison with other programs" is seen to be of some value for a variety of purposes but is not as inexpendable as some other sources.

Looking at the table column by column shows which sources are useful for providing certain kinds of information. The special place of discussions with teachers has already been mentioned as being the only key source for the second column. All other columns have more than one key source; these should be the ones used if at all possible. Finally, it must be emphasized that this is intended as a generalized guide. It may well be in a particular project that an important internal document was written about how to help teachers understand objectives, which would be a valuable source of information in the case of that project. Since it is not a general pattern for such documents to be in existence, however, there is no entry in the corresponding cell of the table. Ideally each evaluation would consider its own sources of information and construct a table of its priorities.

Identifying Major Areas of Change in the Existing System

The part that evaluation plays in preparation for large-scale use of materials involves, as has been suggested, studying the situation existing before changes are made, identifying the intentions of the new program, and finding places where the gaps are large and unlikely to be closed by use of materials alone. The previous section suggested ways of identifying intentions; some of the sources discussed have relevance also in this section, which is concerned with describing the situation in which changes are to be introduced.

Curriculum changes may seem to concern directly only what happens in a classroom; but classrooms do not exist in isolation. Changes there can both affect and be affected by changes in the educational system and beyond—to the social and political climate of the country. Restricting ourselves to those parts of the system that exist in large part to serve the work in schools, there are still a number of elements to consider. Among the most important are initial training institutions, examinations boards, in-service agencies such as teachers' centers and local advisers, the inspectorate, teachers' professional bodies and unions, parents, and logistic systems. Again the evaluation can check that necessary activities in the system have been carried out satisfactorily.

Initial Training

The evaluative role with regard to initial training may well be carried out by developers and evaluator working together with representatives from teacher-training institutions. It will involve looking at the nature and outcomes of existing training, indicated by course content and examination questions, and comparing these with what the developers consider necessary. A teacher's preparation is not determined, of course, only by her college work, but also by her previous education; the total picture may present quite a problem. For example the Papua New Guinea Three Phase Primary Science (TPPS) evaluator reported the following situation at the beginning of the project, despite the existence of a detailed Department of Education syllabus for science in primary grades: "Most teachers' colleges at the time of planning of the TPPS course had little science equipment and science laboratories were practically unknown. Thus the typical teacher came through a primary school in which no science was taught, a very few went to high school for one or two years where the science taught was minimal, then on to a teachers' college which usually did not have the facilities to teach science. With this background teachers were expected to teach science using a syllabus which, while comprehensive in coverage, offered them little help" (Wilson 1972). Early in the development of this curriculum, TPPS courses were introduced into teacher training, and the developers were able to insist that TPPS be taught in schools only by teachers who had undertaken such a course.

In-service Training and Equipment Requirements

The subject of in-service courses, either for tryout or dissemination, is taken up in detail in a later section, but at this point it is relevant to underline the connections with other elements in the system that have to be made before courses on a large scale can be run. In the case of science curricula the availability of suitable equipment is essential. Elementary science projects in many countries find that there is no existing science equipment in the elementary schools and that the equipment produced for secondary science is inappropriate. One such project therefore produced prototypes in its own workshops and began negotiations with equipment manufacturers for large quantities. Of course, manufacturers have to be convinced of the commercial viability of such enterprises; backing at ministry level is helpful. TPPS provides a further solution: "The problem of equipment was tackled by providing each school . . . with a kit of simple materials supplied by UNICEF in a locally made, substantial (and lockable) wooden cabinet. . . . In addition further equipment mostly of a consumable nature was to be supplied by the D.E.O. . . . Finally the teacher is expected to make considerable use of locally available materials, both natural materials and manufactured items, which he can collect, such as bottles, tins, rocks, etc. There are also some simple pieces of equipment which the teacher is expected to make himself" (Wilson 1972).

School Inspectors

Rarely is implementation of an innovation successful without the support of the school inspectorate. Their influence may be direct, as in the case where they are in a position to control in-service work; or indirect, where the promotion and career of the teachers is dependent upon them. Representatives of the inspectorate should be involved in, or consulted about, curriculum development work from the beginning. Efforts should be made to ensure that inspectors know what is going on and will not be offended by decisions being taken, as they see it, "behind their back," or feel that the developers are usurping part of their role. Evaluation has a function in systematically mapping out the influence and responsibilities of inspectors and providing information that will enable these to be used in cooperation with the developers.

External Examinations

Examinations boards have a tight grip on what is taught in many countries, especially at the secondary level. Not only is the content of subjects examined determined by the examination syllabus but also the attention given to general studies and previously nonexamined activities may be changed by the introduction of new methods of assessment. "The effect of examinations has been so far unavoidable because the expectation of many people and institutions—schools, parents, employers, the universities and professions, the world of technical education—have led curriculum in the secondary school to be something which fits the process of assessment rather than the other way round" (Owen 1973). This somewhat depressing statement refers to the situation in England, where external examinations rule the secondary curricula, and where it is essential for curriculum development teams to begin negotiation with examination boards at an early stage so that examinations for new syllabuses are prepared in time for pupils who are taking part in trials. If such arrangements are not made, new materials will not be acceptable to teachers, who will continue to prepare pupils for existing examinations in existing ways. Malaysian experience is that in an examination-oriented system, even if developers succeed in changing teachers' attitudes and teachers accept the value of inquiry learning and desire to implement it, these same teachers are compelled by the examinations to be content-conscious and to teach most of the time by exposition.

Conditions within the School

Though changes in the total system must go along with changes in the classroom, it is in the school that the ultimate effect of innovation must be shown. The teacher is the main resource of learning; changes in teacher behavior determine the impact of innovation and the job of evaluation at the implementation stage is in part to provide information about what changes and support are required for teachers to establish the intended kind of learning environment in their classrooms. Foci of evaluation for this purpose will be such factors as the extent of teachers' knowledge of subject matter and use of new equipment, the general pattern of existing teaching methods, the implicit and explicit objectives demonstrated in present classroom practices, and the availability of materials and equipment that will be necessary for the implementation of the program. However, project teams have repeatedly found that these "surface" elements are not the central problem and that a genuine change in teaching and learning requires some deeper change in teachers' sensitivity and attitudes. For example, the evaluator of the Scottish Project Phi,* which was a modification of the Scottish Integrated Science project aimed to meet the needs of small isolated schools in the Highlands and Islands, concluded: "The Project's experiences support the idea that the implementation of curriculum materials does not rest simply on the provision of adequate equipment and supply of suitably trained teachers. Ultimately, it depends on an acceptance by the teachers themselves that the materials can enhance their teaching" (Roebuck, Bloomer, and Hamilton 1974). The trials of Project Phi materials were not preceded by any appreciable in-service preparation; the result, as the evaluator saw it, was that "in the Project's case the majority of teachers saw the materials as the basis for updating their existing syllabuses, not as a model for restructuring their teaching methods."

Logistic Systems

One important step at the implementation stage is to ensure that the materials and equipment are mass-produced on schedule and that they actually reach the schools and classrooms in working order. For equipment there is the further problem of ensuring appropriate maintenance.

At the planning stage the curriculum developers will have been in touch with the educational planners to ensure that correct budget estimates for the materials and equipment have been made. It is at the planning stage that negotiations will be undertaken and adjustments made both by the planners and the curriculum developers on the type of paper and the standard of equipment to be used. For example, what type of microscopes should be purchased, how many children to one microscope, are spare parts easily available for a certain brand, and so on? Should the purchase be put out for cheapest tender across the world or should it be restricted to companies having maintenance facilities within the country? What are the delivery times? These are the sorts of questions to be tackled conjointly by the curriculum developers and the ministry's planning personnel.

Again, it is important to discover whether delivery of certain recurrent items can be made to schools. In Israel one biology lesson required that a number of a certain type of live fish be delivered to all secondary schools in

*PHI's title is "Independent Learning Materials and Science Teaching in Small Schools in the Highlands and Islands of Scotland"; based at the University of Glasgow, Glasgow, Scotland. A research supported by the Scottish Education Department, 1970-74, that conducted a survey into the provision and use of audiovisual equipment in the Highland and Island countries, developed multimedia materials for use with parts of the Scottish Integrated Science scheme, then conducted trials of these materials and evaluated their impact.

a certain school week. A trial run was undertaken to establish whether this was possible and the types of difficulties that might be encountered. Another new curriculum required a different organization of space within the classroom and different-shaped desks for four or five children to sit at one desk. This was tried out in two schools, and it was discovered that in some cases walls between classrooms had to be knocked down and that the expense of the desks was of a certain order. At this point adjustments had to be made both in the curriculum program and the ministry's budget in terms of the eventual implementation.

Where textbook materials are printed only weeks before the beginning of a school year, the books must reach the school in time. Several tales tell of books not reaching the schools until several months after the beginning of the school year or, where modular learning units were used, of units being in the wrong order in the bound book, or when delivered separately to the school, of their arriving in the wrong order. A recent study (Falayajo et al. 1975) showed that in one school system some schools never received the books, others received limited quantities (only 5 per class instead of 30 per class), and in some cases books arrived in the schools but the teachers did not know they were there. The organizational problems of delivery are complex and extremely difficult, especially in countries with poor transportation and communication systems. Given the circumstances in some countries, it is common to experience delays and losses.

All these examples point to the fact that work at the planning stage is required to formulate (and in some cases try out) a logistical plan for the delivery of books, equipment, and information about their use to the schools. At the implementation stage it is important for the checking mechanisms to be utilized by either the curriculum center or the central or local education administrations so that there is immediate feedback from the schools on the arrival or nonarrival of materials. Only when such information exists can action be taken to remedy shortcomings in the delivery system. Not only should mechanisms be set up, but care should be taken to estimate the workload for such mechanisms and the appropriate staffing.

PROVIDING INFORMATION ABOUT TRAINING TEACHERS FOR USING THE PROGRAMS

The task that faces the development team, or the implementers if they are not the developers, when large-scale use of the new curriculum is planned, is one of drawing together relevant data and experience already gathered and of designing or redesigning strategies and methods for preparing teachers. In doing so it will be necessary to take into account special problems that will not have been faced at previous stages, problems that arise on account of four main factors:

1. The wider range of teachers who will receive the materials
2. The necessity to communicate at a distance
3. The need to be explicit and comprehensive in all aspects of preparation
4. In some cases, because of changes required in the total system of which the teacher and class are elements

Teachers who take part in small-scale tryouts are usually only a handful in number and are chosen from the locality of the development center. Quite often, more able teachers are deliberately selected for these early trials, since they are able to handle materials in an unformed state and to provide the required feedback. They are not generally representative of the total population of teachers. Even if they were, their number is so small that they can receive individual treatment from the team members. Such individual treatment is not possible on the large scale, and it is very likely that the difficulties of presenting the program to the less able and more reactionary teachers will not have been met in practice.

Communication at a distance invariably involves some "loss of signal." In most cases direct communication from project team to teachers will not be possible on a large scale, and some intermediary persons or institutions must convey the material from one to the other. It will be necessary to choose forms of communication where the attenuation will be minimized—perhaps using TV or other mass media channels if possible—or to use organizations such that the message is passed on through capable and informed hands.

Many of the more subtle aspects of a program's philosophy are conveyed informally in small-scale trials. Team members work together with teachers in classrooms and have discussions also at other times. In these contacts many points of misinterpretation or lack of understanding can be cleared up on the spot. Teachers who do not benefit from the firsthand contact will also need similar points clarified and will not have the same opportunity for discussion and questioning. Some points may be covered by revision in the material, but it is unlikely that all queries will be eliminated. Careful documentation of teachers' problems at all stages will help to ensure that small but significant problems are anticipated in the preparation given to teachers.

Some programs require changes that extend to the system outside the classroom, from team teaching to the involvement of parents, changes in the support given by head teachers or local inspectors, or the provision of teachers' centers. While on a small scale these changes may be readily effected through firsthand contacts, on a large scale more formal steps have to be taken to inform and organize those involved. The development and organization of in-service courses is the concern of the whole team, and probably persons beyond the team have parts to play in the implementation of innovations.

Many different aspects of training will be required by teachers and identified by procedures suggested in the preceding section. A comprehensive course might try to provide teachers with the following:

1. Knowledge of the material, including background in the subject matter, experience of working through the activities for themselves, information about how the materials were developed
2. Understanding of the objectives and appreciation of the relationship between learning experiences and objectives
3. Understanding of the teacher's role in using the program, of the principles of class organization and the kind of interactions intended
4. Ability to monitor the progress of pupils, with insight into their way of learning
5. Opportunity for continuing self-development

Not all these aspects will be relevant or necessary in all cases, and one major role of the evaluation will be to provide information about priorities and relative emphases that should be given to different items in this list— and perhaps to add to the list. A few words should be said to enlarge upon these things and explain the reasons for their inclusion where it is not self-evident.

Training Relating to the Activities and Background Information
Many new curriculum projects founder because not enough attention is paid to updating teachers' background knowledge. Indeed, in the case of some new science and mathematics programs for primary teachers, "upgrading" is too delicate a word since relevant background may be totally

lacking. Some project teams, aware of this problem, have attempted to provide background knowledge as part of the material; others have suggested that it is not so important since the teacher can learn at the same time as the pupil, e.g., Nuffield Junior Science Project, England (see *Teacher's Guide 1,* 1967).* In most instances this is unsatisfactory because it ignores the role that background knowledge plays in giving teachers confidence. Some background knowledge should be provided so that the teacher can try the material in the certainty that she will be able at least to direct the children to useful information sources or productive investigations. A danger that must be guarded against in providing knowledge at the teacher's level is that teachers may confuse this with the teaching content; any tendency for this to happen must be opposed by careful explanations of the pedagogic principles of the program. A Malaysian example illustrates how easy it can be for any information provided by a project to be interpreted as essential rather than as enrichment. In this case the background information was provided in pupils' books. Acting on the reactions to an earlier project that had been criticized for providing only a thin book of background reading for pupils, a later project, Modern General Science, provided much more background reading. Subsequently both teachers and pupils complained that the additional material, which was interpreted as necessary information for examinations, was "over their heads."

Some knowledge of how the materials were developed is helpful to teachers for several reasons. It assists in understanding certain features of the program, both in terms of content and processes, and such understanding makes for intelligent use of materials. It may also give guidance as to which aspects of the program are essential to follow and which can be modified to suit certain situations or the preference of the teacher. For example, in the Korean Mastery Learning Project** it was essential for a teacher to follow a sequence of diagnosis, use of compensating programs, teacher instruction, formative tests, and so forth. A teacher might have some choice in other matters but not in the sequence of using these strategies; they were basic to the program. An understanding of the

*Nuffield Junior Science Teaching Project, London, 1964–66, developed guides for teachers to start scientific discovery from children's interests. It was mainly concerned with the age range 7 to 11. No children's books or kits of materials, but project materials were published by W. Collins Ltd., Glasgow, Scotland.

**Begun in 1969 at the Korean Educational Development Institute, Seoul, Korea, the project has produced instructional, diagnostic, compensatory, and enrichment materials to operate a modified mastery learning strategy. Covers most areas of the curriculum and all primary and middle-school grades.

reasons for the sequence, in such a case, certainly adds to the confidence of the teacher in following it and helps to ensure that she will not depart from it in normal circumstances (Kim et al. 1970).

Working through activities for themselves frequently helps teachers to understand the point behind them. Written descriptions can in some cases seem trivial until personal involvement shows how much thinking, skill, insight, and the like is required. Firsthand experience of the program helps teachers to appreciate, and be better prepared to exploit, the potential learning opportunities in the activities. This need not always be through experiences during courses provided by the developers. In the African Primary Science project,

> an effort has been made to see whether it is possible to help teachers teach in this way without having to spend very large investments in training and follow-up by skilled science teachers. The initial indications from these attempts are that good teachers who have had experience themselves in teaching this way can help other teachers teach in the same way at very little cost to the Ministry. In some cases, a good teacher has been released from his classroom teaching in order to be free to help other teachers in his area to start teaching in this way. In other cases, teachers have remained in their own classes but have helped other interested teachers in the same school. In both these cases, independent evaluation of the work of these teachers has shown that training of this sort can be very effective. (Duckworth 1970)

During courses, lengthy experiments or investigations can be covered in a shorter time if slides or photographs of stages in the inquiry and of results are provided. In this way teachers can have the opportunity of interpreting results that it would not be possible to achieve in the time available during a course (e.g., conditions of growth experiments in biology and rural studies).

Training Relating to the Program's Objectives

Participation in activities of the program is also an effective way of introducing or illustrating the program's objectives. One aim of the courses preparing teachers for using new materials must be to interpret the objectives in terms of children operating within the context of the program; without this the written statements of objectives may seem no more than platitudinous remarks.

The role of evaluation in this part of the training stems from its concern with clarifying objectives; evaluation should be able to provide information about ways of helping teachers to understand the meaning of the objectives. In the first place it should be said that having to communicate to teachers objectives devised independently is a situation that is best avoided. When teachers are involved in identifying objectives the communication gap is not created in the first place. Tyler (1964) made an important point about the value of teacher involvement—the danger, he wrote, is that the teacher will not recognize effective ways of reaching the necessary objectives if in fact she has not formulated these objectives for herself. This emphasizes the value of this participation not just to the understanding of objectives but to the teaching-learning process as a whole. The common assumption that teachers are unwilling or unable to take part in this activity is not borne out by experience. For example, in the Science 5/13 project the evaluator discussed the objectives of primary science during a series of meetings with several separate working parties of teachers. In successive revisions of the objectives a closer specification of intentions developed as the groups began to see the value of thinking beyond diffuse aims and analyzing what changes they would really like to produce in children. Progress toward a complete behavioral specification was limited, however, by the need to keep the statements short and simple, to avoid jargon, and most of all, not to narrow the meaning of their intentions. Thus the final list was peppered with words such as "awareness," "knowledge," "appreciation," which are frowned upon by purists. Nevertheless, teachers knew what was meant.

In New Zealand, too, experience has been that teachers have found the writing of objectives of great help in "promoting their understanding of the new programme and giving them increased appreciation of priorities." This resulted from groups of teachers being brought together to study the content of a mathematics program with a view to preparing objectives and eventually writing test items for each objective (New Zealand 1973).

Even if some teachers are able to take part in the planning, the problem of communicating to others still remains unless the whole structure of program development is changed. In many projects the problem is there from the start; the objectives are defined by the team, and ways have to be found to help teachers understand them. Discussions with teachers and observation of any previous preparatory courses are sources of help here, to which might be added the experience of other teams in attempting to solve this problem. Again the Science 5/13 project provides an example. This team found that the best way was not the logical one, i.e., to begin with the objectives and show how the learning activities help children achieve them. This was the approach tried in early in-service courses, but it seemed to fail because teachers had to be given a chance in the first instance to realize the value of clarifying objectives before discussion of them seemed relevant. Therefore, in later courses the first experiences were of activities; after working for a while the teachers were asking questions about the point of the activities and then the time was right to discuss what children might achieve from the experiences. A second look at the same activities led the teachers to see further potential for achievement of other abilities, attitudes, or concepts, and the subject of what the whole range of objectives for the program should be was then introduced. Discussions of this kind enabled teachers to appreciate what objectives mean in the context of actual activities and at the same time to see the role of objectives in this whole area of the curriculum (Harlen 1973).

Training Relating to the Teacher's Role and to Class Management

Certain aspects of the teacher's role in the program have already been mentioned under other headings; the same happens in a course, the subject permeates many aspects of the program. It is important that these are drawn together and a teacher receives an account of his or her role that is convincing and practicable. Teachers have to be clear about their own objectives in using the program: In what respects must the program be followed closely? To what extent is adaptation to suit particular circumstances desirable? Is the teacher primarily a guide or an instructor? Should teacher interaction take place mainly with the class as a whole, with groups, or with individual children? Problems in changing the teacher's role may be far-reaching, since expectations in this respect are often culturally embedded. For instance, in Malaysian schools generally, and it is suggested in most Asian settings, students expect teachers to know all the answers. A teacher who does not show that he is well-informed is nearly always regarded as a mediocre instructor. Therefore, if a new program calls for a radical change in both content and approach, there is a double job for the in-service courses to tackle. In such cases it is necessary to proceed by stages and not expect a rapid change in teacher behavior.

Projects able to produce films or videotapes to demonstrate the teacher's role find these of great value in giving concrete form to general description, and these visual aids can also be used to inform parents and the public in general about changes going on in the school.

In practice, understanding of the teaching-learning processes and of the teacher's role is probably inseparable from the understanding of objectives. Teachers will grasp the essentials of the program more readily if they see the implications of the objectives for the way they interact with their pupils, the experiences they make available, and for their own role in the classroom. There is much that evaluation can contribute here, on account of its concern throughout the material development with the extent to which objectives are embodied in the activities.

As with objectives, it is best if teachers can experience some of the thinking that led to the statements in the material about the activities and the approach to them. By considering selected objectives against the background of the values of the project and the ideas about children's learning it embraces, it is possible to define the kinds of activities that will fit the description. For example, one goal of the APSP is to develop in children "ability to find out for themselves—to see problems and to be able to resolve them for themselves." This indicates problem-solving ability as an objective, but it also expresses the value of firsthand experience and the opportunity to find as well as to solve problems. Illuminated by other goals of the project, the conclusion can be drawn that, for instance, the children's activities will involve concrete things that they can investigate firsthand, the immediate environment will be the major area of enquiry, the problems may not all be readily solvable, different children will work in different ways, children will mostly be working independently. Similarly it is possible to deduce certain things about the teacher's role: that it will not primarily be a role of information supplier, but one of enabling children to find out for themselves; that the teacher may have to allow children to make mistakes rather than impose a "correct" procedure; that he or she will be interacting with children individually or in small groups.

The very practical subject of class management might seem to be the easiest to approach, but many teachers criticize in-service courses particularly for not giving enough help in this matter. The difficulty frequently stems from the course tutors using traditional, often formal, teaching methods in the courses while trying to explain that the teachers should use quite different methods in their schools. Too often, courses attract the kind of remark made by Clegg (1968): "the trainers try to convey fire-lighting techniques by themselves using pot-filling methods."

In an attempt to avoid this criticism some trainers are introducing courses in which the teachers can have experience of the new activities within a setting that reflects the organization for learning intended by the program. In Macquarie University, for example, a new course for trainee teachers was introduced in 1972 with the objective "to develop a knowledge, understanding and empathy with the concept of individualization as the desirable basis for curriculum development" (Cohen 1973). Students taking this course arranged their work program individually with the course lecturers, and only about three out of twenty-four hours per week of study on this course were used for class meetings. "For each task, students could formulate their own individual objectives within a broad framework established by the lecturers. For at least one of these assignments, students worked in a group. Thus the rate of work depended on a group effort, while for at least three of the other assignments, they could set their own dates for completion of the work. . . . The students were also requested to state the criteria by which the work was to be evaluated. . . ." (Cohen 1973). Thus students studied the subject of individualized learning at the same time as experiencing what it was like for the objectives and learning experiences to be tailored to their individual needs.

Training in Applying New Criteria for Monitoring Pupils' Progress

New programs often cut teachers off from established ways of monitoring the progress of their children. This might arise, for example, when teachers are told in a new mathematics program that the ability to count is not as important as the concept of an "ordering relation" between numbers, e.g., Nuffield Mathematics Teaching Project, England (1967).* Recognizing whether or not children can recite numbers is no longer a valid criterion of progress teachers can use; but what replaces it? If there is no adequate replacement teachers become uncertain about whether the children are learning, about whether the program is "any good." Should they fall back on previous methods of checking progress and use inappropriate criteria, their worst fears may well be realized.

If the materials do not provide new methods and criteria for assessing progress, it will be necessary to supply teachers with tools for this purpose during training courses. Where the materials do provide tests it is nonetheless relevant for preparatory courses to help teachers understand the reasons behind their presence and the principles of their use. Teachers require information about their pupils' progress for two main purposes: (1) to assess their development so that activities can be chosen to match individual needs as far as possible, and (2) to assess achievement at various points throughout and at the end of the program. Where possible, a single tool should be provided to cover both purposes so that teachers and pupils are not overburdened by testing. Generally this means that formative assessments are used to indicate the developmental level to which the next activity should be adapted and at the same time form a cumulative record of achievement.

The role of evaluation in this matter is to provide teachers with the tools for evaluating their pupils' progress, or to give them the knowledge so

*The Nuffield Mathematics Teaching Project, sponsored by the Trustees of the Nuffield Foundation 1964–71, produced guides for teachers to convey a modern approach to mathematics for children from 5 to 13 years. The guides place an emphasis on concrete experience and understanding rather than mechanical manipulation. Based at the Centre for Science Education, Bridges Place, London SW6, England.

that they can themselves construct instruments and define achievement criteria. In either case the teachers become evaluators. They have to be clear about what it is that they are evaluating, i.e., about the objectives of the program, how to collect information about their children, and how to assess this information and interpret it in terms that help both their pupils and themselves to operate more effectively.

Generally a program's objectives are wide-ranging, including attitudes, various kinds of skill and mental ability, as well as knowledge and concept attainment. Comparing these with what is assessed in the traditional kind of test question makes the case for widening the range of evaluation tools. The important point is that when the teacher is acting as evaluator, he or she has to take seriously the task of assessing progress toward all the objectives and not just those for which traditional methods provide ready tools.

The problem, and a hint of the solution, is expressed in the case of APSP by Duckworth:

> They (teachers) have realized that there are important things for children to learn which are not tested by written examinations. These are such things as whether children develop confidence in themselves and their abilities, whether they respect the ideas of other children, whether they like learning and want to learn on their own, whether they know important things about their own localities which are not included in the syllabuses . . . There are no memorized answers the children must know how to give. It is mainly by what happens every day in the classroom that the teacher can tell his progress. (Duckworth 1970)

Thus it is important that methods of monitoring pupils' progress should be supplied, preferably built into the material, but otherwise provided in in-service courses. What Duckworth did was to provide guidelines so that teachers could use their observations of children during lessons to find out whether the children were benefitting:

> here are some questions a teacher can ask himself as he watches a child's work from day to day—
> 1. Does he make suggestions about things to do and how to do them?
> 2. Can he show somebody else what he has done so they can understand him?
> 3. Does he puzzle over a problem and keep trying to find an answer even when it is difficult?

4. Does he have his own ideas about what to do, so he does not keep asking you for help?
5. Does he give his opinion when he does not agree with something that has been said?
6. Is he willing to change his mind about something, in view of new evidence?
7. Does he compare what he found with what other children have found?
8. Does he make things?

. . .

23. Does he ever watch something patiently for a long time?
24. Does he ever say, "That's beautiful"?

I think you will agree that if a child does even five or six of these things, he is benefitting. (Duckworth 1970)

In a more detailed way the project Progress in Learning Science (1974)* is providing teachers with check lists, and training in using them, for interpreting observations of their children's behavior during normal learning activities in science. Interpretations are related to development of a list of attitudes, abilities, and concepts that are among the major goals of science for primary and middle school pupils. Two lists have been produced, one for the earlier and one for the later stages of development in the age range five to thirteen years. The list of items for "early" development contains the following:

observing	the concepts of:	curiosity
raising questions	causality	originality
exploring	classification	perseverance
problem solving	time	willingness to
interpreting findings	weight	cooperate
communicating verbally	length	open-mindedness
communicating	area	self-criticism
nonverbally	volume	responsibility
applying learning	life cycle	independence

In the construction of the check lists behaviors have been identified for each item that indicate progressive levels of development. Thus, for

*Based at the University of Reading, Reading, England, 1973–77, this project is sponsored by the Schools Council. Materials are produced for teachers and group leaders to use during in-service courses, aimed at helping teachers "match" learning experiences to children's development of attitudes, abilities, and concepts relevant to learning science in the age range 5 to 13 years.

"problem solving," three levels of development are described by the statements:

Problem solving
0. Generally unable to approach a problem without help, or gives up if his first ideas do not succeed.
1. Tries one or more ways of tackling a problem without much forethought as to which is likely to be relevant.
2. Identifies the various steps which have to be taken and tries to work through them systematically.

In the case of attitudes the notion of development is not well defined and the meaning of the three statements is different. The first level, 0, indicates that the attitude has not been observed, level 1 that it has been observed at an immature level, and level 2 that a more mature form has been observed. For "open-mindedness" these statements are:

Open-mindedness
0. Tends to stick to preconceived ideas ignoring contrary evidence and behaving as if unaware of the existence of opinions and findings different from his own.
1. Changes from one idea or opinion to another inconsistently, being influenced by the authority behind alternative ideas rather than the strength of the evidence or argument.
2. Generally listens to and considers all points of view and relevant evidence; accepts ideas different from his own if the evidence is convincing.

The check-list statements suggest to teachers what behaviors to look for at the same time as indicating the level at which a child seems to be operating with regard to each concept, ability, or attitude. In the use of the lists it is emphasized that decisions should be based not on a single observation but on the accumulation of observations involving a particular kind of behavior. When observations relating to all the items are brought together the result gives a profile of a child showing his strengths and weaknesses and provides a basis for taking decisions as to how to help the child.

Using these criteria a teacher can record profiles of all pupils in the class at any one time. This shows not only where individual children are in the various aspects of development but also shows the pattern over the class as a whole. Repeating the observations and recording them, in a different-colored ink, on the same record sheet enables the teacher to see where pupils have or have not made progress both individually and as a whole class. Where a few individuals have failed to make progress as expected, the teacher might look more carefully at how well these pupils' activities have provided for their needs. Where the whole class has failed to make progress, a teacher might well reflect upon the balance of the program or the kinds of activities that have been used, and use the class record as a tool for self-monitoring.

Providing for Continuing Self-development of Teachers

Finally, the opportunity for the continuing development of teachers should wherever possible be a guiding principle in designing in-service courses. Rarely can a single course provide this, and it may be necessary to institutionalize the arrangements for in-service training so that there are permanent bases for courses and relatively permanent staff to organize them. Teachers' centers were set up in England and Wales in the first instance so that teachers could familiarize themselves, in their own time, with the products of the Nuffield projects in mathematics and science. Such centers, of which there are at present over 500 throughout the two countries, now provide accommodation for local courses, working groups of teachers undertaking their own developments, and private study by individuals. Workshop, laboratory, audiovisual aid, and technical facilities are provided; and many centers supply musical instruments, scientific equipment, films, and videotapes on loan.

Centers can help teachers develop their knowledge of curriculum materials, but sometimes problems of changing teaching styles require a different approach. In England the Ford Teaching Project has developed through action research a way of helping teachers to monitor their own performance. In the development phase the team members helped teachers to identify and then to find ways of solving problems in their own teaching. Their work was concerned to help teachers who wished to implement inquiry/discovery teaching methods, in any area of the curriculum, to do this more effectively. The methods of the research team were interviews, with teachers and pupils, tape-recording and sometimes video-recording sessions. One of the problems very soon uncovered by the team was that teachers could describe very precisely their intentions with regard to classroom interactions, but lesson recordings showed clearly that few manifested their intentions in the classroom. Interviews with teachers enabled the team to define problems as seen by the teachers (e.g., pupils not expressing their own ideas, unwilling to reason things out for themselves, being too dependent upon the teacher). Classroom observations and interviews with pupils then suggested hypotheses for diagnosing the problems. Aspects of teachers' behavior were identified which seemed to be inhibiting inquiry/discovery learning and teachers then undertook to test these hypotheses by changing their teaching strategies. The methods of the research team, of recording lessons and discussing lessons with pupils, were eventually taken over by the teachers so that the teachers were monitoring their own performance (Ford Teaching Project 1975*).

EVALUATING THE EFFECTIVENESS OF TEACHER-TRAINING COURSES

Although evaluation has a role in providing information for preparing teachers' courses and for making decisions about which of the topics discussed above is important to include in any particular case, its major role is to evaluate the effectiveness of the courses as they are run. Unfortunately this is a neglected area, and little work has been done on improving implementation courses through evaluation. The crucial influence of the teacher in the effective implementation of materials, widely acknowledged, is generally not reflected in the attention given to preparing teachers as compared with preparing materials. Project teams could learn a great deal from one another if more evaluation studies were made of teachers' courses, and they could improve successive courses if formative evaluation were built into these courses.

There is a large variety of types and organizational settings of in-service courses. Leaving aside courses intended to supplement teachers' initial training in a general way, and courses that lead to certificates or diplomas, and concentrating only upon methods of preparing teachers for using new curriculum materials, there are still five distinct types of in-service involvement currently in use. One of the most common is the concentrated workshop type, where teachers come to a center and are familiarized with a new approach or new materials during continuous work lasting several days or sometimes weeks. Another common arrangement is for the preparatory course to be spread over several weeks, or months, during which meetings are held about once a week. This is possible where courses are locally based, and generally means that the

*Based at the Centre for Applied Research in Education, University of East Anglia, Norwich, England, this project was sponsored by the Ford Foundation, 1973–75. It is an action research project that has attempted to help teachers monitor their own work and reflect on their performance, particularly in relation to implementing inquiry learning in all areas of the curriculum and at all school levels.

central team has had to prepare local course leaders for this purpose. A third type of extended course is school based and involves a body of specially trained teachers or advisers who are released at times to work together with teachers in their classes, using the new program, and may also continue at other times to teach their own classes. Action research of the kind described at the end of the last section (see page 144) is another form of in-service training, as yet not widespread. Finally, the involvement of teachers in development groups, devising their own programs, in part or in whole, or contributing to a national project is an important form of in-service work that is not widespread in many countries but is becoming more common.

In some countries part of a headmaster's role is to provide in-service training for his teachers. In Papua New Guinea, for example, one hour per week is devoted to this. It is entirely up to the headmasters what they do in this time though they may get advice from inspectors and curriculum advisers. Some headmasters are able to undertake a course of their own each year, which includes work on recent curriculum developments. In England, too, headmasters are being encouraged to promote school-based study of new ideas involving all their staff. The project Progress in Learning Science has devised a scheme in which headmasters receive materials and preparation for their role as study-group leader during courses given by local advisers or teachers' center leaders. The local leaders in turn receive information and materials through a central course run by the project. Combinations of the arrangements mentioned here add to the varieties of in-service work, and of course the list is not intended to be exhaustive.

The main foci of evaluation during a course are teachers' reactions to the course and the effect of the work on the teachers. As has been seen, the aims of the various elements within a teachers' course are concerned with knowledge of the subject matter and activities of the materials, understanding aims and objectives, acceptance of classroom practices that are congruent with these aims, and change in the attitude of teachers toward different kinds of pupil behavior.

In many instances evaluation of these things may not require sophisticated instruments and quite simple ones can be used to find out whether a course is having any immediate effect of the kind intended. Instruments that can be most readily used are interviews, schedules or check lists, questionnaires for collecting reactions from course participants, informal tests for checking on knowledge of subject matter, attitude scales and follow-up observations of classroom practices. In addition most course leaders collect impressions through informal discussions with participants and could make a useful record of reactions by using a check list of questions to be raised in informal contacts. Ongoing evaluation of reactions led one course organizer to appreciate the strains involved when teachers have to endure being taught; he perceived a preference among teachers for creating things rather than receiving information, and subsequently made provision for teachers to find out information for themselves instead of receiving it through instruction.

Yoloye (1970) devised methods for investigating teachers' reactions to training courses. Part of the study was to try to assess the teachers' involvement in their training by asking them to write reports of their investigations; the reports were graded in four categories by judges who were not involved in the training and who were provided with a list of factors to be used in making their judgments.

Many courses aim to improve teachers' own knowledge of the subject matter. The inclusion of formative tests that help the participants to check their own progress could do much to improve the efficiency of these courses. Such test results would also enable those who run the courses to identify areas where teachers find the ideas difficult, or where misunderstanding is found.

Attitudes of various kinds—toward a change in their role, toward encouraging children to learn in different ways, toward catering for differences between individual children—can be measured by devising simple scales or questionnaires. The instrument devised for measuring changes in teachers' attitudes while using trial materials of the Science 5/13 project was used in a separate study of the effect of different arrangements for teacher preparation upon teachers' attitudes. Pre- and post-measurements were compared for four groups of teachers; one group was given a condensed Science 5/13 course, one an extended course, one the materials and no course, and the fourth had no course and no materials. The results showed that the greatest improvement in attitude toward the child-centered learning on which the materials were based was found for those teachers who were given an extended course; next best the condensed course. Teachers having no course and only materials suffered a decrease in attitude, while for those with neither there was no change. These results, even though tentative, point to the importance of materials being supported by courses and the greater effectiveness of the course being spread over a considerable time (in this case ten weeks) rather than condensed into a full week's work.

The end product of all courses is for teachers to use a project's ideas and materials effectively in the classroom. Observations in the classroom are thus an important part of the evaluation of in-service courses. Both immediate and long-term effects should be studied, and some of the techniques that can be used are described in chapter 9. The importance of teachers being able to use the material in the way intended in order to give it a fair trial has been mentioned many times. If the preparatory course fails to help teachers to understand and use the materials, then the results of later evaluation of outcomes or processes may possibly lead to a false conclusion that the material is failing to achieve its objectives. Thus it is important to monitor classroom practices early in the trial period, soon after the course, in order to see whether the preparation has enabled teachers to use the material in a way that will allow its effects to be explored.

Systematic investigations should also be carried out to relate the outcomes of courses, in terms of changes in teachers' knowledge and behavior, to the content and organization of the course. Events and processes of the course should be recorded, and relevant conditions and constraints documented. Then it should be possible to relate the outcomes to the experiences and opportunities provided for the teachers in the courses. Some form of cluster analysis or multivariate analysis will show associations or correlations between sets of variables and provide firm evidence to guide course planning. It may then be possible to plan courses using evidence about the efficiency of different forms of organization, which is at present lacking. For example, extended courses may be more successful than concentrated ones for changing attitudes, while the reverse may be true in the case of improving background information. This knowledge of the effectiveness of different courses and of the relationship of the changes produced in teachers to other variables is generally lacking and will be supplied only if project teams recognize the importance of evaluating this stage of their work. The absence of any appreciable amount of this kind of evidence means that a vital stage in curriculum innovation is based on tradition, hunches, and guesswork. New materials alone will not bring about advances in education. Methods of preparing teachers to use new materials should be subject to the same close evaluation as is the development of materials themselves.

REFERENCES

Armstrong, J. E., ed. "Sourcebook for the Evaluation of Instructional Materials and Media." Madison: University of Wisconsin, Special Education Instructional Materials Center, 1973. Mimeographed.

Clegg, A. "Improving Methods of Communication and Implementation." In *Curriculum Innovation in Practice,* edited by J. S. McLure. London: Her Majesty's Stationery Office, 1968.

Cohen, D., and Deer, C. E. "A New Australian Approach to Curriculum Studies: Part 2, An Individualized Curriculum." Macquarie University, North Ryde, Australia, 1973. Mimeographed.

Duckworth, E. "Evaluation of the African Primary Science Program." Educational Development Center, Newton, Mass., 1970.

Eraut, M. R. "Analysis of Curriculum Materials." University of Sussex Centre for Educational Technology, Brighton, January 1974. Mimeographed.

Falayajo, W.; Yoloye, E. A.; and Bajah, S. R. "The Mid-western Nigeria Primary Science Evaluation Report." International Centre for Educational Evaluation, Ibadan, 1975. Mimeographed.

Ford Teaching Project. "Unit 2 Research Methods." Centre for Applied Research in Education, University of East Anglia, Norwich, 1975. Mimeographed.

Harlen, W. "The Effectiveness of Procedures and Instruments of Use in Formative Curriculum Evaluation." Ph.D. dissertation, University of Bristol School of Education, Bristol, England, 1973.

Harlen, W. *Science 5/13: A Formative Evaluation.* London: Macmillan, 1975.

Kim, Hogwon, et al. *The Mastery Learning Project in the Middle Schools.* Seoul: Korean Institute for Research in Behavioral Sciences, 1970.

Malaysia Curriculum Development Centre. "Comments on the Integrated Science Project." Report sent to IIEP, 1975.

New Zealand, Department of Education. *Item Bank: Mathematics Levels 1-6.* Wellington, 1973. Mimeographed.

Nuffield Junior Science Project. *Teacher's Guide 1.* London: Collings, 1967.

Nuffield Mathematics Project. *Various Teachers' Guides.* London: Chambers & Murray, 1967.

Owen, J. G. *The Management of Curriculum Development.* Cambridge, England: Cambridge University Press, 1973.

Progress in Learning Science Project. *Check-lists for Observing and Recording Children's Abilities, Concepts and Attitudes Relevant to Learning Science.* Reading: University of Reading School of Education, 1974.

Roebuck, M.; Bloomer, J.; and Hamilton, D. *Project PHI.* Glasgow: University of Glasgow, Department of Education, 1974. Mimeographed.

Shipman, M. D. *Inside a Curriculum Project.* London: Methuen, 1974.

Tyler, R. W. "Some Persistent Questions on the Defining of Objectives." In *Defining Educational Objectives,* edited by C. M. Lindvall. Pittsburgh: University of Pittsburgh Press, 1964.

Weiss, J.; Edwards, J.; and Dimitri, D. "Formative Curriculum Evaluation." Ontario Institute for Studies in Education, 1972. Mimeographed.

Wilson, M. "Research Report 14." Faculty of Education, University of Papua New Guinea, 1972. Mimeographed.

Yoloye, E. A. "Evaluation for Innovation: African Primary Science Program Evaluation Report." Educational Development Center, Newton, Mass., 1971. Mimeographed.

Yoloye, E. A. "A Study of Teacher Reaction to Training on APSP Materials." *Journal of the Science Teachers Association of Nigeria* 9, no. 1 (1970): 21–25.

7

Quality Control of Implemented Curriculum over Time

Evaluation is always concerned in one way or another with the improvement of educational programs. Through formative evaluation a set of new curriculum materials, innovative teaching methods, and procedures are tried out in a preliminary version and revised and improved to form a final version. Through summative evaluation, the overall effectiveness and quality of a new curriculum is assessed, and further improvement and adjustments are devised and introduced in the nation's schools. When a final decision is made to introduce new materials, methods, and procedures, the role of evaluation becomes even more important in maintaining the effectiveness and quality of the new educational program in action. In general, the effectiveness and quality of an educational program are not determined solely by the educational program. They are mainly determined by the interaction among (1) the nature and appropriateness of the program, (2) how it is used by teachers and students, and (3) under what conditions it is used. Therefore, the continuous improvement of an educational program is undertaken not only at the formative and tryout stages but also during and after the large-scale implementation stage.

This chapter was written by Hogwon Kim.

In the systematic pattern of curriculum development given in this handbook, quality control comes at the final stage. The problem of quality control is how to maintain the effectiveness of an implemented curriculum over a period of time for the intended student population.

THE NEED FOR QUALITY CONTROL

When a new curriculum or educational program is implemented, the general expectation is that its effectiveness will increase with the passage of time. Teachers gain experience and adjust to new programs or teaching methods. Students may also become aware of what they are expected to learn from a new curriculum.

In some cases, however, a new curriculum that proved effective in the earlier stages of tryout and field trial may turn out to be less effective once it is implemented throughout the system. A seemingly successful innovation at one point in time may be less attractive to students at another point in time. Indeed, both positive and negative changes may alter the effectiveness of an educational program. Negative change in the effectiveness (that is, a decrease in the effectiveness or a deterioration of the educational program over a period of time after its implementation) is important to assess.

Total and Differential Deteriorations

A curriculum may be said to have "deteriorated" when the curriculum loses its effectiveness to a significant degree either in the total student population or in some subgroups of the population for which the program is intended. For example, when a new social studies program intended for the fifth grade in elementary school loses its effectiveness more or less *equally* among the various subgroups of students in the target student population of the fifth grade, the program can be said to have suffered *total deterioration*. When this phenomenon of total deterioration occurs to a serious degree throughout the entire student population, the typical inference is that the program requires a thorough revision.

In other cases the effectiveness of a curriculum deteriorates only in some schools and only with some subgroups of students. For example, a curriculum may lose its effectiveness very quickly with students in rural schools, but continue to maintain about the same degree of effectiveness with students in urban schools after the curriculum is implemented, as illustrated in figure 7.1.

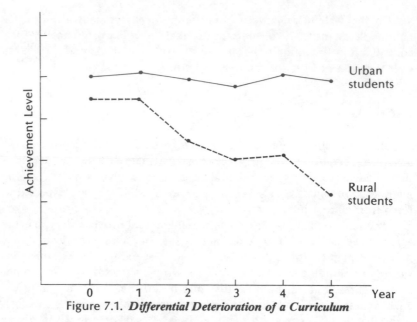

Figure 7.1. *Differential Deterioration of a Curriculum*

Here, the curriculum continues to work well with some students and some teachers and schools, but works less well in certain respects with other students and teachers. The term *differential deterioration* is used to indicate such partial or differential decrease in the effectiveness of particular curricula, methods, or procedures.

In other cases, it may be found that students learn as effectively as in the pilot or tryout stage in the knowledge and comprehension part of the learning outcomes but learn less well in the higher mental processes such as application, analysis, and synthesis. A hypothetical example is shown in figure 7.2.

A new educational program, curriculum, or method can sometimes produce unintended and often undesirable effects on student-learning in the long run. For example, a new science program that works well as far as cognitive learning is concerned may, over time, decrease student interest in science. In other cases, certain teaching methods or learning procedures may produce undesirable study habits, competition, or anxiety among students. Such unintended learning outcomes are important to assess and can form another kind of deterioration of an educational program.

Roles of Evaluator in Quality Control

Evaluation is an effective and sometimes very powerful quality-control process for educational innovations introduced into schools. The

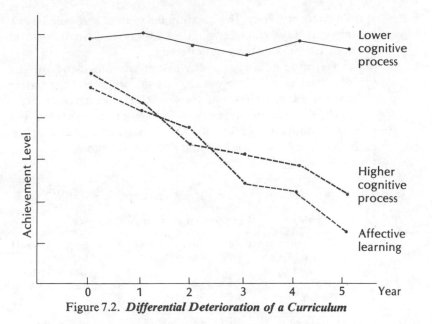

Figure 7.2. *Differential Deterioration of a Curriculum*

evaluator should assume a major responsibility for improving educational programs in their formative stages as well as in their postformative stages. In other words, carefully selected samples of students, classrooms, and schools should be periodically and systematically surveyed to find out whether a new curriculum that worked well at one time continues to work well. More specifically, the role of the evaluator for the purpose of quality control may be stated as follows:

1. The evaluator should assume a major responsibility in discovering whether or not a particular program continues to be effective in attaining its specified educational objectives. When any significant deterioration is observed, the evaluator should determine whether it is total, differential, unintended deterioration, or any combinations of these.
2. The evaluator should be able to identify the cause or source of deterioration, if any, through careful data collection and analysis. Sometimes, the cause of deterioration may be evident, e.g., teachers failing to implement the new method in the intended ways. In other cases, deterioration may be caused by some built-in but hidden characteristics of the educational program itself. Without knowledge of the cause and source of deterioration, it is very difficult to work out any relevant, effective solutions and prescrip-

tions for remedy. Here, the question the evaluator should be able to answer is why and under what conditions is a particular curriculum or teaching method not effective.

3. When the cause or source of the deterioration is identified and measures are taken to improve the effectiveness of a deteriorating program or method, the evaluator should take the necessary steps to investigate how well the remedial actions or measures work. The evaluator should keep providing the decision makers and curriculum developers with relevant and appropriate information as to which measures are effective.

A schematic representation of these three roles appears in table 7.1.

Table 7.1. **Quality Control of Implemented Curriculum over Time**

	1. Identify Need for Quality Control	2. Find cause of Deterioration	3. Apply Corrective Measures and Investigate Effectiveness
A. Problem	Find out if an implemented curriculum continues to be effective Identify where quality control is needed	Understand why and how deterioration originated	Apply appropriate quality-control measures Find out whether a particular measure is effective
B. Process	Compare student achievement data in the current term with those in the previous terms or years	Survey how the curriculum is implemented, under what conditions, to what student groups Analyze and compare a series of formative tests Derive hypotheses which explain why the effectiveness of the curriculum is decreasing	Organize appropriate quality-control measures Verify if these measures are effective under small-scale experimental situations Apply the verified quality-control measures to the target population

Table 7.1. continued

| C. Data | Summative assessment programs or summative achievement tests administered every year

End-of-course examinations

Standardized achievement tests

Expert and teacher judgment

Attitude and interest survey

Questionnaires

Other unobtrusive measures | Formative tests

School survey data

Interviews and questionnaires

Expert and teacher judgment

Classroom observation | Formative and summative tests

Attitude and interest survey

Other unobtrusive measures |

THE PROCESS OF QUALITY CONTROL

The three roles of the evaluator described in the previous section may be considered as the necessary steps an evaluator should undertake in the process of quality control for any implemented educational programs, curriculum, or methods.

Identifying the Effectiveness and Deterioration

In order to identify whether a new program is deteriorating in one sense or another, some base-line data should be collected in advance against which the current effectiveness (i.e., the achievement level of the students after the implementation stage) can be compared. This requires that a sufficient amount and variety of information about the effectiveness of the new program be collected carefully when the program is still in the field-trial stage. When some significant discrepancy is found between the base-line achievement data obtained in the field-trial stage in Year X and the current achievement data gathered in Year X-plus-a, we may conclude that deterioration has occurred.

Comparability of Base-line and Current Data

It is important to ensure the comparability of the base-line data and current data. If comparability is violated to a significant degree, the discrepancy may be attributed not to deterioration in the program but to the differences in the way these two kinds of data are collected. One way of ensuring the comparability is to collect the current data under conditions that resemble as closely as possible the original conditions under which the base-line data were collected.

Systematic Stock-taking of Implemented Curricula

After a new curriculum or teaching method has been implemented, it is essential to undertake regular and systematic assessments of its effectiveness on a half-yearly or yearly basis.

Summative tests. Systematic assessment programs of student achievement such as the National Assessment of Educational Progress are one type of assessment that can be used as a form of quality control.* Through these regular stock-takings, we can follow up whether the effectiveness of a new curriculum or teaching method is improving or deteriorating.

To insure comparability, the repeated administration of the same summative test is desirable. However, it is often more desirable to administer parallel forms of the same achievement test than to use the same form of the test repeatedly.

Standardized achievement tests can also be used to find out whether the effectiveness of a particular curriculum is changing. One should be careful in using standardized tests, however, because in most cases they do not reflect the objectives of the new curriculum in a balanced way. The processes used for developing standardized tests focus on eliminating items on which there are differences for students of a particular characteristic (e.g., sex, urban, rural, residential). Thus, test standardization procedure will often eliminate items on which students of the new program would perform better (Shoemaker 1972).

Nevertheless, for examining general outcomes such as reading comprehension, basic arithmetic, or proficiency in a foreign language, the utilization of standardized tests may be recommended, since such general

*The National Assessment of Educational Progress is a large-scale evaluation study of educational attainments in the United States. Its purpose is to furnish information to all those interested in American education regarding the educational achievements of children, youth and young adults, indicating both progress made and problems faced. The assessment is being made in ten subjects: art, career and occupational development, citizenship, literature, mathematics, music, reading, science, social studies, and writing. Results in each subject are reported by age level, community type, geographical region, race, and sex (see Womer 1970).

objectives appear in all curriculum programs. Standardized tests provide either national or local norms; we can compare the student performance of particular classrooms and schools against these norms.

If the same standardized tests are administered successively year after year, the results will allow us to find out whether the curriculum is still adequate for the new groups of students in terms of previous norms.

End-of-course examinations. Teacher-made achievement tests given at the end of a semester or course may be useful data for the purpose of quality control. Selected teachers can be requested to use the same achievement tests over several years and compare the results year after year. This is, of course, a less systematic way of stock-taking, but it is most powerful for quality control since the final responsibility of quality control rests with individual classroom teachers. When the same tests cannot be used repeatedly for reasons of confidentiality, teachers may use anchor items in their tests to equate the test scores.

Additional data. Additional data may also be collected through careful observation and other measurement devices (such as interest and attitude scales), especially when the deterioration is of the type of unintended outcomes. Unobtrusive measures such as library withdrawal records, the number of enrollments in optional courses, and anecdotal records are also useful additional information (Webb 1966).

Identifying Causes of Deterioration
When signs of deterioration are observed in any implemented curriculum, it is important to determine their underlying causes. This involves testing various hypotheses to explain why such deterioration occurs.

Major Sources of Deterioration
Failures in implementation. A new curriculum may not be effective under any conditions. Each program has a set of intended effects, and these effects can be accomplished only when the program is used in appropriate ways. Thus, the first source to be examined is how the program is actually implemented in schools. A teacher using the new program may miss the important steps inadvertently or use some materials wrongly. Observation of classroom activities, and questionnaires and check lists used unobtrusively, may reveal what actually took place in the classroom.

Changes in the conditions of implementation. The effectiveness of an educational program is also dependent on the conditions under which it is implemented. Thus, for example, if the level of teacher morale is now significantly lower than it was in the field-trial stage, and if other variables remain about the same, it is safe to infer that the discrepancy in student achievement levels between the initial field-trial stage and the later implementation stage may be accounted for by the difference in the levels of teacher morale. In actual situations the problem is not as simple and straightforward. Frequently, causes for the discrepancy in the results are multiple and compounded. Nevertheless, the underlying logic should remain the same.

This underlying logic makes it clear that the evaluator should have systematically collected in advance some basic information about the conditions under which the new curriculum or methods were initially implemented in Year X in order to identify which variables under the present conditions in year X-plus-a differ significantly. A systematic collection of relevant information about the conditions of initial implementation is indispensable for quality control.

In this connection, some general variables are suggested for the evaluator. Information about these general variables should be collected in the field trial and initial implementation stages:

1. *Teacher variables:*
   Teacher morale and motivation
   Teacher perception and attitude toward new curriculum
   Teacher perception of his/her role in the new curriculum
   Teacher knowledge and understanding of the contents of the new curriculum
2. *External variables:*
   Geographical location of schools: urban, rural, remote, etc.
   Size of classroom
   Availability of various facilities and teaching equipment
   School climate, etc.

Changes in the target population. Sometimes a new curriculum is tried out with some deliberately selected groups and schools and then diffused to much wider ranges of student groups and schools. The deliberately selected schools usually have more experienced teachers and better facilities and teaching equipment. Since the tryout and field trials are usually conducted with small samples of students and teachers, it may be more feasible to organize activities such as intensive teacher-training and close supervision. In addition to these variables, the student samples for which a new curriculum is intended may change over a period of time in general characteristics such as ability levels, ranges of ability, and attitude and value-orientation toward schooling. No doubt, these changes in the target student population could be associated with decreased effectiveness of the curriculum after it is implemented.

Some may argue that this is the problem of biased sampling in the tryout stage and that the effectiveness of the curriculum is not really decreasing. It is desirable, of course, to select the tryout and field-trial samples so as to represent as closely as possible the target population for which the new curriculum is to be implemented. In some cases, however, the problem is not merely one of biased sampling. Where student enrollments are increasing rapidly and population migration is frequent, one needs to adapt the curriculum continuously to changes in the student population and to undertake quality control of its effectiveness. This is also true for communities and countries where teacher attrition rate is especially high or school admission policy is changing.

Methods of Analysis

Analysis of formative tests. Probing the formative test results can help us understand where a particular curriculum is especially weak and why. Very roughly, we may say that summative achievement tests tell us whether a curriculum is improving or deteriorating, but most summative tests cannot pinpoint where the difficulties originated and why they originated (see chapter 10 for a more detailed definition of these concepts). Since one of the principal purposes of formative tests is to diagnose learning difficulties of students (Bloom et al. 1971), formative test results may be another source for identifying the causes of curriculum deterioration.

One way of analyzing formative tests is to compare test results in the current year or term with those obtained in the previous year or term. If the results for the current term appear as good or better than those of the previous term, teachers may be persuaded to seek ways of further improving their teaching process. If the results appear lower than those of the previous term, teachers should be urged to find out where the difficulties lie and how to remove them.

Another way of analyzing formative test results is to compare the results of successive formative tests given to the same group of students over a particular period of time. Three possible curves of results on a series of formative tests are shown in figure 7.3.

Curve *A* represents a series of formative tests in which the same proportion of students attain mastery on each test. In curve *C* the proportion of students attaining mastery decreases over the successive tests, and it

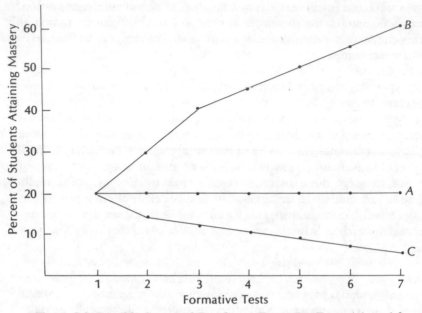

Figure 7.3 *Possible Curves of Results on Formative Tests.* Adapted from
B.S. Bloom et al. *Handbook of Formative and Summative Evaluation of Student Learning* (New York: McGraw-Hill, 1971).

is obvious that the rate of failure will be very high on the summative test. When the observed curves are of the *A* or *C* type, we may infer that the students were not motivated to undertake the necessary additional learning and that the formative tests were not properly used for feedback in the teaching-learning process. Curve *B* is one in which formative tests were used effectively for feedback, and each student attempted to learn what he had missed on each of the tests.

A third way of probing the formative tests is to analyze the errors of students in a particular class on each item in the test. Through item analysis, teachers can discover in what particular items the majority of students have difficulties. Once these difficulties are identified, it becomes easier to develop hypotheses about the possible sources of difficulties.

Other methods. Various modes of evaluation and measurement may be utilized in the process of data collection. For example, classroom observation may be a powerful device for the identification of weak points. Scales and inventories for attitude, perception, motivation, and the like are also useful devices. Carefully structured group discussions, interviews, and case studies can reveal underlying difficulties of program implementation, but these methods are expensive in time and cost. Structured as well as open-ended questionnaires are inexpensive alternatives that can be used in certain situations.

Applying Corrective Measures and Investigating Their Effectiveness

When the causes of deterioration are identified and the specific difficulties pinpointed, appropriate corrective measures must be devised and applied. Analytically, at least, these corrective measures for quality control of ongoing curriculum may take several diversified forms.

In some instances, alterations and revisions can be inserted directly into the curriculum and teaching strategies. For example, minor revisions may be made in the learning materials with which the students continuously manifest learning difficulties, or the intervals of formative tests may be shortened to provide students with more frequent feedback.

In other cases, steps can be taken to change the conditions under which a new curriculum is implemented. This may lead to an improvement in working conditions in the classrooms, or adjustments in the way the curriculum is implemented. For example, students in a classroom could be divided into several small groups in remedial learning sessions so that they have closer interactions with teachers and other students.

In still other circumstances, corrective measures may take the form of in-service as well as pre-service training programs for teachers. Teachers may lack cooperative interactions with their colleagues. Through carefully planned workshops and conferences, teachers may learn a great deal from others' experiences (for example, how problems are handled by other teachers in other schools).

The samples of classrooms and schools to which corrective measures will be applied need not be very large, especially for the purposes of experimentation. It is desirable and sometimes more effective to apply a quality-control measure to a few small groups of students and make an intensive investigation of how the measure actually works and under what conditions it works effectively. The evaluator may then move to a larger group; his problem now becomes how to relate the knowledge and experience gained in small samples to a larger group of students and schools.

When corrective measures are applied, the evaluator is responsible for investigating their effectiveness. If there are alternative measures, the evaluator must assess the relative merits and values of such alternatives.

In investigating the effectiveness of any quality-control measures, either pre-post design or experimental-control-group design may be used.

If the experimental-control design is used, assignment of student groups to either experimental or control conditions should be random. When there is a doubt on the comparability of the samples, appropriate statistical procedures should be applied to control the initial differences.

Formative and summative types of achievement test results may be used for investigating the effectiveness of particular corrective measures. Attitude and interest scales as well as other unobtrusive measures may also be used when the criterion of effectiveness is other than student achievement.

CONTINUITY IN THE PROCESS OF QUALITY CONTROL

In many curriculum centers throughout the world, evaluation is regarded as a quality-control measure for curriculum, instructional methods, and procedures. Evaluation is increasingly being seen as a continuous process of information collection and supplying feedback for improvement rather than as a process of passing judgments.

It is very important to recognize the fact that the processes of curriculum development and quality control are important public enterprises; the education of millions of children in a nation is dependent on them. Continuous quality control of any ongoing curriculum may require an enormous amount of effort, time, and money. But this expenditure and effort eventually pay off when they enable the early detection of problems during the implementation of a program.

This is also why we need a stable curriculum center to undertake a continuous and systematic stock-taking of implemented curriculum at regular intervals and apply appropriate quality-control measures. Quality control should be seen as a built-in process in curriculum development work. Through such control the ongoing curriculum can be regularly adjusted to make it more relevant and responsive to the needs of the individuals and of the society as a whole. Where a central or local curriculum center does not exist, much responsibility for quality control will rest with individual schools. In each society or country those responsible for curriculum development must find ways and means by which quality control of implemented curricula can be continuously and systematically exercised.

REFERENCES

Bloom, B. S., et al. *Handbook of Formative and Summative Evaluation of Student Learning.* New York: McGraw-Hill, 1971.

Shoemaker, D. M. "Evaluating Effectiveness of Competing Educational Programmes." *Educational Researcher* 1 (May 1972): 5–8.

Webb, E. J., et al. *Unobtrusive Measures; Non-reactive Research in the Social Sciences.* Chicago: Rand McNally, 1966.

Womer, F. B. *What Is National Assessment?* Ann Arbor, Mich: National Assessment of Educational Progress, 1970.

PART III

Evaluation Instruments and Strategies

8

Expert Judgments as Evaluation Data

At various stages in curriculum development expert judgments are needed as input data by the curriculum decision makers. Many competencies must be integrated to produce a new curriculum; no one person would possess all the expertise required. For a specific curriculum area we define an expert as one who is competent and experienced relevant to a particular aspect of the curriculum development process. Thus teachers in a subject area, subject-matter scholars, educational supervisors and inspectors, philosophers, psychologists, sociologists, parents, and informed citizens may serve as experts in the curriculum development and curriculum evaluation process.

This chapter deals only with expert judgments collected and summarized formally, i.e., a distinction is made between the expert's participation in the process of curriculum development as a consultant or team member and the systematic collection of expert judgments to be utilized as curriculum evaluation data. As a matter of fact, all members of a curriculum team are experts. But the opinions or views they express during the regular course of their work are not considered evaluation data. Only judgments expressed in response to some standard stimulus or question are considered as such in this chapter. In other words, evaluation data implies

This chapter was written by Göran Leide. **167**

multiple responses to a given stimulus and some formal summary of these responses, either quantitatively or qualitatively.

The chapter covers questions of the following type:

1. In which situation should expert judgments be used?
2. What types of decisions are facilitated by summarizing expert judgments?
3. What kinds of experts should be used as data sources?
4. What means and ways of working should be used to elicit judgments?
5. What kind of methodological problems may arise in connection with using such data?

WHEN SHOULD EXPERT JUDGMENTS BE USED?

Expert judgments can be used in various stages of curriculum development. In some cases there is no alternative to their utilization in the evaluation process. This may be true if one wants to evaluate some features of the instructional materials, such as their scientific accuracy, the correctness of their language, and their relevance to contemporary life. For these purposes expert judgments constitute the most adequate data for determining the quality of the materials.

Empirical tryout of the materials may be less useful for verification of such aspects of the curriculum than expert judgments. In addition, several types of judgments are needed at the initial stages of curriculum development, such as: desirable objectives, important subject-matter topics, and the relevance of particular materials for a particular age group or grade.

There are also cases when the evaluator may have a choice between utilizing experts' judgment and trying out the new materials in the actual class situation. Given such cases, expert judgments are to be preferred in the following circumstances:

1. When there is no time for the lengthy trials required in gathering empirical evidence. This may happen if the materials are unfamiliar and the time required to prepare or train teachers for program tryout would delay program development.
2. When there is no possibility of trying out all the recommended variations of a new program. In such a case the experts may suggest a few promising alternatives, which will then be tried out empirically.

In both cases expert judgment is used to save the time and labor required by an empirical tryout (Lewy 1973). Experts may also be asked to predict the attitudes of children, parents, and teachers toward a certain innovation program; the level of mastery that various groups of students will reach at the end of a certain time period; the most effective way of sequencing the learning experiences; the types of difficulties students will encounter during the study of *particular materials;* and so on. Most commonly, program elements recommended or positively judged by experts will later be submitted to empirical tryout. Thus certain positive errors resulting from the judgments can be corrected later by empirical evidence. That is, if the experts approved a basically deficient program, *empirical tryout will detect its flaws* and will enable the program writers to eliminate the errors. On the other hand, *negative errors committed by the experts may never be detected.* That is, if the experts did not approve a certain program or part of it, it will probably never be tried out; and the possibility of correcting the erroneous judgment of the experts will not arise. Caution should therefore be exercised to prevent the early and possibly unjustified elimination of innovative program features without allowing for their being tried out. Rejection of some program component is justified only if the experts possess sufficient evidence regarding its deficiency.

TYPES OF DECISIONS

Expert judgments are most frequently used to facilitate two types of decisions: selection of program elements, and modification of program materials.

Selection of Elements
At an early stage of program development decisions have to be made as to what elements should be included in the program. Frequently the program writers have to select among a large pool of desired educational objectives or attractive content units. In such cases expert judgment may serve as the basis for decision making. Table 8.1 is an example of a form used to elicit relevant data.

One special form of an evaluation study used to select educational objectives or to determine priorities among competing objectives is the Needs Assessment Study. Hoefner (1973) specifies four stages of needs assessment studies. The first step is the identification of goals that are considered by various sections of the society to be important. Often and erroneously, this single stage is referred to as *the* needs assessment study, but in reality it is a more complex process and consists of several stages. The second stage is the determination of the students' actual and desired achievement levels. The "discrepancy" between current achievement level

Table 8.1. **Form for Rating Program Units**

Instructions: Please mark your answer for each cell of the following matrix, according to a scale ranging from 0 to 5. 0 means "not at all important" and 5 means "highly important."

	The name of the unit	*Its importance within the domain of the subject matter*	*Necessary prerequisite for later units*	*Relevance to life outside school*	*Fits major program goals*
Unit 1					
Unit 2					
Unit 3					

and the level desired or expected should serve as one, but only one, criterion for setting priorities. The third stage is the determination of the significance of certain increases in achievement. It may well be that a small increment of achievement in one educational objective is more highly valued than a greater increment in some other objective. The fourth step in the selection of goals is assessing the probability that a given achievement increment can be obtained. All four stages entail judgment.

An example of the instruments used in a needs assessment study is given in table 8.2. The respondent is asked to indicate to what extent a particular objective is and ought to be included in the school program. The discrepancy between the desired and the actually practiced educational goal in the school system identifies an educational need.

Modification of Program

Experts may be used to review program materials, to criticize them, to point out and suggest program modifications. In many curriculum centers a formal judgment of the curriculum materials by experts is required before the materials are released for print. Tables 8.3–8.4 illustrate this. Table 8.5 contains some questions related to the evaluation of an educational television program. Similar types of questions can be used for the evaluation of school radio programs. Table 8.6 gives an example of a program monitoring form to elicit reactions from teachers concerning their use of a new program.

COMPETENCY OF EXPERTS

The expert is a person who possesses thorough knowledge and a high level of competence in a certain domain of human endeavor. In the context of

Table 8.2. **Form of a Needs Assessment Study—Affective Objectives**

| Description of Behavior | Behavior Developed in School | | | Behavior to Be Developed | | |
	Not at all	To some extent	Highly	Not at all	To some extent	Highly
Students should have rational control over their emotional reactions						
Students should regard love of others as the main motive in human behavior						

Source: S. Eden, "The Translation of General Education Aims into Functional Objectives: A Needs Assessment Study," *Studies in Educational Evaluation* 1 (1975).

curriculum evaluation there are several types of expert. In the initial stages, when the program rationale and objectives are determined, the contributions of the philosopher and the sociologist are very important (Eden 1972). Subject-matter specialists are asked to judge the scientific significance and accuracy of the curriculum materials. Educational psychologists are asked to examine the fit of the curriculum materials to the readiness level of the target student population, and the adequacy of the learning strategies employed in the program for helping students to develop in the desired direction. Experienced teachers may be asked to pass judgment on the teachability of the materials.

It should be emphasized that the competency of the expert in this connection is considered confined to his speciality. Bloom (1966) writes: "The special problem here is to determine the proper role of the specialist. His understanding of his own subject does not mean that he is an expert on the teaching of this subject." Eden (1972) states: "An expert who is a specialist in a defined area sometimes sees the problem only from his point of view." Bruner (1966) adds: "It is reasonably plain to me as a psychologist, that, however able psychologists may be, it is not their function to decide upon educational goals, any more than the ablest general decides whether a nation should or should not be at war." In selecting the expert, the major consideration should be his professional competence. The evaluator should search for experts whose value and integrity are fully recognized by the curriculum team.

One crucial issue in the selection of experts is their neutrality. Should they, or can they, be neutral? Eden (1972) writes that even if the expert only prepares the data for the decision-making authority, his personal judg-

Table 8.3. **Social Studies Curriculum Analysis, Short Form**

*Answer each of the following questions using this rating scheme and give
an explanation for your judgment after each question.*

0	1	2	3	4	5	6
Not at all		*To a moderate extent*			*To a great extent*	

Explanation _____

To what extent are *pictorial sources* such as maps, graphs, charts, tables,
and other illustrative materials *interpreted and utilized* with textual
material and questions arising from it?
To what extent are *key terms and concepts defined* for the student in the
materials?
To what extent are *adequate data readily available in the materials* for the
student to be able to answer questions?
In general how *accurate do the factual data and their interpretation
seem to be* in all parts of the program?
To what extent is a multiethnic approach integrated into the materials?
List ethnic groups included _____
To what extent do the materials and the suggestions in the teacher's
guide encourage development of the following cognitive processes:
(a) Observing or perceiving
(b) Listening
(c) Discussing
(d) Defining and expanding key terms and concepts
(e) Contrasting, comparing
(f) *Recognizing a problem for further inquiry*
To what extent do the materials or the suggestions in the teacher's guide
encourage students to explore, clarify, and act:
(a) on *their own values*
(b) on values held by *others*
(c) on the *presentation of alternative and conflicting points of view*
To what extent does the testing program, or the other evaluation means
made available with the program, test the students' factual recall?
To what extend does the testing program take into account the learning
abilities and capacity of:
(a) slow students
(b) average students
(c) gifted students

Source: Selected questions from "Social Studies Curriculum Analysis, Short Form," in
Teaching American History, ed. A. O. Kownslar (Washington, D. C.: National Council for
Social Studies Yearbook, 1974).

Table 8.4. **Evaluation of a Multielement Instructional System**

A. OBJECTIVES

1. Does the system include a *statement of instructional objectives?*
   _____ yes _____ no
2. Is this statement *detailed enough to be helpful?* _____ yes _____ no
3. Is this statement directed: _____ to the teacher only, or _____ to both teacher and students?
4. *If the system's objectives are unstated, are they obvious:* _____ to the teacher only _____ to both teacher and students _____ to neither teacher nor students?
5. Are the objectives readily compatible with individualized or self paced instruction? _____ yes _____ no
6. Do the objectives *invite the student's affective involvement?* _____ yes _____ no
7. Do the objectives appear to involve only cognitive development? _____ yes _____ no
8. Are the objectives conceived in a tight relation to the subject matter only _____ yes _____ no; or are they conceived in relation to a student's human development? _____ yes _____ no

B. MANNER OF USE

1. Are all elements of the system reasonably easy to use? _____ yes _____ no; only some elements _____ yes _____ no
2. Is the system *flexible?* _____ yes _____ no; or is it a *tight, step by step program?* _____ yes _____ no
3. *Are special skills or extensive preparation required before* the teacher can employ the system? _____ yes _____ no
4. If *equipment* is included, is it *easily used* by the teacher _____ yes _____ no; by the students? _____ yes _____ no
5. Are the system's materials readily used by the students? _____ yes _____ no
6. Do you know of evidence of the system's successful use in other educational settings? _____ yes _____ no
7. Does the system *present any unusual storage problems* _____ yes _____ no; or *problems of distribution to students?* _____ yes _____ no
8. Does using the system actively involve the students? _____ yes _____ no
9. Does the *system offer adequate evaluation procedures* for the teacher _____ yes _____ no; for the student? _____ yes _____ no
10. Is there a good match between the evaluation procedures and the systems objectives? _____ yes _____ no
11. Did you find the evaluation procedures adequate? _____ yes _____ no

Acceptability scale
   1 _____ unacceptable 2 _____ acceptable with reservations
   3 _____ acceptable 4 _____ more than acceptable 5 _____ excellent

Comments?

C. QUALITY OF CONTENT
1. Is the system's *content authentic* (and, if applicable) *accurate?*
   _____ yes _____ no
2. *Is the content timely* (if applicable) _____ yes _____ no
3. Are the *illustrations and examples apt* for your students?
   _____ yes _____ no
4. Does the *content communicate effectively?* _____ yes _____ no
5. Are the system's sensory aspects (sound, colour, visuals, etc.)
   appropriate? _____ yes _____no
6. Is the system designed for ease of student progression? _____ yes
   _____ no
7. Is the system's *vocabulary appropriate* for your students?
   _____ yes _____ no
8. Is the *content presented clearly?* _____ yes _____ no
9. Did your students find the content *relevant* and *interesting?*
   _____ yes _____ no

Acceptability scale
   1 _____ unacceptable 2 _____ acceptable with reservations
   3 _____ acceptable 4 _____ more than acceptable 5 _____ excellent

Comments?

D. QUALITY OF CONSTRUCTION
1. Does the system present any unusual problems? _____ yes _____ no
2. Did you find the system sufficiently durable? _____ yes _____ no
3. Are the system's elements well-designed? _____ yes _____ no
4. Did the system present any safety problems? _____ yes _____ no
5. If the system contains equipment, does it operate reliably?
   _____ yes _____ no
6. If equipment repairs were needed, was the repair service adequate?
   _____ yes _____ no
7. Were such repairs required frequently? _____ yes _____ no
8. Were such repairs made easily and quickly? _____ yes _____ no

Acceptability scale
   1 _____ unacceptable 2 _____ acceptable with reservations
   3 _____ acceptable 4 _____ more than acceptable 5 _____excellent

Comments?

Source: Prepared by Educational Facilities from J. R. Armstrong, ed., "A Sourcebook for the Evaluation of Instructional Material and Media" (Milwaukee: University of Wisconsin, 1973). Mimeographed.

ments are part of this process: "As a person he shares hopes, dreams, frustrations and prejudices with other human beings." This implies that practically no expert is absolutely neutral. Stake emphasizes the need to include in the evaluation report the opinions both of experts who favored a

Table 8.5. **Questionnaire for the Technical Quality of TV Information Shows**

Audio-video balance
Were the oral/visual parts in balance?
Would some material presented visually have been better left to imagination?

Production quality
Is there adequate motion in the telecast? (e.g., drawing map or chart rather than showing one previously prepared)
Was there too much narration?
Rate language delivery: conversational quality
                         change in volume, pace, pitch
Is there enough variety in show?
Was music well used?

Visual
Titles: Was lettering large enough and distinct?
Were color tones pleasing?
Did photographs help tell story?
Were too many stills (photographs) used?

Lighting
Do lights illuminate subjects adequately?
Do lights model subjects to make them stand out from background?

Camera action
Did cameras show subjects high enough to ensure instant recognition?
Were there good transitions between close-ups and long shots?

Source: W. B. Levenson, and E. Stashoft, *Teaching Through Radio and Television* (New York: Greenwood Press, 1969).

given program and of those who did not (Stake 1967). Nevertheless, program writers benefit mainly from the judgments of experts who basically accept the program rationale. Thus, for example, it could hardly be useful to collect judgments concerning an integrated science course from experts who strongly oppose the integration of various branches of science into a single course of studies and who prefer their separation as individual courses. Likewise, it hardly seems profitable to have a course in new mathematics for elementary school grades judged by experts who openly oppose the teaching of such materials in elementary schools. Program writers have to consult experts holding divergent opinions before they make decisions concerning the program's rationale, but as soon as they reach a decision about the general principles of the program, they will benefit mainly from the judgments of those experts who subscribe to their rationale.

Table 8.6. **Geography Program Monitoring Form**

Please tick the most appropriate response to each question
Tick box 1 for *Definitely Yes*
Tick box 2 for *Probably Yes*
Tick box 3 for *Don't Know*
Tick box 4 for *Probably No*
Tick box 5 for *Definitely No* → 5 4 3 2 1

1. In general did you find teaching the unit(s) interesting? ☐ ☐ ☐ ☐ ☐

2. Was there enough guidance on the unit(s)? ☐ ☐ ☐ ☐ ☐

3. Did you find the layout of the unit(s) satisfactory? ☐ ☐ ☐ ☐ ☐

4. Would you prefer to have the objectives more precisely stated? ☐ ☐ ☐ ☐ ☐

5. Did you find basic resources (including books) easy to find? ☐ ☐ ☐ ☐ ☐

6. Would you like more ancillary materials given to you? (If so, specify at end of questionnaire) ☐ ☐ ☐ ☐ ☐

7. Did you think the unit too difficult for your pupils? ☐ ☐ ☐ ☐ ☐

8. Was there an interest in the unit throughout? ☐ ☐ ☐ ☐ ☐

9. Did you think the units in the course restricted your teaching style? ☐ ☐ ☐ ☐ ☐

10. Did the units in this course encourage you to alter your S1/2 syllabus at all? ☐ ☐ ☐ ☐ ☐

11. Do you think meeting with other teachers attempting these units would help you in your teaching of it? ☐ ☐ ☐ ☐ ☐

12. Do you think the course of units is generally too long? ☐ ☐ ☐ ☐ ☐

Source: B. J. McGetterick, "Geography Programme Monitoring Form" (Scottish Centre for Social Subjects, Jordanhill College, Glasgow, 1975). Mimeographed.

WAYS TO ELICIT JUDGMENTAL DATA

Judgmental data is elicited either in the form of *oral* or *written* responses to some series of questions. The responses can be given *individually* by each respondent alone, without his considering responses given by others, or in

Table 8.7. **Types of Judgmental Data**

Respondent	Form of Responses	
	Oral	Written
Individual	interview hearings	questionnaire, free responses, essay, content analysis
Group	reference group remiss	Delphi technique hearings

a *group situation,* where the respondents may interact with and be affected one by the other. Accordingly, one may distinguish four different types of data collection, as outlined in table 8.7 and discussed in the following pages.

Oral—Individual Responses

Interviews

The easiest way to get information from experts is to question them directly in an interview situation. An interview may be fully prestructured, i.e., several respondents may be asked a standard series of questions. Alternatively an interview may be entirely unstructured, i.e., the respondents are asked to react freely to certain ideas related to the curriculum development or to some specific curriculum materials. The advantage of a structured interview is that it provides many responses to one particular question and thus enables assessment of consensus among the experts concerning a certain issue. The advantage of the unstructured interview is that it may call to the curriculum writer's attention some unconsidered aspects of the program. Here is an example of an unstructured interview:

A group of experts were asked to criticize a program in home economics for seventh-grade girls. In a series of unstructured interviews the following remarks were made: (1) "The program strongly emphasizes the table manners of middle-class groups and does not pay attention to working-class table arrangement habits." (2) "The program does not present the table manners of ethnic minorities." (3) "The program should deal with situations where the children themselves assume responsibility for arranging meals, such as meals in the school cafeteria, meals during school excursions, etc."

An example of a series of questions in a structured interview is given in table 8.8.

Table 8.8. **Interview Schedule from the Malaysian Curriculum Centre**

Section C.
C1 One of the major objectives of the second Malaysian Plan is the "Orientation and expansion of education and training programmes towards meeting the manpower needs of the country."
—Do you think that the programme contributes towards this goal?
—Why do you think so?
C2 Another major objective is to promote integration and national unity.
—Do you think the programme contributes towards this goal?
—In what way?
—Does the programme contribute towards closing the disparity in educational opportunities between regions and races?

Hearings

A more formal way of setting up a series of individual interviews is sometimes called "hearings." In the "hearing technique" members of the curriculum team arrange meetings with representatives of various groups and organizations that have an interest in the new program.

A hearing technique was used in developing syllabuses for the Swedish *Gymnasium* (higher secondary education). The evaluator arranged meetings for each subject team with representative university specialists in the same subject, as well as with specialists in commerce and industry. The experts were chosen by *the team* as being able to represent the range of issues that it felt required discussion. The experts were then asked to what extent they thought these issues were to be known by the students. Afterward the team had an opportunity to clarify its own point of view and to ask for the experts' motives and for alternative solutions. Depending on circumstances, a hearing could be confined to a series of individual interviews or could develop into group discussions.

The team had the final responsibility of balancing the requirements and interests of the different experts in order to reach a realistic and acceptable syllabus.

Oral—Group Responses

Reference Groups

The previous sections dealt with data collection from individuals responding alone. The present section describes a method of eliciting data in a group situation.

In the initial stage of curriculum development, especially in national curriculum reforms, there is a need to involve representatives from several interest groups in the planning. Sometimes the curriculum center will take the initiative for inviting such representatives, but usually this will be the responsibility of the leaders of the curriculum reform. Here is an example:

> In planning the Swedish Reform of Higher Education, several high level reference groups were associated with those in charge of the project. In the course of developing objectives and programs, plans and implications were discussed within these groups. The groups had regular meetings. This procedure secured a continuous evaluation of goals and materials produced by other expert groups also associated with the project staff. From the political point of view it was a guarantee of essential support from influential groups.

The "Remiss" System

This system is widely used in Swedish administration to collect expert judgment on government reports. With suitable modifications it is applicable to curriculum development. It could be used, for instance, when the team has constructed some written materials, such as lists of objectives, syllabuses, instructions, teaching aids, or detailed plans for the implementation of a new curriculum. The idea is that the report should be criticized and, if necessary, corrected before it is finally approved. To some extent this procedure will safeguard the team from substantial troubles later. It is therefore to be considered as a step in formative evaluation when it is still possible to alter project details.

In Sweden the reports are sent to all organizations and institutions that might be concerned. Political parties and labor unions are usually involved. In most cases major organizations will in their turn send the materials to a number of local institutes or departments under their administration. Among other recipients of a report by the Ministry of Education will be the National Board of Education responsible for administering the school system. The National Board of Education will send copies to teacher-training colleges and some schools. A school requested to analyze the report usually appoints a group to prepare its comments. The material is then discussed in meetings and probably revised before it is accepted as the school's opinion. In such a case the National Board of Education will usually issue new report based on the comments received from the schools but including its own views. Finally the Ministry will analyze all "remiss replies," discuss them, and publish selected comments and arguments. This, together with the original report, is the basis for a final decision on the project.

Some technical details may be of interest to curriculum developers elsewhere. When the Ministry has received all comments, these are arranged according to issues. It is therefore desirable that the report be highly structured, so that nonspecialists can take care of the collation. The Ministry is not obliged to follow recommendations, although a very strong opinion against a proposal will often lead to modifications.

Individual Written Responses

Questionnaires

A common way to collect expert judgments is to use questionnaires. Examples of questionnaires were given in tables 8.3–8.6. These questionnaires were of the short-answer or multiple-choice type. The advantage of using such questionnaires is that they require relatively little time and effort on the part of the respondent. They can also be summarized easily, either manually or with the aid of a computer.

A variation on using a questionnaire for examining the adequacy of curriculum materials is given in table 8.9. In this example answers were recorded in the text of the curriculum materials to be evaluated. In the course of developing a manual for a science apparatus kit, it was considered too time-consuming and costly to produce a preliminary version and try it out in a number of classes. To ensure that their approach was generally acceptable, the authors tried a few experiments in some schools. They then tried out the remaining experiments themselves in order to make

Table 8.9. **Guidelines for Comments, Kenya Institute of Education**

For each experiment:
1. Is the topic relevant to the syllabus?
2. Is the subject content correct?
3. Is the language correct and adapted to the level of the students?
4. Are the diagrams correct?
5. Is the description of the procedure logical and easy to follow for pupils at this level?

For the manual as a whole:
6. Are important topics from the syllabus missing?
7. Do the materials allow for individual differences?
8. Do the materials provide for a variety of learning activities?
9. Are the materials in line with the objectives of the syllabus?

All suggestions should be recorded at the appropriate place in the text.

certain that the sequencing and the instructions were technically correct. Finally, three experts were invited to judge the manuscript. This team included experts on the subject matter, on teaching, and on apparatus construction. Each expert was given a copy of the draft manuscript and asked to note the corrections he wanted made. Each was given a check list of the salient features he was to look for. The list is shown in table 8.9.

After completing their task, the group members discussed the manual together with the evaluator, who in this case was also one of the authors. Usually they reached a common conclusion on corrections, although the experts made very different suggestions originally.

Unstructured Free Responses

Frequently evaluators are interested in eliciting from experts fully detailed and justified free responses concerning various issues and including both positive and negative comments. A summary of such responses is given in table 8.10.

A suggestion to invite essay-type responses on intricate questions was made by Weinberg, who claimed that group discussions and conferences are sometimes inefficient ways of obtaining information from experts. He writes:

> Now committees in my view can no more produce wisdom
> than they can design a camel. The atmosphere of a committee
> is too competitive, too verbal. Wisdom is a very personal kind of
> thing: it flourishes best when a single mind thinks quietly and
> consistently—more quietly and consistently than is possible when
> one is engaged in the rough-and-tumble of committeeship with its
> often tendentious and personal exchanges. Thus, I have felt that
> some of the most troublesome questions ought to be thought
> through by individuals who would then set their thoughts down
> in essays. Out of many such essays, written by different people,
> could come, if not clarity and guidance, at least a common language
> and framework in which to conduct the discourse. (Weinberg 1967)

The method suggested by Weinberg could be adopted for curriculum development, especially in the initial and implementation stages when problems are complicated.

Content Analysis

A unique way of using expert judgments is to perform a content analysis of the study material. Though content analysis is considered a highly objective way of describing the traits of some communication materials, it does involve the judgments of well-trained persons.

Table 8.10. **Free Comments on Educational Programs**

MUSIC
Aims: To increase awareness of classical, folk, and pop music; to
             contrast the music of North, South, and Central America. A
             course for developing understanding of music, not for
             developing the skills of the musician.
Sketch: Musical sensitivity grew with exposure to ethnic music and
             basic concepts in musicology. Work with ensembles.
Comments: Course content excellent; studio facilities inadequate. Staff
             contributed little to other fine arts courses or total Institute;
             no real ties to Woodstock Nation.

WILDERNESS LEADERSHIP
Aims: To combine the skills of camping, canoeing, backpacking,
             etc., with the responsibilities of leadership and organization,
             so that students can guide others into the wilderness safely
             and with a sensitivity to its social, aesthetic, and ecological
             aspects.
             Practical experience.
Sketch: Students practiced making plans for trips, assisted groups on
             Cannon River canoe outings, etc., learned the problems in
             looking out for others in ordinary as well as hardship and
             deprivation conditions, and constructed own pack frames
             and other items of equipment.
Comments: A very popular and worthwhile educational experience, it
             should be expanded for forthcoming Institutes, but should
             be changed to provide more instruction in guiding and
             wilderness living.

Source: R. Stake and E. Craig, "An Evaluation of TCITY, the Turin City Institute for Talented Youth 1971," in *Four Evaluation Examples,* ed. R. Stake (Chicago: Rand McNally, AERA Monograph Series on Curriculum Evaluation, 1974).

"Content analysis involves systematic, replicable quantification in analysis, and a description of communication content (written, verbal or visual) with a particular focus on the purpose of description" (Grobman 1972). One may add to this definition that patterns of motor behavior can also be submitted to content analysis.

To perform content analysis one first needs to define a series of relevant categories, e.g., factual information, explanatory sentences, and open questions. Second, one has to *determine the unit of analysis*. It may be a specific learning activity, a paragraph, a sentence, or even a single word. On the basis of classifying the units according to predetermined categories, one may produce objective profiles of different curriculum materials. An example of such profiles is given in figure 8.1.

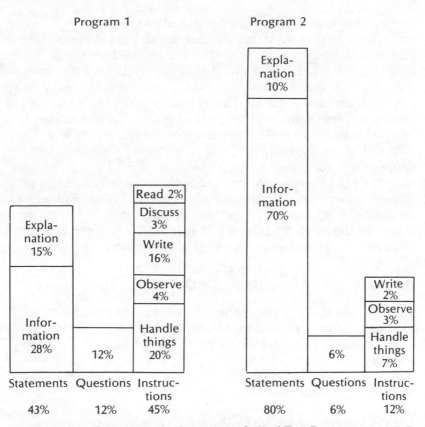

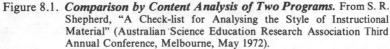

Figure 8.1. ***Comparison by Content Analysis of Two Programs.*** From S. R. Shepherd, "A Check-list for Analysing the Style of Instructional Material" (Australian Science Education Research Association Third Annual Conference, Melbourne, May 1972).

Grobman writes that content analysis can be used to describe the presence of selected characteristics in curriculum material such as the compatibility of the material with specific aims, the nature of presentation, and the value orientation of the materials.

Group—Written Response
The Delphi Method
The Delphi method was generated to facilitate the utilization of experts' advice in making policy decisions. The proponents of this method suggest avoiding group meetings, where one dominating person may easily impose his view on the others (Kaplan et al. 1950). Instead of having group

meetings, the experts are given written questions and asked to answer in writing. The responses are then collected, tabulated, and summarized by the leader of the study, and this summary is circulated among the respondents. They are asked to reexamine their position and restate their opinion, given this body of original responses. The Delphi method is in fact a group process carried out in writing. The reiterations employed in this method increase the consensus concerning certain issues. At the same time they bring out the controversial issues where consensus can hardly be obtained. This method has frequently been used in the context of curriculum evaluation, mainly to determine worthy educational goals. Thus, for example, Rasp (1974), using this technique, studied the relative importance of 67 different educational goals as perceived by American educational experts. He also examined regional differences, and differences between groups of experts in terms of their readiness to change their judgment on subsequent interactions and administrations of the questionnaire.

PROBLEMS IN SUMMARIZING JUDGMENTS

Since the evaluator collects responses from several experts, it is necessary to summarize the data in such a way that they are useful for decision making. Clearly, if all the experts are in complete agreement, the task of summary does not create any difficulties. Most often, the data contain controversial opinions; guidelines are needed to translate such data into operational recommendations.

Consensus and Reliability

Evaluators are inclined to search for elements of consensus in a multiplicity of data, and they sometimes strive to increase consensus among the judges artifically. It should be emphasized, however, that consensus is not a necessary prerequisite for utilizing expert opinion. On the contrary, in the context of curriculum evaluation the evaluator may be very interested in collecting the range of views and opinions held by persons of divergent approaches (Stake 1967). It is important to know the range of opinions concerning a particular issue prevailing in a society, as well as the limits of consensus that can be obtained. Evaluators frequently postulate consensus among experts concerning judgmental data, but consensus should be postulated only when there is certainty of the possible application of well-defined criteria to obtain highly objective descriptive data. Thus, for example, one may strive to obtain consensus among experts concerning the classification of sentences into such categories as factual statements, explanatory statements, generalizations, and so on.

But, it may be totally unrealistic to believe that consensus could be obtained concerning social goals and ambitions. The attempts to increase consensus among experts described below do not refer to issues of values; rather, they refer to the meaning of terms and to the application of certain principles to concrete situations.

In the context of judgmental data, consensus among experts is frequently considered an index of reliability. In the case of grading essay-type examinations, for instance, one postulates that several persons, who have already agreed on common criteria for grading the essays, will assign similar scores to a particular essay. This does not mean that aiming for consensus justifies imposing the one set of criteria on all the judges. The attempt to increase consensus, at least in evaluation studies, starts only after agreement concerning the criteria to be used has been obtained. Some recommendations for increasing consensus among experts may be derived from Kaplan's recommendations (Kaplan et al. 1950).

1. The task should be clearly stated in advance and all terms should be fully defined and illustrated by examples.
2. The expert should be given time to examine the questions thoroughly and if possible to retrieve from his previous experience any material necessary to support his view.
3. The experts should meet as a group to discuss the questions and only then be asked to state their opinion.
4. The group should not be prohibitive in size.
5. The group should be asked to justify its views and predictions.

Statistical Methods to Evaluate Consensus

Frequently it is necessary to obtain a numerical measure of consensus. One has to differentiate between two cases: consensus in rating and consensus in classification.

Consensus in Rating

If experts are ranking a number of entities, e.g., a number of different methods or a number of pupils, there will usually be some agreement between their lists; but the agreement may not be complete. It is then possible to estimate the degree of agreement using the Kendall coefficient of concordance W (Siegel 1956). A high value of W, as judged from a table of critical values, indicates that the agreement between the experts is not due to chance. If the agreement is significant, one usually considers the order of the sums of the scores as the best estimate of the true order between the entities. It should be emphasized, however, that a high value of *W* does not mean that the ordering is *correct,* only that the judges agree. Before the results may be used and accepted, it is necessary for the evaluator to ensure that the judges are using the same criterion for their ordering. In the process of calculating the coefficient, it is sometimes discovered that some experts' lists deviate considerably from the final list. This indicates strongly that value scales have been different. It still remains for the evaluator to find if the majority or the minority is correct and to decide whether the ranking should be repeated or some of the lists should be discarded.

The details of the use of the Kendall coefficient of concordance are available in standard textbooks on statistics (e.g., Siegel 1956).

Consensus in Classification

An easy way to express consensus in classification is to indicate the percentage of items concerning which consensus had been reached in their classification. A more sophisticated formula to indicate degree of consensus is provided by Scott (1955; see also Medley and Mitzels 1963). A method of presenting the full map of agreements and disagreements in the classification by different experts is suggested by Lewy (1974).

Adversary Models of Evaluation

In contrast to the search for consensus, the use of adversary models implies the presentation of the full array of contradictory arguments related to the problems of curriculum development. To obtain the maximum information, a process modeled after legal proceedings is followed. In this approach a supporter and an adversary are attached to the curriculum team. The first has to collect evidence in favor of the program, while the second tries to refute the validity of this evidence and to present arguments against the program. The decision maker has to pay attention to both the supportive and the antagonist arguments when he determines the direction of further action.

Kourilsky warns against paralyzing any possible innovations by paying too much attention to adversary arguments (Kourilsky 1973). She emphasizes the need to synthesize supportive and adversary views in reaching sound decisions.

THE STATE OF THE ART

Recently utilization of expert judgment has become a widely used strategy in curriculum evaluation. Some examples of the many variations on this theme in various curriculum centers have been presented in this chapter.

Judgment has become one of the three most frequently used data types in education, the other two being observation and cognitive or affective achievement measures. Highly formalized techniques were developed to construct, analyze, and summarize the data collected in using achievement measures and observational schemes. At the same time *no well-formulated theories exist concerning the utilization of judgments.*

While this chapter has presented the state of the art in this field, it has probably served more to highlight the relevant problems than to resolve them.

REFERENCES

Armstrong, J. R., "A Sourcebook for the Evaluation of Instructional Materials and Media." Madison: University of Wisconsin, Special Education Instructional Materials Center, 1973. Mimeographed.

Bloom, B. S. "Role of the Educational Science in Curriculum Development." *International Journal of Educational Sciences* 1 (1966): 5–16.

Bruner, J. *Toward a Theory of Instruction.* Cambridge, Mass.: Harvard University Press, 1966.

Eden, S. "The Translation of General Aims of Education into Functional Objectives for Curriculum Construction." Ph.D. dissertation, University of Chicago, Chicago, 1972.

Eden, S. "The Translation of General Education Aims into Functional Objectives: A Needs Assessment Study." *Studies in Educational Evaluation* 1 (1975): 5–12.

Grobman, Hulda. "Content Analysis as a Tool in Formative and Summative Evaluation." Paper presented at the Fourth Asian Regional Conference in Biological Education, Jerusalem, 1972.

Hoefner, R., et al. "National Priorities for Elementary Education." Center for the Study of Evaluation, University of California, Los Angeles, 1973.

Kaplan, A.; Skogstad, A. L.; and Girshick, M. A., "The Prediction of Social and Technological Events." *Public Opinion Quarterly* 14 (1950): 93–110.

Kourilsky, M. "An Adversary Model for Educational Evaluation." *Evaluation Comment* (University of California, Los Angeles) 4, no. 2 (1973): 3–6.

Kownslar, A. O., ed. *Teaching American History.* Washington, D.C.: National Council for Social Studies Yearbook, 1974.

Levenson, W. B., and Stashoff, E., *Teaching Through Radio and Television.* New York: Greenwood Press, 1969.

Lewy, A. "Utilizing Experts' Judgement in the Process of Curriculum Evaluation." Report No. 87, Center for the Study of Evaluation, University of California, Los Angeles, 1973. Mimeographed.

Lewy, A. "Types of Examinations in History Studies." *Journal of Educational Measurement* 11 (1974): 35–42.

McGetterick, B. J. "Geography Program Monitoring Form." Scottish Centre for Social Subjects, Jordanhill College, Glasgow, 1975. Mimeographed.

Medley, D. M., and Mitzel, H. E. "Measuring Classroom Behavior by Systematic Observation." In *Handbook of Research on Teaching,* edited by N. L. Gage. Chicago: Rand McNally, 1963: Pp. 247–328.

Rasp, A. F. "Delphi: A Strategy for Decision Implementation." *Educational Planning* 1 (1974): 42–47.

Scott, W. A. "Reliability of Content Analysis: The Case of Nominal Scale Coding." *Public Opinion Quarterly* 19 (1955): 321–325.

Shepherd, S. R. "A Check-list for Analysing the Style of Instructional Material." Australian Science Education Research Association Third Annual Conference, Melbourne, May 1972. Mimeographed.

Siegel, S. *Non-parametric Statistics for the Behavioral Sciences.* New York: McGraw-Hill, 1956.

Stake, R. "The Countenance of Educational Evaluation." *Teachers College Record* 68 (1967): 523–40.

Stake, R., and Craig, Gjorde, "An Evaluation of TCITY, the Turin City Institute for Talented Youth, 1971." In *Four Evaluation Examples,* edited by R. Stake. AERA Monograph Series on Curriculum Evaluation. Chicago: Rand McNally, 1974. Pp. 99–139.

Weinberg, A. M. *Reflections on Big Science.* Cambridge, Mass.: MIT Press, 1967.

9

Observational Techniques

One way of obtaining information about the progress and outcomes of an education program is to observe directly selected aspects of its implementation as they occur. For example, one might observe activities in classes where the program is being used. Such observation may be related to students' behavior, teachers' behavior, or both.

Compared with techniques such as tests and questionnaires, observation is a relatively expensive way of gathering data. It is time-consuming and its coverage is often limited by practical considerations such as the number of trained personnel and school schedules available. There are also problems of observer reliability. Nevertheless, there are certain situations during curriculum evaluation in which observation is particularly useful and even indispensable.

Observational techniques have been extensively treated in educational literature. A series of volumes describe in detail the best-known models of class observation (Simon and Boyer 1967). Several excellent reviews discuss merits of different observed teacher behaviors (Rosenshine 1971, 1973; Dunkin and Biddle 1974). This chapter concentrates on issues related to the utilization of observational techniques in the context of curriculum evaluation. It presents a brief description of the following issues:

This chapter was written by E. Ayotunde Yoloye. **189**

1. The variety of situations in which observational data seem to be useful
2. Major types of observational techniques, including some particular models of observation that have been used in the context of curriculum evaluation
3. The role of observational data at different stages of program development

SITUATIONS THAT MAY BE SERVED BY OBSERVATIONAL DATA

Measuring Classroom Process Variables

Observation may provide information about important process variables that characterize work in the classroom. It may indicate how the lesson time is divided between a variety of activities such as individual work, small-group work, and whole-class activity, or how time is divided between teachers' talk, students' talk, and nonverbal activities in the class. Observational techniques may be used to answer a variety of other questions, for example: To what extent do students actively participate in class activity? What elements of the program increased participation of the students and what elements did not elicit participation? Who are the active participants? Did the lesson arouse interest? How much class time was devoted to task-oriented activities and how much to irrelevant activities?

Measuring Attainment of Program Objectives

Observation may provide information about the attainment of certain program objectives. This may be the case in evaluating the attainment of certain psychomotor skills, such as using certain tools properly, performing activities that require muscular coordination and body movement, and so forth. Often the attainment of cognitive skills can be best evaluated by observing student activities; for example: Can the student observe accurately the movement of an animal? Can he perform the separation of elements in a chemical compound? Can he build an electric circuit? Can he carry out written instructions? Aspects of social functioning also lend themselves to measurement by observational techniques; for example: How does the child interact with other children or with the teacher or with materials?

Measuring Program Implementation

Observation may serve the purpose of measuring the degree of program implementation. Not all teachers carry out program instructions in the way intended by program writers. Frequently the program writers prescribe learning by inquiry; instead, many teachers overload lessons with explanations of an expository type. In such classes one can hardly expect that all program goals will be attained, since the activities designed to lead to the attainment of these goals were not performed in the class. This need to examine the degree of program implementation can be illustrated by the following case: In the 1930s a study was planned in the United States to evaluate the outcomes of the Activity School Project. It was planned to compare the outcomes in activity schools with outcomes in a matched group of nonactivity schools. In order to increase the meaningfulness of the comparison, the evaluators decided to examine first the extent to which the activity schools maintained an educational environment that fitted the principles of the treatment. They identified 61 traits that were supposed to characterize an activity school. It was found that only one-third of the classes in the activity schools showed as many as 50 of the required 61 traits and, surprisingly enough, that one-fifth of the classes in control schools revealed 50 or more of these traits (Tyler 1975). These findings suggest that one cannot assess the effects of a program merely by measuring outcomes in all the schools that formally introduced it. It is necessary to examine the degree of program implementation in each school and to determine to what extent differences in outcomes between schools are affected by differences in the level of program implementation. Stake attaches great importance to the measurement of program implementation and describes it as an examination of the congruence between planned and observed program transactions (Stake 1967).

Identifying Difficulties in Program Use

Observation may help to identify portions of the program that created difficulties in the classroom. Difficulties may emerge as a result of misunderstanding of some content element by the teacher, or of improper application of the suggested teaching-learning strategy. Often such misunderstanding is a consequence of erroneous or insufficient explanations in the textbook or in the teacher's guide.

Students sometimes encounter difficulties in performing certain activities or in following certain reasonings presented in the textbook because of the complexity of the text or the students' lack of necessary skills. Observation is very effective for detecting such difficulties in a program.

Identifying Changes Introduced by Teachers

Frequently teachers introduce changes in the program. For example, they may omit some elements of the program or may add elements that do not appear in the original program version. Program writers are interested to know what changes were introduced by teachers, and why. Information of this type may help them in revising the program, or in formulating specific recommendations for adjusting the program to the particular needs of subgroups of the target population.

Identifying Typical Instructional Pathways

Frequently an educational program is not fully structured, and teachers are given the option to select from a variety of content elements in a certain unit. Consider the following example of a unit on the history of the Roman Empire in the first century. Three topics are suggested for class discussion: (1) the enlightened emperors, (2) the policy of defence, and (3) the power of the provinces. The teacher's guide also suggests six learning strategies to be employed in connection with these topics. A two-dimensional chart of topics and strategies is presented in table 9.1.

Where cells are crossed out, this indicates that the strategies were not considered appropriate in teaching the particular topics in the teacher's guide. The observer may note what strategies were in fact employed in a particular class and how they were sequenced. By comparing records

Table 9.1. **Class Observation Sheet**

Strategy \ Topic	The enlightened emperors	The policy of defense	The power of the provinces
Picture analysis			✕
Analysis of map	✕		
Analysis of historical sources			✕
Comparison			
Evaluation		✕	
Role play	✕	✕	

collected from several classes, it became possible to determine which pathways of action were typical or appeared with a high frequency.

Observation of class activities may reveal which program elements were most frequently selected by teachers and which were least frequently selected. It may also reveal which pathways of activities were selected by teachers in different types of schools. Such information may be useful in the revision of the program, in eliminating or modifying infrequently used elements, and in making more definite recommendations to teachers.

Support for Data from Other Sources

Observational data may provide support for data obtained from other sources, such as experts' judgments, answers to questionnaires, or tests. For example, this may be necessary when the validity of students' responses to questionnaires about their interest in some subject matter may be questioned on the basis of the "social desirability effect," i.e., the student may be inclined to respond in a way that pleases the teacher or fits the standards of the school. Observational data can be used to cross-validate such responses. In the social sciences generally, convergency of results obtained by instruments of different types is used as support for the validity of the different measures (Campbell and Fiske 1959).

Unintended Outcomes

Educational evaluation is often criticized for concerning itself exclusively with the attainment of specified outcomes. Indeed, evaluation often means the examination of congruence between explicitly stated program objectives and measured educational outcomes. Many writers consider this meaning of evaluation restrictive and unsatisfactory. They point out that unintended outcomes of a program may also be significant in determining the merits of a program (Scriven 1972). It may happen, for example, that an educational program achieves excellent results in teaching the correct spelling of several hundred basic words, but at the same time has unplanned disruptive effects, such as decreasing students' interest in studying the mother tongue or creating a negative attitude toward school in general.

Unintended outcomes of classroom practices associated with the utilization of a program are often best detected through observation. The observer should pay attention to any event he considers significant, and not only to the types of behavior or transactions defined in advance for the program.

TYPES OF OBSERVATIONAL DATA

Observation normally aims at making an objective record of events as they occur. Although the eventual objective is to be able to make some judgment about the observed events, the process of making and recording observations is meant to be merely descriptive and not evaluative. It is like taking a still or movie photograph of the event. What judgment is made later depends on the purpose for which the observation was made.

In general there are four stages of effective observation:

1. Paying attention to the relevant event
2. Making an objective record of the event
3. Presenting the records in such a way that they can yield meaningful interpretation
4. Interpreting the records

Occasionally an observer may go straight from stage 1 to stage 4, as in cases where *rating scales* are used. In such a case the observer is expected to make a mental record of the event or series of events, do a mental analysis of the events, and record his interpretation or judgment in the form of a rating.

Observation data are of three main kinds: (1) data from rating scales, (2) data from systematic observation, and (3) data from unstructured observation.

Rating Scales

Rating scales are useful for behaviors that cannot be easily recorded in discrete terms and therefore cannot be easily quantified by counting procedures. For example, an observer may be required to provide information on the following attributes of the teacher:

1. Mastery of the content being taught
2. Provision of reinforcement to students
3. Paying attention to the need of slow learners
4. Proper utilization of curricular resources, etc.

Similarly, an observer may be required to rate student attributes such as:

1. Paying attention to the lessons
2. Following instructions
3. Cooperating with fellow students, etc.

In each of these cases, the observer needs to observe over a period of time several attributes that may be occurring simultaneously and later quantify these attributes in terms of ratings, using for example a scale of 1 to 5, where 1 is the lowest rating and 5 the highest. Ratings are necessarily subjective, and it is difficult to achieve high interrater reliability.

Systematic Observation

This includes all techniques in which predetermined events are observed and recorded in a systematic way according to predetermined schedules.

In order to develop a systematic observation method one should take the following steps:

1. Some aspects of the situation to be observed should be defined in advance. For example, in a class situation an observer may decide to focus on the verbal statements only.
2. Major variants of the selected aspect should be defined. For example, one may classify verbal statements of the teacher into praise, question, reprimand, etc. Besides defining each of these terms clearly, it is advisable to provide examples of activities, behaviors, or events pertaining to each category.
3. A special recording sheet should be prepared and convenient recording rules worked out. In designing a recording sheet, the aim should be to make recording as simple and informative as possible. Number or letter codes are often used to designate each category and so make recording faster.
4. A summary procedure should be worked out for quantifying the records. For example, it may be possible to create a quantified variable by computing the ratio of teacher's praises to teacher's reprimands. Another quantified variable may be the ratio of teacher's questions to the total verbal statements. A third variable may be the proportion of student talk in the total verbal statements. As a rule, the quantification of variables is dissociated from the act of data recording. It may also be that different researchers will be interested in deriving different varibles from a single set of records.

Contrary to the case of rating scales, with systematic observation no high-level inferences should be made concerning general traits of the object of observation. The behavioral categories are closely related to easily recognizable features of the observed phenomenon. Systematic observation schemes are divided into two groups: sign systems and category systems.

Sign Systems

In a sign system attention is focused on a certain set of phenomena, such as: the teacher uses the blackboard, the teacher praises a student, a student helps his fellow student, a student speaks about some task-related experience he had outside school.

If such an event occurs, the observer puts a sign in the column corresponding to that particular phenomenon. It may well be that during a whole period, the observer did not make any sign on the observation sheet. This may happen if none of the events included in the observation system occurred in the class during the period of the observation.

Category Systems

In the category system the object of the observation is divided into component units, and each unit is classified into a certain category of the system. The units may be uniform time periods, paragraphs of the transcript of the teacher's explanation, and so forth. The categories may vary according to the focus of the observation. Thus, one may define a number of categories for describing verbal activities going on in the class.

These categories could be, for example, "teacher gives directions," "student poses questions," or "student answers questions." In category systems it is advisable to define a category as "uncertain" or "unclassifiable" or "other" to take care of units which cannot be classified by the observer. Of course such provision is not needed in the sign system.

Some examples of systematic observation schemes are presented as follows:

The African Primary Science Program (APSP) Observation Scheme

Within the framework of the APSP an observation scheme was developed to fit the special interests of the program developers (Yoloye 1971). The observation scheme borrowed some elements from Flanders' (1970) and Bellak's (1966) schemes, but its major function was to determine whether program goals were attained. In order to understand the fit of the scheme to the characteristics of the program, a list of program objectives and learning strategies is presented below.

Objectives

The APSP should aim at developing the following characteristics in children:

(1) Firsthand familiarity with a variety of biological, physical and man-made phenomena in the world around them

(2) Interest in further exploration of the world around them on their own initiative

(3) Ability to find out for themselves—to see problems and to be able to set about resolving them for themselves

(4) Confidence in their own ability to find out for themselves and do things for themselves

(5) Ability to share in a common development of knowledge, through collaborating on problems, telling, listening and discriminating use of secondhand sources

Strategies
The science program should have the following characteristics:

(1) The focus of study should be on the concrete phenomena themselves.

(2) The materials selected should capture and hold the attention and interest of children.

(3) The materials should reveal that there is not always one right answer.

(4) Materials should allow opportunities for a variety of different ways to find out.

(5) The classroom experience should lead to social interaction among children.

(6) To a large extent, the materials should be simple and familiar.

(7) The materials should encourage children to do things on their own, in their own ways.

Based on these two sets of specifications, three observational instruments (among others) were developed to assess the attainment of the objectives. The first, *The Child Observation Check List,* assesses outcomes related to the child. The other two, *Class Activity Sheet* and *Verbal Interaction Sheet,* sought to monitor teaching procedures and assess to what extent they were in conformity with the stated objectives.

The Child Observation Check List is an example of a sign system scheme. It contains 22 different behavior types divided into four major groups. Whenever a certain type of behavior appeared in the class, the observer put a mark in the appropriate line of the sheet. The sequence of marks was not recorded however. (See table 9.2.)

While objective 1 above is most readily assessed by tests, objectives 2 to 5 lend themselves to assessment with the observation check list. This scheme may be used in two different ways. First, it may be used for keeping a cumulative record for each child. Second, it may be used for recording samples of behavior of several children. Either procedure would yield some information as to whether or not the curriculum program is yielding the outcomes envisaged.

The Class Activity Sheet is an example of the category system scheme. (See table 9.3.) The learning period is divided into units of one minute. Each minute should be classified according to one of the five categories appearing in the scheme.

Categories *A–D* are the most common in any classroom. *E* is to take care of other events, for example: "Teacher writes notes on the blackboard

Table 9.2. **Child Observation Check List**

DATE....SCHOOL........CLASS...UNIT OR LESSON...TEACHER ....

Behavior Category	Specific Behaviors	Tally of Separate Instances of Behavior	Remarks
Social inter- action	1. Compares his findings with those of others		
	2. Cooperates with other children to solve a problem		
	3. Disagrees with a point of view and offers alternative		
	4. Shows what he has done for others to see		
	5. Suggests what to do and how to do it		
Originality	6. Compares things that seem at first different		
	7. Has ideas about what to do with new materials		
	8. Makes or constructs something		
	9. Notices something new		
	10. Pursues his own idea		
	11. Raises a question about common occurrences		

Table 9.2 continued

Persistence and sustained interest	12. Brings materials to school to show or investigate		
	13. Continues his work outside normal class period		
	14. Persists in thinking about and tackling a problem		
	15. Repeats an activity with greater carefulness or to check previous findings		
	16. Tries more than one way of doing the same thing		
	17. Watches something patiently for a long time		
Experimentation and attitude to investigation	18. Changes his mind about something in view of new evidence		
	19. Confesses ignorance when he does not know an answer		
	20. Designs ways to solve problems or checks prediction		
	21. Makes predictions		
	22. Records his activites or findings		

Recording Instructions: 1. Make a tally 1 in the appropriate row each time you observe a new display of the behavior.
2. After 4 tallies in the same row put the fifth tally across thus ⌿⌿⌿.
3. Some behavior may need further specification or description. Indicate this under "Remarks."

and children copy." In a recent evaluation exercise this particular event occurred so often that it was found necessary to create a distinct category.

Interpretation of the records is based on the following rationale:

1. Children should be learning more from interaction with materials than from the teacher's lecture. For most of the time, therefore, the science class should consist of activity with materials by children.
2. Much of this activity should be on an individual or small-group basis.
3. The teacher should be playing a supportive, integrative role rather than a dominative one.
4. The interaction of the teacher at most times should be with individual children and small groups.

One way of getting a picture of the pattern of the lesson is to count the number of tallies in each category and plot a profile. If the teaching objectives of APSP are being met, a profile such as that presented in figure 9.1 should be obtained. Note that the important criterion is the shape of the profile.

This instrument is thus useful for assessing the extent to which a teacher is correctly interpreting the philosophy of the program. It also comes in useful for teacher-training purposes, since a teacher can monitor his progress toward the ideal profile.

A second use of the instrument is of course that it gives a quick visual picture of the sequence of organization during the lesson.

A third use of the instrument is to make inferences on the basis of double tallies. Simultaneous tallies often occur for categories A and B or A and D. The frequency of such double tallies is another indication of inappropriate interpretation of the approach suggested by the program. Ideally, once children have got into individual or group activity, the teacher should work with them as individuals or small groups only. Attempts to force back the attention of the whole class often run into trouble, especially if the activities are interesting.

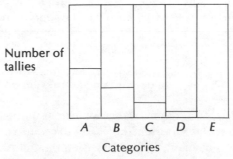

Figure 9.1. *Profile of Lesson Pattern*

Table 9.3. Class Activity Sheet

DATE.......... SCHOOL.............. CLASS........ UNIT OR LESSON .... TEACHER.........

	1	2	3	4	5	6	7	8	9	10	11	12	13	14	15	16	17	18	19	20	21	22	23	24	25
A. Group or Individual Activity																									
B. Whole-class Discussion																									
C. Transition																									
D. Teacher Lectures																									
E. Other																									

Notes on Categories:

A. *Group or Individual Activity:* Children are working by themselves with materials on problems set either by themselves or by the teacher. Discussions involving small groups that may include the teacher may also be going on.

B. *Whole-class Discussion:* A question-and-answer session involving the teacher and the whole class whether every child is participating or not.

C. *Transition:* Periods when teacher is handing out materials or rearranging children's seating, etc.

D. *Teacher Lectures:* When teacher is talking to the class not in response to a question, and not requiring verbal answer from the children.

E. *Other:* Whatever interaction does not fit into A–D.

Instructions for Recording:

1. The numbers in the top line represent minute intervals since the beginning of the lesson. Make a tally in the appropriate row after each interval of 1 minute.

2. The categories imply what the class as a whole is involved in. Thus if the teacher lectures to a small group while the class as a whole is involved in group or individual activity, the tally should still be under A, i.e., Group or Individual Activity. Similarly, if the teacher hands out materials while children are working on their own, it counts not as Transition but as Group or Individual Activity.

3. However, sometimes the teacher attempts to get the attention of the whole class away from group or individual activity for transition, lecture, or discussion. In such a situation, the coding changes either to the category the teacher is trying to impose, or (if some children still continue their own activity regardless of the teacher's efforts) to A and the new category.

In some comparative evaluative studies, a single index of departure from the ideal can be obtained by the ratio: D/T number of tallies, where D indicates the number of tallies in category D, and T indicates the total number of tallies. The higher this ratio, the wider the total departure. Teacher training can thus aim at systematically reducing the value of this ratio for individual teachers.

The Verbal Interaction Sheet tells only part of the story of what goes on in the class. Much of the stimulation of the child depends on the verbal statements of the teacher. Table 9.4 shows the Verbal Interaction Sheet used for monitoring the teachers' verbal statements and for assessing to what extent they conform to APSP ideals. The sheet describes seven categories of verbal interaction. The teaching objectives of APSP place a premium on the statements of the categories *b, d,* and *f,* as the most likely to stimulate inquiry and original work in the child.

Table 9.4. **Verbal Interaction Sheet**

DATE.............................. SCHOOL ....
CLASS........... UNIT OR LESSON .... TEACHER ....

T																	
C																	

T																	
C																	

Recording Instructions: (1) Record only Teacher-Child (*T*) or Child-Teacher (*C*) interactions
(2) Record interactions in the appropriate box in the sequence in which they occur
(3) Indicate the type of interaction by using the symbols *a, b, c, d, e, f,* or *g*
(4) When concentrating on teacher talk only, do not bother to categorize child's statement. Indicate a child's statement simply by a dash (—)

a. Direct instruction (e.g., use only one battery to light the bulb)
b. Open-ended question (seeking information, e.g., what are you making?)
c. Close-ended question (requiring a specific predetermined answer, e.g., what is the boiling point of water?)
d. Suggestion (e.g., there is no torch available; would you like to try a kerosene lamp?)
e. Giving information or expressing opinion
f. Supportive action (e.g., agreement or approbation)
g. Comment implying that the child's statement is unacceptable (e.g., no; you are wrong; yes . . . but)

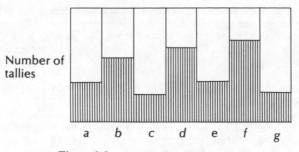

Figure 9.2. *An Ideal APSP Profile*

For purposes of interpretation, therefore, one way of assessing the teacher's performance is to total the number of entries in each category and draw a profile. An ideal APSP profile is presented in figure 9.2.

The peaks are on *b, d,* and *f.* Once again, the important thing here is the shape of the profile rather than numerical values.

Other kinds of interpretation can also be made from the entries. For example, one might count the number of *b* or *c* or both that are followed by a student response.

Unit-related Observation Schemes

In the context of curriculum evaluation, observation focuses frequently on the way a program is used by the teachers and on the reactions of the learners to some suggested program activities. The observer is interested in knowing how students react to various elements of the program and whether their reactions are congruent with the "intents" of the program and/or with generally approved pedagogical principles. Thus, for example, a learning activity may be designed such that students should be able to perform it without the teacher's help. Another activity may be designed to motivate students to relate the study materials to out-of-school events and experiences. The curriculum team wants to know whether these aims were actually achieved. For this reason the team devises a special observation scheme for each learning unit, in which specific questions are related to particular activities appearing in the program.

In most observation schemes of this type questions will be posed as to whether the teacher omitted some learning activities or added new ones not suggested by the program. But in addition to these general questions specific questions related to the particular unit will also appear in the observation scheme. An example for such an observation scheme is presented in table 9.5.

Table 9.5. **Unit-related Observation Scheme—Religion in Ancient Greece**

This observation scheme has been developed for observing a particular unit in a history program. The questions relate to the suggested activities in a single lesson.

Slides [Slides of statues, public buildings, pictures from everyday life in ancient Greece]
 Clarity of pictures . . . .
 Could students describe differences between the characters appearing on the slides? . . . .
 Did students make comments on the beauty of the items? . . . . Specify . .
 . . . .
 How much time was devoted to this activity? . . . .

Cassette-tape recorder [A story about Delphi is recorded.]
 Could students follow the plot? . . . .
 Was the voice clear enough? . . . .
 Did the students appreciate the performance of the actors? . . . .
 After the first stop, did students suggest ways for continuing the story? . . . . Give examples . . . .
 In the discussion following the story, did students give reason for their arguments? . . . .

Homer's Poem [Supplementary reading material]
 Did students understand the content? . . . .
 Did they relate the details of the poem to the pictures presented to them? . . . .
 On the basis of the poem, did they make comments on the differences between monotheism and polytheism? . . . .

Sorting Game [Students were asked to sort picture cards of statues in two piles: gods and human beings.]
Did students show interest in this activity? . . . .
Did they explain their decision? . . . .
 Give examples . . . .
 Did this activity generate discussion? . . . . What arguments came up? . . . .
 Did this activity help students grasp the anthropomorphic character of the gods? . . . .

General Questions
 Did small-group activity take place during the lesson? . . . .
 Did the teacher allow students to pose questions or to react? . . . .
 What percentage of time was devoted to expository verbal explanations by the teacher? . . . .

Unstructured Observation

Sometimes it is informative to record observed behavior or events as they occur and not according to any predetermined coding system. Such observations are referred to as unstructured observations, or *anecdotal records*.

For example, one might be interested in how a particular child reacts when given interesting materials to play with in a class situation without any specific instructions from the teacher. An observer might come up with a record like this:

John spent the first minute not paying attention to the materials given him, but looking at what his neighbor was doing. He next picked up the materials one after the other and inspected them. He then went back to observing his neighbor. After two minutes, he arranged his materials in imitation of those of his neighbor.

Anecdotal records provide an informal and largely qualitative picture of an event. They are useful for describing the interactions of a child with other children in the room, such as signs of aggression or withdrawal, acceptance or rejection, and so on.

A good anecdotal record should have the following features:

1. It should provide an accurate description of a specific event.
2. It should describe the setting sufficiently to give the event meaning.
3. If it includes interpretation or evaluation by the recorder, the interpretation should be separated from the description.

Anecdotal records are more difficult to use than systematic observation, but they are more flexible and often more useful for identifying difficulties that emerge in the execution of a program and for identifying unintended outcomes.

Videotapes or audiotapes are more accurate for anecdotal records. Nevertheless, they are limited in that they are nonselective and may include events not relevant to the recorder's purpose. Subsequent analysis may be difficult. Recording by tape is also relatively expensive.

OBSERVATION AT VARIOUS STAGES OF CURRICULUM DEVELOPMENT

In the process of curriculum development, observational data are used at all stages except at that of defining general outlines of the program. An overall scheme of the uses of observational data is given in table 9.6.

Table 9.6. **Observation at Various Stages of Program Development**

Stage	Purpose	Type	Frequency
Planning	Examine prototype elements		a
Preliminary tryout	Detect flaws Observe effects	Unstructured Unit-related	b
Field trial	Support findings of previous tryout Support findings from other sources	Rating Unit-related Systematic	
Implementation	Adequacy of teacher training Changes in class activities	Unit-related Systematic	
Quality control	Accuracy of implementation Reason for deterioration Efficiency of corrective activity	Unit-related Unstructured	b

a Considerable frequency.
b High frequency.

As can be seen, observational data are most frequently used at the stages of preliminary tryout and quality control. In both cases observation is carried out on a relatively small sample. In the preliminary tryout the whole sample is small, and observation may encompass the whole sample; at the quality control stage the sample is relatively large, and observation is performed on a subsample only. As a general rule it can be said that whenever the sample is large, observational data will be collected only from a selected subsample.

Planning Stage

Besides the brainstorming exercises that planning a curriculum often involves, it is sometimes necessary to have preliminary trials of ideas and materials, if not in the actual classroom, at least in simulated learning conditions. Certain series of materials may appear to the curriculum developer to have high potential for stimulating learning, but before deciding to include these materials in the preliminary tryout package one may wish to test some prototypes of these materials on a small group of students in class or in simulated conditions in the curriculum center. In such a situation, *anecdotal records* come in very useful. Not only could these procedures help in identifying the learning potential of materials, but they could also help identify difficulties that may face the teacher and behavioral impact on children.

Preliminary Tryout

At this stage observation constitutes the most powerful instrument of evaluation. The curriculum team has brought a new program to several classes and is highly motivated to observe the operation of the program in the classes. Very frequently the team members themselves will be the observers, and since only a few classes participate in the tryout, the members will observe some lessons in all classes. Mostly they will use unstructured or unit-related observational forms. The great advantage of this method is that such forms provide immediate feedback for the team, and the gradually accumulated data provide easily interpretable information about the success of the program. The observation focuses on all details of the program, but the team's major effort is to collect data related to specific learning experiences of the program in order to correct any weak points and to produce a new improved version.

Field Trial

In the field trial relatively less weight is given to observational data. Because of the large size of the sample, observation cannot be made in all schools; any attempt to collect observational data should be restricted to a subsample. The major role of evaluation at this stage is to provide further evidence to support the findings of the previous tryout stage, and also to support data of other types, such as teachers' self-reports, students' questionnaires, and tests. A great variety of observational schemes can be used at this stage depending upon the purpose of the evaluation study, although it is unlikely that a large quantity of data of these types will be collected.

Implementation

Implementation has been defined in this book as dissemination of the new program in the system; activities related to implementation are described as taking stock of available records, adapting the system to the conditions required for program implementation, and preparing the teachers to use the new program. In this connection observation can be used to examine the adequacy of the teacher-training program. Additionally, observation may deal with the examination of changes taking place in the management of the class and in the monitoring of student learning.

Quality Control

At this stage observation may be concerned with the accuracy of program implementation. Quality control is intended to determine whether the program is executed well and whether it remains as effective over time as it was when first implemented. Observation of subsamples may focus on the examination of possible reasons for program deterioration and also on the adequacy of suggested corrective treatments. For the first purpose unit-related observation schemes are mainly used, while for the last two purposes unstructured observation is more adequate.

REFERENCES

Bellak, Arno. *The Language of the Classroom.* New York: Teachers College Press, 1966.

Campbell, D. T., and Fiske, D. W. "Convergent and Discriminant Validation by the Multitrait-Multimethod Matrix." *Psychological Bulletin* 56 (1959): 81–105.

Dunkin, M. J., and Biddle, B. J. *The Study of Teaching.* New York: Holt, Rinehart & Winston, 1974.

Flanders, Ned. *Analyzing Teaching Behavior.* Reading, Mass.: Addison-Wesley, 1970.

Rosenshine, Barak. *Teaching Behaviours and Student Achievement.* Slough: National Foundation for Educational Research in England and Wales, 1971.

Rosenshine, Barak, and Furst, N. "The Use of Direct Observation to Study Teaching." In *Second Handbook of Research on Teaching,* edited by R. M. Travers. Chicago: Rand McNally, 1973. Pp. 122–83.

Scriven, M. "Pros and Cons about Goal Free Evaluation." *Evaluation Comment* 3 (1972): 1–4.

Simon, A., and Boyer, E. G., eds. *Mirrors for Behavior: An Anthology of Classroom Observation Instruments.* 14 vols. Philadelphia: Research for Better Schools, 1967–70.

Stake, R. E. "The Countenance of Educational Evaluation." *Teachers College Record* 68 (1967): 523–40.

Tyler, R. W. "The Activity School Project." *Viewpoint* 51 (1975): 12–31.

Yoloye, E. A. "Evaluation for Innovation: African Primary Science Program, Evaluation Report." Educational Development Center, Newton, Mass., 1971. Mimeographed.

ADDITIONAL READINGS

Amidon, E. J., and Hough, J. B., eds. *Interaction Analysis: Theory, Research and Application.* Reading, Mass.: Addison-Wesley, 1967.

Anderson, S. B.; Ball, S.; and Murphy, R. T. *Encyclopedia of Educational Evaluation.* San Francisco: Jossey-Bass, 1973.

Furst, N. J. "Systematic Classroom Observation." In *Encyclopedia of Education,* edited by L. Deighten. New York: Macmillan, 1971. Pp. 168–83.

Medley, D. M., and Metzel, H. E. "Measuring Classroom Behavior by Systematic Observation." In *Handbook of Research on Teaching,* edited by N. L. Gage. Chicago: Rand McNally, 1963. Pp. 247–328.

Roberson, E. E. *Developing Observation Systems.* Tucson, Ariz.: Educational Innovators, 1972.

Thorndike, R. L., and Hagen, E. P. *Measurement and Evaluation in Psychology and Education.* New York: Wiley, 1969.

10

The Use of Tests and Scales in Curriculum Evaluation

INSTRUMENTS

The subject of this chapter is very extensive. Tests and scales have been used in different ways at various stages of curriculum development and implementation. Educational measurement itself is a complex topic, and many excellent books have been written on single aspects of it. This chapter can do no more than provide a brief overview, giving special emphasis to the applications of different types of tests and scales in curriculum evaluation, and introduce and define some of the more frequently employed technical terms. The chapter concludes with a list of suggestions for further reading for those who require more detailed information on one or more aspects of testing.

The team responsible for developing a new curriculum, or indeed for bringing about any educational reorganization or innovation, must constantly be making decisions as to the exact direction and detailed content of their work. The information on which these decisions are based comes from several sources. First, an important part is played by expert judgment derived from personal experience and knowledge of the subject. For example, a curriculum team developing some new materials in agricultural

This chapter was written by Bruce H. Choppin.

science may decide to include a unit on plant nutrition because in their judgment this is essential for an understanding of modern farming techniques. Second, decisions may be based on observations, either structured or unstructured. To continue the example, this same curriculum team may decide to include a substantial part of experimental work in the unit because they have previously observed that students who were offered only lectures in plant nutrition became confused when faced with real-life practical farming situations. Third, decisions may follow from information provided by student performance on tests and scales. To push the agricultural science example a little further, the curriculum developers may decide which of several alternative nutrition experiments to include, based on the ability to generalize results displayed in the test results of groups of students who have carried out different sets of experiments.

In this handbook we use the terms *test* and *scale* to describe formal measurement instruments designed to gather information about student characteristics in an organized way. The characteristics concerned may be abilities, interests, attitudes, aptitudes, and so forth, although most frequently we shall be concerned with achievement.

In general, a *test* may be thought of as a set of questions to which there is an accepted set of "true" answers. The usual method of scoring is to allot marks according to the number of correct responses obtained, although more complex procedures may occasionally be appropriate. The word *scale* is usually used to describe an instrument for whose questions the true-false classification does not apply—such as questions regarding personal attitudes. More complicated marking schemes for such sets of questions yield a score on a "scale" relating to an attitude, an interest, a behavior, and so on.

Two key concepts that we shall associate with the instruments are standardization and objectivity. *Standardization* concerns our control of the situation in which the information is collected. It is because we can get students to react differently to the same stimulus presented in the same context that we can begin to make different interpretations about their characteristics. Where uniformity of conditions does not exist, interpretation of results is very difficult.

Tests given under standard conditions enable the compilation of guides to their interpretation. For example, tables may be developed to describe the average levels of achievement of children of different ages in a particular country. This serves as a framework against which the performance of any single child can be interpreted. It is rare, however, for the curriculum evaluator to be concerned with a completely standardized instrument, because the achievement in which he is interested will usually be concerned with the set of instructional objectives. Existing standardized tests are unlikely to be valid for this purpose. Nevertheless, standardization of the conditions under which test data are *collected* is important whenever the results of a number of different children are to be compared.

Objectivity concerns the extent to which a particular piece of student behavior yields a unique interpretation. In many fields of human inquiry where measurement has been applied, objectivity causes no real problems. Measurement of weight, length, or time can usually be agreed upon by various observers. Human behavior, however, is extremely complex, and the measurement of mental abilities faces special problems. Evidence is always indirect and may be subject to different interpretations. As an example one may cite the perennial controversies over the assessment of literary skill. With tests and scales, attempts are made to elicit unambiguous responses to unambiguous stimuli so as to increase objectivity.

The use of tests and scales in curriculum evaluation implies a collection of information from students in an organized way. In general, the greater the degree of standardization and objectivity that can be built into a testing procedure, the better.

ADVANTAGES AND DISADVANTAGES OF TESTS AND SCALES

When compared with expert judgment or unstructured observations, tests and scales have both advantages and disadvantages. When a decision has to be made, the balance of advantage and disadvantage in the particular circumstances will determine the best approach to gathering information.

An obvious disadvantage of the use of tests or scales, or indeed any structured instrument, is that the investigator must know in advance what it is that he is trying to measure, observe, or assess. Since testing is an organized activity, the goals that have been prespecified will determine the type of information that may flow from the testing. By contrast, expert judgment may employ divergent thinking techniques, and the method of unstructured observation is powerful in that the observer may discover, in the course of the observation, new and important aspects of the phenomenon under study. A trained observer may visit a school classroom for example to determine how "well" a particular curriculum unit is progressing without having to define further the concept "well." If the observation is successful, then the concept "well" will gradually come to be defined during the observation; and the observer in his report may be able to comment on a wide variety of effects, both central and peripheral, that were observed. By contrast, the tester, faced with providing information on the same problem, will have to decide in advance how the concept "well" is to be defined. If it means that at the end of the unit the students will be able to solve a particular sort of problem, then the specifications for the required test can be drawn. If the criterion for success is that the students will be sufficiently interested to continue further study on their own, then again, the evaluator has a measurement problem that can be solved.

If the criteria of success cannot be specified in advance, perhaps because the objectives have never been clearly formulated, then tests and scales cannot be appropriate means of gathering relevant evidence.

A further drawback to the use of tests and scales is the very considerable cost of these methods in terms of time and effort. Tests and scales must be prepared in advance; and the amount of work involved can be considerable. It can well be argued that, unless a test is carefully constructed, it may yield much less information than could be inferred from accumulated observations in the same amount of time.

On the other hand, an observer who wishes to gather information on a particular point may have to observe for a very long time until the particular situation relevant to the behavior in which he is interested occurs. The advantage of a test is that by controlling the situation, it can elicit the specific behavior that it is desired to assess. An example may make this clear. If one desires to discover whether a particular group of children have mastered the concept of conservation of volume for a liquid, then an observer could watch the children's behavior for a period of days or even weeks without seeing anything particularly relevant to the question. With a test composed of tasks like those used by Piaget in his studies, one could stimulate the children on exactly the desired topic so that from their results one could deduce whether or not they had mastered the principle.

Another advantage lies in the ideals of standardization and objectivity mentioned above that facilitate the comparability of information. Evidence collected from several children can be directly compared. The performance of a child on a standardized task in one week may be compared with his performance the next week. Information obtained from tests, as with other forms of measurement, is subject to a certain degree of uncertainty or error; but where a test or scale is composed of a number of comparable items, measurements theory provides a way of checking the degree of precision of measurement, and these data can be included in any assessment of the results. Within this degree of accuracy, test information is usually consistent. In theory, any investigator using the same tests should obtain the same results. This is extremely valuable when it is necessary to obtain comparable assessments on a large number of children.

Measurement is a scientific activity that can be applied to a very wide range of problems. Mental testing procedures have developed greatly in sophistication in recent decades and now have firmly established places in the fields of psychology, psychiatry, and sociology. In the field of education, tests have been found to be of special value. Tests and scales can be used for measuring a wide range of educational outcomes, for example, knowledge, skills, aptitudes, interests. A great deal is known about the construction of suitable tests for specialized purposes; in particular, we have accumulated a great deal of knowledge about the construction of particular test items to assess performance on particular educational objectives. Test and scale results are readily quantifiable, which eases the difficulties otherwise inherent in a complicated investigation of behavior.

In general, we shall recommend that when the information required is of a specific or quantitative nature, tests and scales will usually be more appropriate than the use of unstructured observation techniques. Such situations occur to some extent during the early and formative stages of curriculum development but are most frequently met during field trials in summative evaluation and in quality-control procedures. At the different stages the type of evidence required is different. This has implications for the design of the test or scale to be used.

THE NATURE OF THE INFORMATION TO BE GATHERED

Norm-referenced Measures

We must now consider the nature of the information provided by tests and scales. By far the most frequent type of information is essentially a rank ordering of the students who have taken the test. A mathematics exam that yields a score in the range zero to 100 will probably tell nothing explicitly about the level of mathematics achieved by a student who scores 50, only that he knows more mathematics than another student who scores 40, but less than a third student who scores 70. Such *norm-referenced* information is extremely valuable when one is concerned with grouping students for particular courses or for ranking students in some order of merit. Norm-referenced measures can also be used in research situations where the set of scores from one group of people can be contrasted with those for another.

In curriculum evaluation, one may wish to investigate whether one group of students who have been studying a new curriculum are learning more than another group of students who have been studying the corresponding part of the old curriculum. In this case it is possible to administer the same norm-referenced test to each group and to compare the two sets of scores they obtain. Differences between the two curricula, however, place serious obstacles in the way of this approach. It is usually difficult to design a test that is fair in that it equally represents the teaching objectives of both old and new curricula. If the test matches only the objectives of the new curriculum, then it is hardly a fair test for students who have studied the old. The exception to this would be a case where the new objectives were clearly and generally accepted as being the only ones that mattered; in this case a "biased" test would be appropriate.

If the particular curriculum topic is a new one (i.e., it did not appear at all in earlier curricula), then norm-referenced tests face another limitation, as their results can be interpreted only in relation to other scores on the same tests. In this case the only scores available other than those of people who have studied the new material are those from people who have not studied the topic. Comparisons based on this information will not yield much insight into the detailed learning of the experimental group.

The nature of the information provided by norm-referenced tests is essentially quantitative, but quantities expressed in terms of test scores not immediately transformable into quantities of learning.

Criterion-referenced Measures
These provide a more qualitative type of information about what a student can actually do. A good example is a swimming test. If a student can swim for 50 meters through deep water from one point to another, then we can say he has passed the test and we have some information on his swimming ability that can be related, but does not have to be related, to the performance of other students on the same test. Many performance tests are of the criterion-referenced kind, but so far few cognitive tests have been constructed in this way. Standardization, as discussed, is the procedure of obtaining referencing information—either norm or criterion. Although it is usually more difficult to do this within a criterion-referenced framework, the results will often be much more useful for curriculum evaluation. A test whose items can provide unambiguous information on a student's success or failure in attaining specific curricular objectives is ideal in this context.

Problems relating to criterion-referenced tests are discussed at length in volumes edited by Popham (1971) and by Alkin (1974).

Criterion-referenced measures are becoming increasingly important in the evaluation of *mastery learning schemes* (Block 1971). In this type of class, the teacher's objective is to bring *all* the students to a level of mastery of the main objectives. Success is measured by how many students achieve what objectives rather than by some comparison of average scores with another group. In this situation, criterion-referenced measurement that relates performance directly to achievement of the specified objectives is clearly extremely relevant; in consequence, criterion-referenced methods are now commanding more attention from educational testing specialists. To date, the work has been almost entirely confined to the measurement of cognitive achievement, but the development of criterion-referenced measures of attitude and interest will no doubt be developed in the near future.

Test items used within a norm- or criterion-referenced framework may look the same. The differences lie in the different data needed to establish the satisfactory working of a test item, and in the different interpretations that are placed on results obtained with it. Curriculum workers may often find that the test materials they have available were constructed with a norm-referenced framework in mind. They should then consider whether, with a little care, valid criterion-referenced interpretations may be made.

The existence of separate methodologies for interpreting norm-referenced and criterion-referenced measurement is extremely unusual. Most measurement systems use a common framework, but in mental testing, and particularly educational testing, the special difficulties that were encountered led to the development of alternative referenced frameworks. This duality creates new problems, however, as frequently a particular test may be needed for use within both systems. In general, it would be far more convenient if there were a unified approach to mental measurement.

In recent years, considerable work has been done on the problem of developing and calibrating a measurement system that was simultaneously norm-referenced and criterion-referenced. Lord (1968) in the U.S. and Rasch (1960) in Denmark are two individuals whose research has been most influential. Rasch has shown that truly consistent mental measurement can be achieved only by the use of tests that conform to certain rules. These rules lead to novel methods of analyzing tests and interpreting results. His approach is particularly well suited to the use of item banks and item sampling techniques (discussed later in this chapter) and may, in time, come to be the normal method of test analysis, at least in the quality-control stage of curriculum evaluation.

RELIABILITY AND VALIDITY

Reliability and validity are the two most important properties of measurement; of the two, validity is certainly the most crucial. Reliability is concerned with consistency, and tells us to what extent we can expect stable readings from repeated measurements. Validity is concerned with what a test or question really does measure, or, more precisely, whether it measures what it is supposed to measure. For example, a clock is supposed to measure "true" time and to do so continuously. If it does, we say it is perfectly valid and reliable. If it were to show the wrong time, we would say it was invalid. If it were sometimes fast and sometimes slow, we would call it unreliable. Note that it is perfectly possible to have highly reliable measures of poor validity (e.g., a clock that is consistently 15 minutes fast) but that poor reliability inevitably implies a degree of invalidity.

The clock example is one of criterion-referenced measurement. For norm-referenced measurement, reliability is usually assessed in terms of the consistency of the ordering of students who take the test, and validity by the similarity of this ordering to a "true" ordering on the trait being measured. In this case both reliability and validity are usually reported as coefficients or correlations.

Methods of Establishing Reliability

The difficulty in establishing that a mental test is yielding consistent results comes about because administering a mental test to an individual always changes the individual in some nonassessable way, and this change will affect future measurements. We would not really expect that if we gave the same achievement test to a group of students on each of three succeeding days, they would all get the same set of scores on the three occasions. Nevertheless, test-retest as a method of establishing consistency has been applied frequently, and provides at least some information as to the degree of unreliability of an instrument. An alternative approach is to construct parallel forms of a test, that is to say, two forms that are similar in all respects, but in which the learning that takes place during the administration of one form of the test is not likely to have any direct effect on the scores on the other test taken later. A logical application of this idea is to divide a test into two comparable halves—subtests—and to calculate the scores for each subtest separately. The correlation between these scores provides an immediate measure of the consistency with which the test is measuring, and can be transformed into an estimate of the whole test's reliability. This method has been further extended to an examination of the performance on each individual test, and this leads to reliability estimates based on the "internal consistency" of a set of items (for example, the much used Kuder-Richardson formula 20). This type of estimate is the one must frequently used.

It should be noted perhaps that the reliability of test instruments is far less crucial in curriculum evaluation than it is in the assessment and grading of individual students. In general, averaged results for groups of students will be far more reliable than will be the test score for an individual student. This means that it is quite acceptable to interpret group performance on a single item, and such analysis is often employed in curriculum evaluation.

In the case of formative evaluation, estimates of reliability are unlikely to provide much useful information, and it would seem unnecessary to calculate them. For summative evaluation, however (and in the quality-control stage), reliability estimates are useful as they can help in the assessment of any group differences that emerge. Reliability estimates will be most conveniently calculated when the test items are being tried out prior to their operational use.

Methods of Establishing Validity

Validity exists only in terms of a particular context—the context for which it was originally developed or for which it is now being applied. For example, an existing mathematics examination may quite validly assess the performance of students who have studied the traditional mathematics curriculum, but the skills with which it is concerned may not be those required by a new mathematics curriculum. If this is so, then the examination could not be regarded as valid for assessing performance on the new curriculum. Thus, whereas reliability may be of less concern than usual to the curriculum evaluator, validity assumes a special importance.

It must be stressed that however good the psychometric properties of the test may be, it will be of no use for evaluation if its content is not relevant to the particular curriculum.

Various methods of establishing this relevance or validity have been developed. The more sophisticated depend upon measuring agreement between the test and some external criterion—either a more direct measure of performance or another test. For norm-referenced measurement, agreement is usually measured by a correlation coefficient; for criterion-referenced measurement, a variety of nonparametric tests may be used. These methods, however, are rarely appropriate in curriculum work, and the evaluator will almost always have to rely on what has been called *content validity*. This is established by obtaining the agreement of expert but independent judges that the items of the test do measure what is required by the curriculum. The usual procedure is to allow a small group of people who have not been concerned with composing the test to review the items and to judge what each one tests. The evaluator can use the comments received to revise and improve the test.

Two procedures at the test-construction stage will help to achieve good content validity. First, if possible the test should be based on the same curriculum blueprint or list of objectives that the development team has used. Second, careful analysis of the text materials written for the course will yield ideas for relevant test questions and also indicate the appropriate vocabulary and style. Of course, these two procedures cannot by themselves ensure that a new test will be valid, and it should always be submitted to some sort of independent checking or review.

DIFFERENT TYPES OF INSTRUMENTS

In curriculum evaluation we use tests and scales in order to collect detailed information on what the students have learned. A number of different types of test are in common use (e.g., essays, multiple-choice, practical), and as we are concerned with the measurement of various educational outcomes (e.g., knowledge, skills, attitudes, and interests), it is appropriate to consider the extent to which different types of test and scale provide relevant information.

Essays

Examinations based on the writing of essays have a very long history. For more than thirteen hundred years, essays have been used in China as the regulators of academic and professional promotion.

The ability to write a clear essay has proved to be a valuable guide to the selection of professional personnel, particularly at the highest levels. Nevertheless, it has become clear, in recent years, that essays are of much less value when our concern is to measure the amount of learning that has taken place. For curriculum evaluation, the unreliability of essay marking and the difficulty of focusing a question on to a specific curricular objective means that frequently an essay examination is not the best approach.

The exception to this general rule lies in the need to test certain more complex objectives that cannot be easily covered by more objective techniques. Examples of such objectives contain behaviors such as "ability to marshal evidence," "ability to present an argument logically," and "ability to evaluate the effects of alternative courses of action." If such objectives are to be tested by the evaluator, then it will probably be necessary to accept the inaccuracy and inconvenience involved and to use an essay test.

When compared with other types of examination, the chief distinguishing feature of the essay is the multiplicity of information about the writer that it contains. Unfortunately, most of the information is not very relevant to the measurement of learning. Students have an opportunity to draw on the full range of their experiences, and different students will choose to write on different aspects. It is very difficult to phrase the wording of an essay question so that it will elicit evidence of learning of a specific point. It is usually not reasonable to assume that the writer is ignorant of matters that are not specifically mentioned in his essay.

A general criticism that has been voiced against the essay examination when it is employed for assessing the performance of individual students is the inconsistency in marking that usually occurs. This unreliability is important when the examination is being used to grade individual students, but it matters less in curriculum evaluation; here our concern is with gathering evidence on the learning that has taken place and not on an exact and accurate ranking of student performance.

Many disadvantages of an essay can be overcome if a question is restructed into a "short answer" form. Here, although the student is not told precisely what the content of the essay response should be, he is guided by a series of questions that suggest what his essay should attempt to answer. Each section can then be separately considered to see if it contains evidence on the attainment of a specific objective. As an example of this, consider the examination question from an advanced biology examination

Figure 10.1. *A Typical Essay Question in a Science Examination*[a]

Noctiluca is a bioluminous (phosphorescent) marine protozoa that is less dense than sea water and therefore floats. The protoplasm has large permanent vacuoles containing a clear fluid. This fluid has been shown to contain ammonium chloride in solution and is acid in reaction (pH 3). When these organisms are in ordinary sea water (which has a specific gravity of 1.024), they tend to float to the surface. They will remain suspended for a short time in sea water diluted to a specific gravity of 1.014, but soon begin to rise again. When placed in further dilutions of sea water, they continue to sink at first, but soon rise, their volume visibly increasing. They finally burst in sea water diluted to a specific gravity of 1.008. Lack of oxygen prevents bioluminescence, but has no effect upon specific gravity or volume of *Noctiluca*.
Explain these phenomena

Source: Joint Matriculation Board, General Certificate of Education, Manchester, 1971.
[a] To obtain evidence on the achievement of a variety of objectives in a biology curriculum.

Figure 10.2. *Structure added to the essay question produces a series of "short answer" questions, each of which is focused*

(a) What inference might be made with regard to the osmotic pressure of the fluid in the vacuoles when the animal is in normal sea water?

....

....

....

(b) As *Noctiluca* has no cell wall, can it be said to develop turgor? Give a reason for your answer.

....

....

....

(c) How do you think adjustment to floating (or specific gravity) is made.

....

....

....

Source: Joint Matriculation Board, General Certificate of Education, Manchester, 1971.

---

presented in figure 10.1. Here the student is given very little indication of what is required and in consequence the answers produced will be difficult to evaluate.

When, however, a series of prompting questions (such as those shown in figure 10.2) is added, the question becomes much more clearly focused. If an understanding of the biological phenomena concerned has been an objective of a particular curriculum segment, then answers to this question will provide more specific and detailed information as to the amount of learning that has taken place.

It is not necessary to restrict the short-answer technique to this type of question. An examination can be composed of separate "short answer" items that are not conceptually linked, but each of which bears on the attainment of one of the curricula objectives. Figure 10.3 contains a sample of such items from a test of physics. Careful rules need to be developed for scoring such a test, but the problem of deciding which answers are acceptable and which are not is less difficult than the comparable problem of scoring an essay examination.

The short-answer approach is particularly valuable at an early stage in the curriculum development process. Trials of new curriculum materials with small groups of students need to be monitored very carefully to identify problems that may be occurring. It is in this situation that the richness of the material in the nonobjective type of test question is most valuable.

Figure 10.3. *Short-answer Questions Designed to Measure the Understanding of Various Scientific Processes*

5.

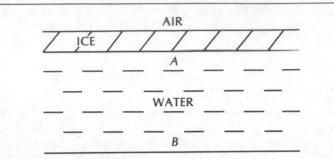

The temperature of the air in contact with a thin layer of ice which has formed on the surface of a pond is just below 0°C.

(a) State the probable temperatures of the water at the positions

     A .... and B ....

(b) What fact concerning the density of water do these temperatures indicate?

. . . .

(c) Why will it take a long time for the pond to freeze solid even if the air temperature falls well below 0°C?

. . . .
. . . .

Source: University of London, General Certificate of Education, 1970.

Student Work Sheets

One particularly useful way of incorporating short-answer questions in the early stages of curriculum trials is to bind special work sheets into copies of the initially printed version of the new material. These work sheets are perforated to enable them to be torn out of the booklet and contain a series of short-answer questions on the topics covered by the unit. Figure 10.4 illustrates such a work sheet.

The sheets are filled in by students as they work through the material, and are collected periodically by the curriculum development team for analysis. This procedure has the advantage of providing similar information to that which would be obtained in a formal examination setting without any of the disturbance or tensions that the latter situation often provokes.

Figure 10.4. *Example of a Tear-out Student Work Sheet*

Experiment A

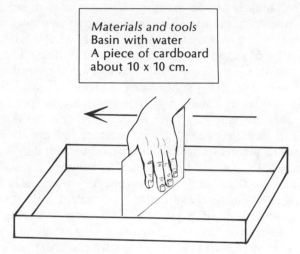

> Materials and tools
> Basin with water
> A piece of cardboard
> about 10 x 10 cm.

Moving the cardboard in the water with its wide surface
placed in the direction of the movement.

Place the cardboard into the basin (don't bend or roll it) and try to
move it in water, with the wide surface placed in the direction of the
movement, from one end of the washtub to the opposite end (see the
drawing). Now repeat the experiment, but this time look for a more
efficient method for moving a cardboard in water (now you may even
change its form).

1. What forms have you made? . . . .
. . . .

2. Of all the forms you have tried out, which is the form most convenient
for moving in water? . . . .
. . . .

Source: Curriculum Center, Ministry of Education and Culture, Israel.

Objective Test Items
A more recent development in examining has been the introduction of
objective test items. These are items for which all possible answers can be
classified into one of two groups: correct and incorrect. People who are
experts in the subject matter should all agree with this classification. The
usual procedure has been to arrange that each item has just one correct
answer with all other answers being incorrect.

The first type of objective item to consider is the *supply* item. In such an item the student is called upon to fill in a missing phrase (often just one word or one number) and an exact right/wrong marking scheme can be applied. Arithmetical problems are commonly met examples of this item type, but others can be found in most subjects of the school timetable. Some examples of supply-type items are shown in figure 10.5.

Tests composed of these items are much easier to score than are essay or "short answer" tests. They suffer, however, from several disadvantages. The most serious is that it is difficult to frame supply items so that they test higher-level objectives. Except for item *D*, which measures skills involved in problem solving, the examples listed in figure 10.5 are all measures of knowledge. The second difficulty is that the question may have several correct answers but not all of them may be relevant to the objective in question. Item *B* in figure 10.5 illustrates this. As written, the item attempts to assess achievement on the objective "the student will know the main component gases of the air" with the desired answer, "nitrogen." Several other possibilities exist, however. The student may respond "invisible" or "an element" or yet again "heavier than hydrogen." All these answers are correct, but none of them is helpful in assessing performance on the objective. Item *C* in figure 10.5 shows a modification of the question that makes it more difficult for the student to give a correct but unwanted answer. Item *D* requires analytic skills, knowledge of principles, ability to apply principles to actual problems, and so on, and it is this multiplicity of behaviors that limits its usefulness in curriculum evaluation. If the student responds correctly, then we have some information of his successful learn-

Figure 10.5. *Supply-type Items to Measure Specific Knowledge (A-C) and Higher Skills (D)*

A. The result of multiplying 12 by 9 is _____.

B. The gas which appears in air in the greatest amount is _____.

C. _____ is the name of the chief constituent of air.

D. A solid element X forms two oxides which contain respectively 71.2% and 62.3% of X. Calculate the equivalent weight of X in each oxide. The specific heat of X is 0.084. Given that the product of the atomic weight and specific heat of a solid element is approximately 6.4, write down the formulae for the two oxides of X. _____ and _____ .

Source: University of London, General Certificate of Education, 1969.

Figure 10.6. *Multiple-choice Items Designed to Measure Knowledge of Specifics (39 and 40), Comprehension (41), and Analytic Skills (42) in Science*

---

39. The amount of heat required to raise the temperature of a body by 1°C is called its
   A. Thermal expansion   B. Heat capacity
   C. Specific heat capacity   D. Thermal conduction

40. When the saturation vapour pressure of a liquid is equal to the external pressure the liquid is at its
   A. Melting point   B. Freezing point   C. Boiling point
   D. Dew point

41. Hot liquid in a vacuum flask loses heat by
   A. Conduction through the vacuum
   B. Convection through the vacuum
   C. Conduction through the cork
   D. Contact with the base on which it is standing

42. When the air temperature falls below 0°C the surface of a pond will freeze while the water below remains at about 4°C for some time. This is because
   A. Convection almost ceases in the pond at 4°C
   B. Water contracts as the temperature falls from 4°C to 0°C and so isolates the 'crust'
   C. The ground is still warmer than 0°C and so heats the pond from beneath
   D. At this temperature radiation is more important than convection

---

Source: J. H. Avery and A. W. K. Ingram, *Objective Tests in Ordinary Level Physics* (London: Heinemann, 1969).

---

ing; but if the answer is incorrect, further analysis will be required to determine in which respect the teaching has failed.

The other class of objective test items with which we are concerned is that which deals with *choice*. Here the student has to select one or more of a set of possible answers that are presented to him.

Multiple-choice items have a fairly standard format. The initial part of the item, called the *stem,* leads to a specific question. This is followed by a series of alternative answers, and the student is directed to select the one that is correct. The correct choice is called the key, and incorrect choices are *distractors*. A typical form of multiple-choice items is illustrated in figure 10.6. Some skill is required to write good multiple-choice items, but this can be acquired through experience. Particular points to note when writing questions are:

1. The questions should not be ambiguous, and one but only one of the alternative responses must be correct.
2. The distractors should be plausible such that they can only be eliminated from consideration by a student who can correctly solve the item.

The chief virtue of this type of test is that it can be administered and scored very quickly. The marking produced is definitive—right or wrong—and it is relatively easy, therefore, to combine results from a large number of students.

Examinations composed of objective questions are usually more reliable and in consequence often more valid measures of attainment than comparable nonobjective examinations.

It is also extremely valuable to be able to analyze the incorrect answers in terms of which distractor has been chosen. If the questions have been well constructed so that the distractors themselves represent particular types of error, then such an analysis will give detailed information about where the teaching has not been fully successful and what remedial action is needed.

Three specific disadvantages may be noted. The first is that such a test item measures the ability of the student to recognize the correct answer when he is shown it rather than his ability to write it for himself. On some occasions this may not be important, but on others it is a rather serious defect. The second disadvantage is that guessing is invited on these questions, as a student who has no ability to solve the problem still has an appreciable chance of choosing correctly by guessing. This may give an exaggerated impression of the proportion of the students who actually know how to solve the problem. The third disadvantage is that although it is easy to construct multiple-choice test items to measure knowledge, it is relatively much more difficult to create items that will measure the "higher order" mental abilities such as analysis and synthesis. Nevertheless, the problems are not insoluble, and the reader is referred to several excellent books of advice on the construction of objective tests.

Practical or Performance Tests

Most educational tests require the students to perform some type of mental activity (e.g., solve a mathematical problem) and write down the answer. There are, however, a number of subject areas in which the most direct evidence of attainment can be provided through some measure of actual performance. The most obvious examples are the science subjects, and others that involve the use of equipment or apparatus. In modern curricula it is typical for great importance to be attached to "practical" objectives. Science courses ideally feature both field work and work in the laboratory. By contrast, examiners have tended to be wary of the practical examination because of the particular difficulties of standardization, reli-

Figure 10.7. *Example of a Structured "Practical" or "Performance" Test*

Instructions to the Student

Assumption: Through transpiration a plant loses as much water as it takes up.
Equipment: Two sealed tubes, plant cuttings, oil.
Question: On the basis of the assumption stated above, and using the
            equipment listed above could you determine:

a. relative to the total fresh weight what is the proportion of water
   loss of cuttings with twigs and leaves exposed to sunshine during a
   fixed amount of time;
b. the same but for cuttings with twigs but without leaves.

If you need more equipment ask the teacher and he will give you what you require.

Describe each step of your work. Ask the teacher's approval after each step of your work.

If you do not know how to proceed, the teacher will give you a slip of paper which contains proper instructions.

Guidelines for the Teacher
On basis of the assumption stated, the student has to plan a series of activities to measure the amount of water loss.

He will measure the amount of water take-up instead of directly measuring the amount of water evaporated.

Actions:
1. The student selects two plants. From one of them he cuts the leaves.
2. He puts each of them into a sealed tube containing similar amounts of
   water.
3. He pours oil on the top of the water in the tubes to prevent
   evaporation.
4. He measures the quantity of the water at the beginning of the fixed
   time period and at its end.
5. He determines the amount of water absorbed by the plant.
6. He weighs the plant with leaves and the plant without leaves.
7. He determines the proportion of water absorbed relative to the weight
   of the plant.

Source: Ruth Zozovsky, "The Evaluation of the Achievement of Inquiry Skills" (M.A. thesis, Tel-Aviv University, 1973).

---

ability, and validity that are involved when a test is carried out in a school laboratory.

When grading students these problems are very real, but in curriculum evaluation standardization and reliability are of less concern. The remaining difficulty, the requirement of validity, can be overcome if special care is taken with the construction and subsequent administration of the test.

Good practical examinations can provide a great deal of information about the attainment of practical objectives. The short-answer form of item has proved to be a valuable means of collecting written evidence of scientific performance. This allows one piece of practical work (e.g., a small experiment) to yield separate information on a number of distinct objectives. An example of a structured practical test question appears in figure 10.7. In general, we would recommend that wherever a new unit of curriculum has objectives that relate to practical abilities or performance, then some feedback for the curriculum development team in the form of practical tests or examinations should be provided. It should be noted, however, that less attention has been paid to developing useful tests of practical abilities than to other types of educational tests, and there is still considerable room for experiment and innovation in this area.

Scales of Interest and Attitude

The team of American educators who developed a taxonomy of educational objectives divided the whole range of objectives into three separate areas or domains: the *cognitive domain*, which concerns remembering and the use of remembered information for the solving of intellectual tasks (Bloom et al. 1956); the *affective domain*, which is concerned with feelings and emotions (Krathwohl et al. 1964); and the *psychomotor domain*, concerned with muscular skills and physical manipulation of objects requiring neuromuscular coordination (Harrow 1972).

Mental tests are usually employed for assessment in the cognitive domain, and practical or performance tests in the psychomotor domain. The interests, attitudes, and values that make up the affective domain are by far the most difficult to assess, and a variety of different approaches have been employed.

It is important to separate the concept of "attitude" from more general personality characteristics or "traits." An attitude is limited in scope and specific, while personality traits are not. Thus "anxiety" is a general psychological condition that will probably permeate most of one's activities (and is therefore a trait), while "hostility to foreigners" is a local reaction aroused only in certain situations and would be considered an attitude. Traits are considered relatively stable personality characteristics, while attitudes are not. The development of particular personality traits is not usually thought to be an appropriate educational goal, whereas the development of desirable attitudes is frequently found among stated curriculum objectives.

The attitudes of the students are often considered very important in the evaluation of a new curriculum, and it may be desirable to obtain measures of these. A particular difficulty attaches to the assessment of the interest of the students in the new curriculum, because of what is known as the "Hawthorne effect." Interest will be stimulated when new materials are being tried out just because the materials are new, and certain positive outcomes observed at the beginning may disappear once the innovation gets past the experimental stage.

The most direct way to obtain information about attitudes is by means of an attitude questionnaire. This consists of a series of questions, each with a list of alternative answers, covering various aspects of a topic. The following is an example:

Would you prefer to teach in a large city, or in a village?
A. In a large city
B. In a village
C. No preference

Do you think that teachers in the rural areas should be paid more than those who work in cities?
A. They should be paid more
B. They should be paid less
C. They should all receive the same salary
D. I am not sure

Such a questionnaire provides a rudimentary basis for classifying students or assessing the popularity of particular options, but frequently a more precise measurement of the attitude is required. Then the research usually turns to an attitude scale.

Unlike tests of achievement where items typically have correct or incorrect answers, a scale for measuring attitudes or values has no right or wrong answers as such, though some may appear more desirable to the curriculum developers. Items are designed to obtain information as to the true feelings of the respondent, and a marking scheme yields a score that gives an indication of the respondent's overall attitude or interest.

Figure 10.8. *Thurstone Scale: Attitudes of Staff toward Economic Projects in Schools*

Instructions to the Teacher:
Check the appropriate box for each statement with which you agree.

                                                                    Agree

1. Supervision of self-reliance projects should be carried out
   by specialist staff.

2. I would enjoy participating in self-reliance projects if my
   teaching load were reduced.

3. I would enjoy participating in self-reliance projects if
   teachers also shared the proceeds from the projects.

4. I would enjoy working in the self-reliance projects if
   teaching were my own choice.

5. I find relaxation in self-reliance projects after a day's
   mental work.

6. I work hard in the school shambas to earn good marks
   for my house.

Source: Report of the African Regional Seminar on Educational Evaluation, Dar-es-Salaam, 1975 (Paris: IIEP, 1975).

There are two major patterns for attitude scales. One, which is illustrated in figure 10.8, consists of a set of statements displaying various degrees of positive or negative attitude toward the chosen topic. Each statement has a numerical value associated with it representing its relative position on the scale. The respondent is invited to check all those statements with which he is basically in agreement. Then his attitude score is the average scale value of all those statements he endorses. This type of scale is called a "Thurstone scale" (Thurstone and Chave 1929). The example given in figure 10.8 is for assessing teachers' attitudes toward cooperation in secondary school "self-reliance" economic projects.

The other common pattern is illustrated in figure 10.9. This is called a "Likert scale" after the psychologist who first described its use (Likert 1932). Such a scale is made up of statements each of which is unequivocally favorable or unfavorable to the attitude being measured. Neutral statements are not included. The instrument is scored simply by giving five points for strong endorsement of a favorable statement, four points for agreement, three points for uncertainty, and so on. The scoring is reversed for the unfavorable statements, with strong endorsement then receiving

Figure 10.9. *Likert Scale to Measure Attitude toward Working in Rural Areas*

Instructions to the Student:
Check one box in each row to indicate how you feel about a statement.

	Strongly Agree	Agree	Un-certain	Dis-agree	Strongly Dis-agree
1. The work in rural schools is most interesting.					
2. I feel relieved when I leave the noise of the town and go to the countryside.					
3. Life in the villages is enjoyable.					
4. The people of the rural areas are not coopera-tive.					
5. Life in the rural areas is barren and monotonous.					
6. People in rural areas need more help than urban people.					
7. One does not know what to do with one's leisure time in the villages.					
8. Working in rural places is not as dull as some people may think.					
9. You can always find a useful way to spend your leisure time in rural areas.					
10. People like city life be-cause there nobody interferes with your per-sonal affairs.					

Source: Report of the African Regional Seminar on Educational Evaluation. Dar-es-Salaam, 1975 (Paris: IIEP, 1975).

Figure 10.10. *Part of a Behavioral Scale of Interest in Science*

Below is a list of things you might do outside school. Look at each one and if it is something you do very often or used to do very often, mark A. If you have ever done it at all, mark B. If you have never done it, mark C.

11. Read a science fiction book.
    A. Often
    B. Sometimes
    C. Never
12. Look at the moon or planets through a telescope.
    A. Often
    B. Sometimes
    C. Never
13. Do chemistry experiments with your own equipment.
    A. Often
    B. Sometimes
    C. Never

Below is a list of some things you may do. If you do, mark A. If you do not, but would like to, mark B. If you are not interested in doing it, mark C.

14. Make a hobby of studying or collecting flowers or leaves.
    A. I do it
    B. I would like to
    C. I am not interested
15. Make a hobby of studying or collecting insects.
    A. I do it
    B. I would like to
    C. I am not interested
16. Make a hobby of studying or collecting rocks or fossils.
    A. I do it
    B. I would like to
    C. I am not interested

Source: G. F. Peaker, *An Empirical Study of Education in Twenty-One Countries: A Technical Report* (IEA) (Stockholm and New York, Almqvist & Wiksell and Wiley, 1975).

---

one point. The attitude score is the sum of the scores on each of the individual statements.

Both types of scale have been found to work well, and to have reasonably high reliabilities. As Likert scales are generally easier to construct (one does not have to determine individual scale values for the statements), they tend to be preferred in curriculum evaluation work.

The chief difficulty with measuring attitudes is that the students may choose to tell you what they think you want to hear rather than their true feelings. The effect can vary from class to class, making interpretations of the results very difficult. In an attempt to avoid this some workers have turned to scales that ask students to report on their behavior rather than their feelings. It has been found that students' behavior is a good indicator of their true feelings, and it has been thought that it might be reported more honestly by the students. An example of such a scale is shown in figure 10.10. This is part of an instrument designed to measure the interest of secondary students in science; it seeks to to this by discovering how many science-related activities these students have chosen to participate in. Unfortunately for curriculum evaluators, such behavioral consequences of attitude change may take many months to manifest themselves, so this technique would not normally be appropriate at an early stage in the curriculum reform process.

An alternative approach is to get the relevant behavior rated by some independent person, such as a school inspector. Figure 10.11 shows such a

Figure 10.11. *Scale for Rating Teachers on Their Willingness to Work in Rural Areas and Willingness to Better the Life of the School Community (to be filled in by inspectors and directors of primary schools)*

	Agree	Uncertain	Disagree
1. He would complain if he were asked to work in the villages.			
2. He would not refuse to work in towns.			
3. He mixes freely with all types of people.			
4. He participates in social activities in the school community.			
5. He volunteers to teach or organize literacy campaigns.			
6. He shows interest to know the social atmosphere around the school.			
7. He has friendly relations with people in the school community.			
8. He is liked by the people living near the school.			
9. He does not refrain from doing manual work.			

Source: Report of the African Regional Seminar on Educational Evaluation, Dar-es-Salaam, 1975 (Paris: IIEP, 1975).

scale developed to assess the extent to which teachers have absorbed the desired attitudes toward working in rural areas. Although it has the form of a Likert scale and could be scored as though it were one, it rests on observed behavior rather than on reported feelings.

Descriptive Scales

It is also possible to get students to report to the curriculum team on the teaching they receive. Although they may appear similar, the scales used are not the same as scales of attitude or interest. Further, it is important to understand that students are not being used as judges either of the curriculum or of the teacher, but rather as a group of observers who can report on activities within the classroom. The method is an alternative to the formal class-observation techniques discussed in an earlier chapter. The basis of the method is that while one student, or indeed one teacher, could provide only a rather unreliable report on what went on in the classroom, the consensus of student reactions should be considerably more accurate. Figure 10.12 shows an example of a descriptive scale designed to gather information about the teaching of biology. The purpose is to discover whether teachers are employing methods appropriate to a new approach to biology. Some of the activities listed may be considered to be characteristic of traditional biology teaching, while others are required by the modern curriculum. All students in all the courses involved in the field trials would be asked to complete the descriptive scale instrument, and the data would be analyzed class by class. The feedback so provided would be extremely valuable to the curriculum team in determining whether teachers were employing the desired strategies.

Semantic Differential

The *semantic differential* technique (Osgood et al. 1957) employs a set of rating scales applied to a particular objective or concept. The scoring is somewhat akin to that used for Likert scales, but as the different items are concerned with different dimensions of affect, the analysis is substantially more complex. An example of a semantic differential instrument is shown in figure 10.13. This set of scales was developed to measure the achievement of objectives concerning values in civic education. The responses are scored to give three separate assessments, defined by factor analysis, of the individuals' feelings toward the local government authority. In other applications, the respondent may be asked to fill in the same set of scales for a number of different concepts about which attitudes are to be compared. Although this may seem to be a somewhat unwieldy approach to the measurement of a simple "liking for" or "interest in" a particular topic, its

Figure 10.12. *Descriptive Scale Concerning the Teaching of Biology*

To the student: for each of the statements below, decide whether they are a true or false description of your biology class and check the appropriate box.

---

1. We students are often allowed time in class to talk among ourselves about ideas in biology.   True   False

2. We seldom or never discuss the problems faced by scientists in the discovery of a scientific principle.   True   False

3. We have a chance to analyze the conclusions that we have drawn in the laboratory.   True   False

4. We often talk about the kind of evidence that is behind a scientist's conclusion.   True   False

5. My teacher asks questions that cause us to think about things that we have learned in other chapters.   True   False

6. If I don't agree with what my teacher says, he wants me to say so.   True   False

7. My job is to copy down and memorize what the teacher tells us.   True   False

8. Much of our class time is spent listening to our teacher tell us about biology.   True   False

9. Most of the questions that we ask in class are to clear up what the teacher or text has told us.   True   False

10. Our tests often ask us to write out definitions of terms.   True   False

11. Our tests often give us data and ask us to draw conclusions from these data.   True   False

12. The data that I collect are often different from data that are collected by the other students.   True   False

13. If there is a discussion among students, the teacher usually tells us who is right.   True   False

---

Source: H. E. Steiner, "A Study of the Relationship between Teacher Practices and Student Performance of Selected Inquiry Processes" (Ph. D. dissertation, University of Texas, Austin, 1969).

Figure 10.13.   *Semantic Differential Scale to Measure Attitude toward*
Local Authority

Here are some words and sentences which have been used by different
people to describe the way they think about your town or city council.
Each time, we give you two words or phrases with opposite meanings and
spaces in between for a tick to show your own opinion. For example:

Friendly: :   :   :   :   :Unfriendly

If you think that your town or city council is very friendly, put a tick next to
"Friendly".

Friendly: √   :   :   :   :   :Unfriendly

If you think that your town or city council is very unfriendly, put a tick next to
"Unfriendly".

Friendly: :   :   :   :   √   :Unfriendly

If you don't know, put a tick in the middle.

Friendly: :   :   √   :   :   :Unfriendly

If you think your town or city council is friendly, but not so very friendly, put a
tick like this:

Friendly: :   √   :   :   :   :Unfriendly

Or if you think it is unfriendly, but not very unfriendly, put a tick like this:

Friendly: :   :   :   √   :   :Unfriendly

How would you describe your town or city council?

1.	Friendly:	:	:	:	:	:Unfriendly
2.	Warm-hearted:	:	:	:	:	:Cold-hearted
3.	Weak:	:	:	:	:	:Strong
4.	Popular:	:	:	:	:	:Unpopular
5.	Rich:	:	:	:	:	:Poor
6.	Cares about me and my family:	:	:	:	:	Doesn't care about :me and my family
7.	Does things for selfish reasons:	:	:	:	:	Does things for the :good of the whole country
8.	Pays attention to complaints:	:	:	:	:	Doesn't pay atten- :tion to complaints
9.	Can have their decisions changed by ordinary people:	:	:	:	:	Can only have their de- cisions changed by :powerful people
10.	Run by a few big, powerful groups:	:	:	:	:	Run by people just like :ourselves
11.	Gets things done:	:	:	:	:	Often doesn't get :things done
12.	Can be trusted:	:	:	:	:	:Can NOT be trusted

Source: A. N. Oppenheim and J. V. Torney, *The Measurement of Childrens' Civic Attitudes
in Different Nations* (Stockholm: Almqvist and Wiksell, 1974).

value in assessing more complicated objectives in the affective domain can be considerable.

TEST-CONSTRUCTION PROCEDURES

The evidence sought from tests and scales is not the same throughout the curriculum development process. At the early tryout stage where the intention is to gather detailed information from a small sample for formative feedback to the curriculum team, the instruments used will require less statistical sophistication. Later, when the evaluative approach is summative rather than formative, different procedures for test construction and analysis become appropriate.

Steps in Formative Testing

1. Definition of objectives. Formative tests at the tryout stage will usually be prepared for a small segment of the curriculum. The first step is to identify what this segment is, and to compile a detailed list of the curricular objectives relating to it. This can be considerably aided by a careful analysis of the curricular materials (e.g., textbooks, teachers, instructions), which relate to this segment. A formative test should reflect both the objectives specified by the curriculum team, and at the same time new materials used in the teaching. (On occasions, careful analysis of the textual material may lead to a clarification and restatement of the curriculum team's original objectives.)

2. Item construction. Test items can be generated from the assembled materials. The set of questions should be comprehensive, in that they should cover the whole range of ideas included in this unit of curriculum. As the number of children to be tested will be comparatively small, the use of nonobjective test items, particularly of the short-answer type, may often be appropriate. In these cases, however, it is important to specify how the answers to such questions are to be marked so that they will provide evidence relevant to the attainment of the objectives. In general, formative test questions should reflect the style and mode of presentation used in the curriculum unit. For example, for a segment of a language curriculum concerned with listening or speaking in a foreign language, an oral presentation, perhaps using tape recordings, may be appropriate. For written tests based on written curriculum materials, care should be exercised to maintain the same linguistic style that has been used in the texts. It is neither necessary nor desirable to repeat portions of the curriculum material in the test itself, but a general rule is to keep the test material fairly similar to that which the students have already met. There is a tendency to

phrase test questions so carefully that they eventually become tests more of
reading ability than of achievement in the particular curriculum concerned. This should be avoided as it would be very difficult to separate out
evidence of reading difficulties from evidence of poor learning in the
required curriculum. Alternative types of test and test items were discussed
earlier in this chapter.

   3. Validity. A key feature of testing for formative evaluation is the
rapid feedback of results to the curriculum development team. As a rule this
will preclude any extensive trials of the test, and statistical checks on its
validity, reliability, and so forth. On the other hand, the validity of the test
is of considerable importance, as the curriculum development team is
unlikely to be much persuaded by evidence from a test that they consider
irrelevant. The validity with which we are here concerned is *content
validity* (i.e., the agreement of independent but expert judges that the
questions in the test are relevant measures of achievement for this curriculum unit). Provided they have not been involved in the generation of the
test items, the members of the curriculum team themselves are well suited
to helping with this validation task.

   4. Administration. An adequate number of copies of the test are then
made, and the test is administered (usually by the normal class teacher,
during regular instruction). The test may be introduced as a separate task
that all the children take together, at the same time, and that is removed by
the evaluator for scoring; alternatively, it may be incorporated directly
into the package of curriculum materials that the children work through
when they get to the appropriate point. Where the former method is used it
is particularly valuable to allow the teacher and students to score the test
themselves to get feedback as to their own performance, although of
course the materials must then be passed on to the evaluator for interpretation. Various techniques for giving rapid feedback to the students have
been tried. One particularly simple method (involving only regular mimeo-
graphic equipment) consists of keying the correct answer to a multiple-
choice-test item with special but invisible ink, which only becomes visible
when the student marks that response with his pencil. Even simpler,
though less immediate, is to allow the teacher to read out the answers while
the students mark their own work.

   5. Analysis and feedback. Analysis of the results from formative test
instruments are often most conveniently done by hand. For these tests the
evaluator will be less concerned with the notions of reliability and item
discrimination than with direct evidence to what each child has learned.
For this reason an analysis of each test question separately is frequently
useful. The curriculum team may wish to hear not merely what percentage

of students responded correctly to each item, but also which mistakes were most commonly made. Indeed, an analysis of the errors will often reveal more about the strengths and weaknesses of the curriculum than will examination of a list of scores based on correct answers. Of course, a large number of errors on a particular question may as well result from the question being badly worded as from a failure of curriculum, and results need to be examined with this possibility in mind.

Steps in Summative Testing

1. Definition of objectives. At the field trial or quality-control stage of curriculum development, it is probable that tests will be required to cover the whole curriculum or at any rate major sections of it. It is not possible in such a situation to administer a test that will assess performance on every detailed objective and every minor topic of the course. Instead, the test will usually aim to assess performance on a sample of the full range of objectives; but in order that this sample may be seen to be a representative one, it is important at the beginning to specify the complete set of curricular objectives in as much detail as is possible. General statements of objectives, such as "the student should understand the scientific method," are not very helpful at this stage. Although it would need relatively few such statements to cover the whole curriculum, they do not give any easy guide to the building of test items. Alternatively, a straightforward list of every small piece of learning included in the curriculum would be very long and tedious to construct. A convenient way of avoiding this problem is to use a grid that serves as a blueprint for the whole course. In many cases such a grid, which contrasts content topics with levels of behavior, will already have been constructed by the curriculum team at the planning stage. (Such grids are discussed at length in chapter 3.)

2. Selecting specifications for the test. The full range of curriculum objectives must now be sampled. In norm-referenced testing where one is chiefly interested in discriminating between the levels of performance of different students, this sampling is not of crucial importance. In curriculum work, however, it should be remembered that the test will provide information to the curriculum team only about those objectives that are actually represented in the test questions. This will make it particularly important to consider *all* the major content topics as well as a range of different behaviors. While a usable test for norm-referenced purposes may be built entirely of "knowledge" items, curriculum workers concerned with criterion-referenced measurement will usually require that a test provide evidence on the achievement of higher-level objectives as well.

3. Item construction. Test items should be assembled to meet the specifications for the test. They may be drawn from pools of items already available, or may have to be specially composed. At the summative evaluation stage the advantages of objective test items over nonobjective types become more pronounced. This is primarily because the numbers of students involved are much larger, and there is a strong need for accurate, reliable marking. In general, the notes on test construction for formative evaluation (see page 237) apply also at the summative stage. If the multiple-choice format for test questions is used, it is important to select good distractors. One way to generate these is to try out the test items in a short-answer or supply format to discover what mistakes are made. Indeed it may be possible to take test materials used for formative evaluation at any early stage of the curriculum project and restructure them into objective items for use in the summative tests.

In summative evaluation, interest will be centered on test scores rather than on performance on individual items, but it is not necessary to restrict the test to producing a single score. Items can be grouped according to the topic with which they are concerned or the skilled behavior they require, and separate scores calculated for each group. Such scores are called *subscores* and the group of items leading to one is known as a *subtest*. Subscores that reflect performance on different facets of the curriculum can be extremely valuable. The number of different subscores to be included is limited, because of the need to retain reliability for each. As a general rule each subtest should contain at least six objective items (or four short-answer questions if the test is of the nonobjective type), but lengths of ten items (or eight) are preferable.

4. *Content validity.* Again, as with formative testing, content validity is extremely important. The test must not only be reliable, it must also be generally acceptable as relevant for measuring achievement on the curriculum. Content validity is usually the only practical way of establishing this, and the methods for developing it were discussed on page 238. If the summative evaluation involves the comparison of performance on several curricula, then it is important to clarify in advance the purpose of the summative test so as to arrive at appropriate measures of validity. It cannot be stressed too strongly that test scores will not be accepted as useful evidence in the evaluation of any curriculum unless the test itself is believed to be relevant.

5. *Pretesting, analysis, and refinement of items.* In summative evaluation it is frequently possible and desirable to include pretesting, analysis, and refinement of items. This step aims at improving the test by identifying questions which are not working satisfactorily and by revising them, increasing the overall reliability and perhaps the validity of the test. In

pretesting it is usual to administer the test to a small number of students who have been studying the appropriate material but who will not form part of the main sample. The number of students will usually be in the range of 30 to 200. The results of the test are carefully analyzed to give the frequency of response and point-biserial correlation of each item with the total score on the test (and with the subscore if applicable). If a multiple-choice format has been employed the calculations should also be repeated for each distractor. Although this method of analysis was developed for use with norm-referenced tests, its application will usually improve the quality of criterion-referenced tests also. The results of the analysis are carefully examined to uncover weak points in the structure of each item. When these have been identified, alterations to the questions can be considered. If an item proves particularly bad, it may be better to discard it at this stage rather than to try to revise it; hence it is often wise to include more items in the pretest than one would eventually expect to use.

6. *Administration.* The comments made concerning the administration of formative tests (see page 238) apply here too, although because of the necessity for standardizing testing conditions in a large number of schools it is usual for the administration of the test to be made a formal class activity. Standardization is, of course, crucial if comparisons between different groups of children in different schools are intended. There is some danger that if the class teacher knows that the performance of his children will be compared with those in other schools, he may be tempted to interfere with the testing process either during the test administration or after the papers have been collected. In particular instances it may prove necessary to introduce independent examiners or other persons into the room where the test is being taken, but a more constructive solution is to persuade the teachers involved beforehand that the testing is not intended in any sense to be an assessment of their competence as teachers, but rather is being made with a view to evaluating the curriculum.

7. *Analysis and feedback.* Analysis of the results of summative testing will usually be statistical. The large quantities of data generated by tests in these circumstances are often conveniently handled by machine. Simple computer programs are widely available, and provide the possibility of extremely rapid analysis of the data and statistical feedback. Even without a computer a great deal of analysis can be performed using other equipment to obtain total test scores for each child together with some estimates for the reliability of the test. Where subtests have been defined, scores and reliability estimates for these will also be needed. Interpretation of results will usually be made on the basis of scores and subscores rather than on the results of individual items, as it will be recalled that the individual items

assess performance on only a sample of the range of behaviors developed by the curriculum and cannot hope to cover it as completely as do tests at the formative stage. Even so, marked discrepancies in performance on individual items between different groups of students merit further investigation. The results and interpretations of the analysis are relayed to the appropriate people. These may be the curriculum team or perhaps some other department of the ministry of education. Most teachers also appreciate some feedback as to the overall performance of their students when related to the results achieved in other schools, but if the testing has been carried out for curriculum evaluation purposes it would be a mistake to encourage teachers to use the results for regular grading of students.

Procedures for the Construction of Questionnaires and Scales

For questionnaires and various forms of scales, the aspect of clarity cannot be emphasized too strongly. It is important that the words used to express questions or statements are not open to misinterpretation, as any degree of ambiguity is liable to invalidate the results. For this reason, if for no other, careful trials and subsequent editing and refinement of questionnaire materials are usually considered essential.

Questionnaires may be open-ended (in that the respondent is asked to compose and write in his own answer) or closed with a series of alternative answers from which the respondent has only to select the most appropriate. The disadvantages of the former pattern are that a considerable amount of effort may be required to code free responses into categories suitable for analysis, and that this coding introduces a subjective element and an additional source of error into the instrument. The disadvantage of the latter pattern is that the alternative answers offered may not be both exclusive and truly exhaustive, so that particular respondents may find it difficult to express their true answers adequately. A frequently employed procedure, and one that seems to work well, is to try a new questionnaire initially in an open-ended form, and then to use this first set of responses to frame what will hopefully be an exhaustive set of answer categories for the second closed form. If circumstances permit, this second form should also be pretested.

For attitude scales, whether of the Thurstone or the Likert type, the basic requirement is an appropriate set of statements. These statements must not only be relevant to the attitude concerned, but they should be worked so as to seem meaningful and realistic to members of the intended population of respondents—whatever their age or cultural background. In order to obtain such a set, phrased in appropriate language, it is usual to record discussions or interviews with relevant individuals on the subject of the intended scale, and to use these records as the source of the statements.

For Likert scales, it is then necessary to sort them into negative and positive statements, discarding those that are neutral or ambiguous. Some subsequent improvement can be effected by pretesting the scale and using item-analysis procedures analogous to those for cognitive tests. Statements for which the responses do not correlate with the rest of the scale should be revised or perhaps discarded.

In the case of Thurstone-type scales, it is desirable to get a group of "experts" to rate each statement according to its position on the attitude dimension—using perhaps a nine-point scale. For each statement the mean of these ratings is calculated and this value is assigned to the statement. The scale should be composed of items with scale values fairly evenly distributed over a range from strongly positive to strongly negative. Pretesting and statistical analysis can also be used to refine this type of scale.

THE USE OF ITEM POOLS AND ITEM BANKS

Test construction can be an extremely expensive and time-consuming process, and since many thousands of good test items on every different subject of the school timetable have already been composed, it would seem desirable to take advantage of these wherever possible. As a result, a number of *item pools* or *item banks* are being set up. The term *item pool* is generally applied to a simple collection of items all in a single subject area or for the assessment of performance on a single curriculum. A good example is the collection of biology test items published by the BSCS Curriculum Team in the United States for use by teachers.* The term *item bank* is generally reserved for pools of items for which are available statistical data on the validity, reliability, difficulty, and discrimination of each item. Both item pools and item banks tend to classify the constituent items in terms of the content area and level of student objective with which they are concerned. Nonobjective-type test items will also require a description of the method of scoring. The item bank is likely to contain additional information as to the precise student behavior being tested; the special advantage of this is that it permits one to select a set of items that have known psychometric characteristics and are immediately relevant for the assessment of learning on a particular curriculum.

Although there seems no doubt that in the future the development of new curricula with new objectives will necessitate the creation of some

---

*BSCS (Biological Sciences Curriculum Study) produced courses in secondary school biology and special materials for low-ability high school students. It is associated with the University of Colorado, Boulder, Colorado.

completely new test items, it is hoped that the widespread introduction of item banks will substantially reduce the labor involved in constructing a test. It is relatively simple to arrange for the transfer of test items together with the psychometric data that accompany them from one country to another. There is no reason why curriculum centers around the world should not cooperate in the provision of item banks and share the material they accumulate. In time, the use of item banks may replace standardized tests for the assessment of achievement.

In curriculum evaluation, the performance of a class of students rather than the scores of individuals is often of interest. If a large pool of items is available (for instance, in an item bank), then it may be useful to set different test items to different groups of students within the class. This encourages individual work by the students and gives a more thorough sampling of the full range of curriculum materials. Provided proper allowance is made for this testing method when the sample of children is selected, it is possible to gather a great deal of extra data on the working of the curriculum and at the same time considerably reduce the time each student spends doing the test.

FURTHER READING

This chapter has been able to give only a brief outline of the present position regarding the use of tests and scales in curriculum information. Readers requiring more detailed information on any of the topics discussed will need to consult some more specialized source. A guide to some of the most generally available books is given below:

General Books on Measurement in Education

The best general introductions are by Thorndike and Hagen (1969), Cronbach (1970), and Ebel (1972). Cronbach has an especially good chapter on test validity, while Ebel is recommended for his discussion of different types of item. More mathematical treatments of classical measurement theory can be found in Gulliksen (1950) or Guilford (1954). Of these, Gulliksen's book is mainly concerned with objective tests, while Guilford's covers the whole range of psychological measurement.

A good introduction to the idea of criterion-referenced testing is the small volume by Popham (1971).

Books on Tests and Scales

Several of the volumes listed above cover the format of various types of test and scale, together with procedures for creating and scoring them.

In addition there are some excellent chapters on specialist topics in Thorndike (1971), while Furst (1964) details the process of test construction. Examples of the application of many different types of test items to the evaluation of achievement in various subjects of the school curriculum can be found in Bloom et al. (1971). Extensive treatment of the theory and practice of assessing "The Practical" can be found in various publications by Schwab, particularly the recent series of articles in the *School Review*. There are few good texts on scale construction, but one that can be recommended is by Oppenheim (1966). This covers the use of the semantic differential as well as more straightforward measures of attitude and interest. The standard sources on the framing of teaching objectives, a key issue in assessment, are Bloom et al. (1956) and Mager (1962), while a full discussion of this topic can be found in Popham et al. (1969).

Item Banks and Modern Developments in Assessment

Wood and Skurnik (1969) offer a general introduction to item banking. Matrix sampling theory which contributes to the practical use of item banks has been developed by Shoemaker (1970). Recent work on test theory is presented in Lord and Novick (1968). An influential book that stimulated a great deal of research into alternative measurement systems was Rasch (1960), but more accessible treatments of the same idea are Wright (1968) and Willmott and Fowles (1974).

REFERENCES

Alkin, M. C., et al., eds. *Problems in Criterion-referenced Measurements.* Los Angeles: Center for Study of Evaluation, University of California, 1974.

Block, J. H., ed. *Mastery Learning: Theory and Practice.* New York: Holt, Rinehart & Winston, 1971.

Bloom, B. S., et al. *Taxonomy of Educational Objectives, Handbook 1: Cognitive Domain.* New York: McKay, 1956.

Bloom, B. S., et al. *Handbook on Formative and Summative Evaluation of Student Learning.* New York: McGraw-Hill, 1971.

Cronbach, L. J. *Essentials of Psychological Testing.* New York: Harper & Row, 1970.

Ebel, R. L. *Essentials of Educational Measurement.* Englewood Cliffs, N.J.: Prentice-Hall, 1972.

Furst, E. *Constructing Evaluation Instruments.* New York: McKay, 1964.

Guilford, J. P. *Psychometric Methods.* New York: McGraw-Hill, 1954.

Gulliksen, H. O. *The Theory of Mental Tests.* New York: Wiley, 1950.

Harrow, Anita. *A Taxonomy of the Psychomotor Domain.* New York: McKay, 1972.

Krathwohl, D. R., et al. *Taxonomy of Educational Objectives, Handbook II: Affective Domain.* New York: McKay, 1964.

Likert, R. "A Technique for the Measurement of Attitudes." *Archives of Psychology* 22, no. 140 (1932): 1–55.

Lord, F. M., and Novick, M. R. *Statistical Theories of Mental Test Scores.* New York: Addison-Wesley, 1968.

Mager, R. F. *Preparing Instructional Objectives.* Palo Alto, Calif: Fearon, 1962.

Oppenheim, A. N. *Questionnaire and Design and Attitude Measurement.* New York: Basic Books, 1966.

Osgood, C. E., et al. *The Measurement of Meaning.* Urbana: University of Illinois Press, 1957.

Popham, W. J., ed. *Criterion-Referenced Measurement: An Introduction.* Englewood Cliffs, N.J.: Educational Technology Publications, 1971.

Popham, W. J., et al. *Instructional Objectives.* AERA Monograph on Curriculum Evaluation No. 3. Chicago: Rand McNally, 1969.

Rasch, G. *Probabilistic Models for Some Intelligence and Attainment Tests.* Copenhagen: Danish Institute for Educational Research, 1960.

Schwab, J. J. "The Practical: A Language for Curriculum." *School Review* 78 (1969): 1–24.

Schwab, J. J. "The Practical: Arts of Eclectic." *School Review* 79 (1971): 493–542.

Schwab, J. J. "The Practical 3: Translation into Curriculum." *School Review* 81 (1973): 501–22.

Shoemaker, D. M. "Allocation of Items and Examinees in Estimating a Norm Distribution by Item-sampling." *Journal of Educational Measurement* 7, no. 2 (1970): 123–28.

Thorndike, R. L., ed. *Educational Measurement.* Washington, D.C.: American Council on Education, 1971.

Thorndike, R. L., and Hagen, E. *Measurement and Evaluation in Psychology and Education.* New York: Wiley, 1969.

Thurstone, L., and Chave, E. *The Measurement of Attitude.* Chicago: University of Chicago Press, 1929.

Willmott, A. S., and Fowles, D. E. *The Objective Interpretation of Test Performance.* Slough: National Foundation for Educational Research in England and Wales, 1974.

Wood, R., and Skurnik, L. S. *Item Banking.* Slough: National Foundation for Educational Research in England and Wales, 1969.

Wright, B. D. "Sample-Free Test Calibration and Person Measurement." In *Proceedings of the 1967 Invitational Conference on Testing Problems.* Princeton, N.J.: Educational Testing Service, 1968.

Teachers, Parents, and Community as Data Sources*

Previous chapters suggested a variety of criteria to examine the merits and the efficiency of an educational program. These criteria included such factors as the scientific accuracy of the instructional materials, their importance in out-of-school situations, the processes taking place in class, and the outcomes of using the program. Most of these criteria, if not all of them, are related to the effect the program has on the learner. However, an educational program may affect not only the learner but also his environment. It therefore seems essential to examine the effect of the program on significant persons in the learner's environment, i.e., on teachers, parents, and members of the community. Moreover, it is not enough to evaluate program effects ex post facto; it is also advisable to proceed with program planning so as to secure wide support from those upon whom the success of any new program is strongly dependent.

Such support is important not only for strategic reasons to convince the public of the need for such cooperation (e.g., for facilitating the implementation of the program), but it also constitutes a legitimate basis

*The information in this chapter that deals with educational planning in Benin (Dahomey) was supplied by Dr. H. Kordes, Münster, Federal Republic of Germany.

This chapter was written by Mario Leyton Soto.

or justification for producing a program of a certain type. A curriculum center, irrespective of the level of expertise of its members, does not have any legal or moral right to impose educational goals and educational materials on a community. Curriculum centers are entitled to suggest educational programs only if their work reflects values prevailing in the society and also represents consensus concerning proposed goals. This means that curriculum centers should seek information about social needs and values and act in a way that is responsive to them, rather than try to find easy ways to convince the community about the adequacy of their programs. This chapter describes some methods of obtaining information from the community about educational needs.

It is suggested in addition that curriculum centers should examine the acceptance of the program by teachers, parents, and other members of the community. Finally, teachers and parents may be utilized as sources of information about the effect of the program on the learners themselves. Thus evaluators may well be interested in obtaining data from teachers, parents, and community members concerning three different issues: (1) their perception of educational needs, (2) the way they were affected by the new program and whether they accept it, and (3) their perception of the learner's reaction to the program. An overall scheme is given in table 11.1.

The table reveals that such data sources may be used at various stages of program development and may be used for the sake of selecting program elements and for modifying the program or specifying the conditions

Table 11.1. **Teachers, Parents, and Community as Data Sources**

Issues Evaluated	Stage	Referents			Roles
		Teachers	Parents	Community	
Perceived needs	Planning	Pedagogical principles	Values	Values	Select elements
Acceptance	Tryout Implementation	Identification	Approve objectives, contents, activities	Differences between subgroups	Modify Specify conditions of use
Learner's reaction to program	Tryout Implementation	In school	Out of school		Modify Specify conditions of use

of its use. Generally teachers will be asked to express their opinion about pedagogical and didactical aspects of the program, while parents and community members will be asked about their acceptance of values, objectives, contents, and the like contained in the program.

PERCEIVED NEEDS

As indicated, educational planners, including curriculum centers, have to suggest educational programs that are in harmony with accepted social values. It is therefore the responsibility of educational planners to obtain information about values predominant in the society for which any particular program is being developed.

The relation of educational planners to the community for which the program is being developed may take one of the following patterns: (1) democratic leadership, (2) neutral inquiry, (3) supportive clarification.

Democratic Leadership

Political and intellectual leaders of a society or community generally suggest a series of goals for the educational system. Their suggestions are based on preliminary study of social needs and values and of the expected reactions of the community to the suggestions. Democratic leaders try to convince members of the society to accept the suggested goals and try to explain the beneficial effects of their plan for the society as a whole. The final test of their suggestions will be the acceptance of the plan by votes on the part of community members or of their representatives.

This type of educational planning is illustrated by the educational reform proposed in France. The reform suggests educational goals of the following types: equality of opportunity for all children; knowledge base common to all students; high average cultural level of the total population; friendly school atmosphere; promotion of all types of learning, including intellectual, aesthetic, physical and manual; close relationship between school and life; ability to work in a group and individually; intellectual energy; and individual effort in school work (Haby 1975).

Such goals were suggested within the framework of the educational reform. The suggestions were widely discussed in the country, and political and intellectual leaders representing various subgroups of the population expressed their opinions about the goals. This debate involved clarification of the meaning of all suggested goals. Nevertheless, the final approval of these suggestions will be determined by some voting procedure that it is hoped will represent the public's acceptance of these goals. While the community's acceptance of them is strongly sought, no evidence of the amount of consensus will be examined through activities conducted by a professional evaluator. The expression of consensus will constitute a political act, and the determination of consensus will be made through actions of a political character.

Neutral Inquiry

Another approach to obtaining information about public opinion is the neutral inquiry that characterizes the work of the social scientist. The social scientist is not trying to influence members of the society. He is interested in conducting an inquiry to find out what values dominate in the society and what specific educational needs are given preference by the members of that society.

While democratic leadership is more concerned with the general educational goals of the educational system, social scientists are more concerned with the translation of these general goals into specific objectives. An example of such an attempt is the work of Eden, who set out to translate a politically formulated general statement about educational goals (the educational act of the parliament) into specific curricular objectives. In order to do this he conducted an inquiry about the interpretation of the general goals by members of the community (Eden 1975).

Eden's work related to the general educational aims of an educational system approved as a legislative act by parliament. In a series of interviews, 22 intellectual leaders formulated some description of concrete behaviors that illustrate the values presented in the act. In this way about 200 behavioral statements were collected. These statements were listed in a questionnaire, and representatives of the community indicated the extent to which they thought the school should be concerned with the development of each specific behavior. As a result of the responses to the questionnaire, Eden divided behavioral statements into four major groups:

1. High acceptance level and a high consensus level. Such behaviors may constitute the basis for educational objectives to be implemented immediately in the system.
2. Low acceptance level and a high consensus. Such statements should be rejected and eliminated from the list of educational objectives.
3. High acceptance and low consensus. Objectives pertaining to this category cannot be implemented in the system before further study of the basis for the lack of consensus is made. It may be that low consensus reflects different opinions of subgroups of the society.

If this is so, there is a case for developing alternative programs, and school communities can then decide which of them best fits their values.

4. Medium acceptance level and medium consensus. Objectives pertaining to this category will usually not serve as program objectives to be implemented immediately in the whole system. They may serve as a pool from which teachers may select objectives responding to particular needs of their students.

Educational evaluators assume major roles in conducting inquiries concerning perceived educational needs in a society.

Supportive Clarification

In communities that are in a transitional stage, for example, from traditional agriculture to a modern industry, and in depressed areas in developed countries, it may be inadequate to utilize the technique of neutral inquiry. The reason for this is that the community members themselves may not be fully aware of the consequences of changes in patterns of life. The cultural background and the life conditions of the social scientist, the educational evaluator, or the educational planner may be quite different from those of the community. In such situations it may be advisable for the educational planner or evaluator to work together with leaders and members of the community and to help them clarify the consequences of ongoing changes. At the same time the evaluator or planner should acquire a better knowledge and deeper understanding of community values, which should then be taken into consideration when planning appropriate educational programs. An example of the "supportive clarification" approach to determining educational needs may be the work of a program development team in Benin (Dahomey).

The Benin Program Planning

An educational program had to be developed for rural areas of Benin. The program had to cope with problems of rural exodus, i.e., the movement of young persons (especially of primary school leavers) from rural to urban areas. Most school leavers in rural areas could not find work and therefore constituted a serious social problem. One of the major objectives of the educational program was to find a way to integrate elementary school leavers into their rural community. The team of evaluators visited the villages; had group meetings with community leaders, village people, and young persons; and tried to identify major causes of the exodus.

Examination of local conditions revealed that family and village chiefs refused to give land to school leavers even when the land was not being used. They refused to give young people the right to marry and did not let them participate in decisions relating to community life. The reason for this, it was claimed, was that village chiefs were afraid to lose their authority in face of a group of educated youngsters.

A solution had to be found whereby leaders maintained their authority and young people gained a sufficient level of autonomy to make them willing to integrate themselves into the life of the rural community.

Group discussions were held in which evaluators helped village chiefs to see various aspects of the situation, and this led to a solution. It was decided to establish agricultural cooperatives for the young school leavers. The educational program of the elementary school then prepared students for life in their rural community where they were supposed to obtain a certain level of autonomy but had to accept the authority of the traditional leaders of the village.

ACCEPTANCE OF THE PROGRAM

A new educational program can succeed only if teachers, parents, and community members accept it. A program that is opposed by the community or by its subgroups is both morally unjustified and strategically inadequate.

Thus, as soon as a program becomes available for tryout, the evaluator should concern himself not only with problems emerging in the classroom but also with the reactions of various subgroups in the community to the program. The major interest of the evaluator is the reaction of teachers, parents, and community members.

Teachers' Acceptance

The acceptance by teachers of an educational program is a necessary precondition for its success. If teachers do not accept the basic philosophy of a program, one can hardly expect that it will be properly implemented. It is the evaluator's task to obtain data about the teachers' acceptance of curriculum materials. The summary of such data will help to determine which beliefs and attitudes of teachers should be changed before the program can be used, or which types of teachers are likely to succeed in using it.

The teachers' acceptance may relate to ideas about the relevance of the materials to the needs of the students and of the society, the values reflected in the material, the nature of science in general or the nature of a particular discipline, and the principles of teaching-learning implied in a particular curriculum.

Relevance. It may be that teachers consider a certain educational program irrelevant to the needs of the society and of the learners. Teachers frequently oppose educational programs imposed on them by central educational authorities. This has happened in several cases where programs were prepared by foreign experts or were merely translations of foreign programs without consideration of local needs and conditions.

Values reflected in the material. Educational material is usually value loaded. Thus, a course in social studies may reflect conservative or liberal values; it may reflect religious values, or it may be neutral toward religion. Programs in science, too, may deal with questions such as the role of science in the society or the contribution of science to the improvement of life conditions.

It seems obvious that teachers are more likely to teach a program successfully if they themselves accept the basic values reflected in the program.

The nature of science. Several recent programs in science emphasize the tentative nature of scientific theories and laws. Science is not a fixed set of eternal laws, but rather a series of continuous attempts to systematize phenomena in an economical way. Accordingly, for a good scientist it is not enough to know a large amount of accumulated knowledge: he also has to be competent in generating knowledge. Again, such ideas will be transmitted to the learner only if the teacher accepts them.

Principles of teaching and learning. Educational programs may be structured according to different principles related to the teaching-learning process. Some programs are organized in a strictly linear way, i.e., the sequence of learning experiences is fully determined by the program writers, whereas other programs allow greater freedom in selecting activities and in determining their sequence. Some programs present a large amount of factual knowledge that the student has to memorize, while others present problems to which the students are expected to generate solutions.

Examining Teachers' Acceptance

Several questionnaires have been developed to assess the extent of teachers' acceptance of educational programs. Some items selected from such a questionnaire are presented here:

—Conducting experiments is an important element in a scientist's work.

—The scientist is willing to share his findings with other fellow scientists.

—We have to accept as unquestionable facts the findings reported by well-known scientists.

—A hypothesis may turn out to be wrong.

—A scientific study has to lead toward findings useful in practical life.

—The application of proper scientific methods will necessarily lead to the solution of any problem.

Utilization of such questionnaires enables curriculum projects to determine in what areas teachers' opinions should be changed before a program is fully implemented in the system, and it also enables the curriculum personnel to identify those teachers who are most ready to utilize the program in their schools.

Parents' Acceptance

The parents' acceptance of the program is mainly related to general aims, contents, and students' activities. Information on parents' acceptance of the program may be used by curriculum teams in two ways. First, they may decide what elements of the program should be modified in order to obtain wider consensus and fuller acceptance of the program. If, for example, for a certain issue there are two opposing views in the community, they may give a more equitable representation in the program to the two different views. In other cases the curriculum team may specify the use of the program and explicitly indicate that its use is dependent on the acceptance of a particular series of values and beliefs.

General aims. As long as students learn traditional content elements that have appeared in educational programs for the past few decades, most parents will not question the legitimacy of the program. If, however, content elements and learning activities of a new type appear in a program, the goals of the new program must be communicated to parents to obtain their support. If new courses in vocational education are introduced in a system, if basic changes occur in teaching a foreign language in school, if a "new mathematics" replaces traditional courses, and so forth, explanations should be given to parents about the new educational goals and evidence should be gathered that parents indeed approve of, or accept, the goals of the new program.

Contents. Parents may indicate interest in specific contents included in students' textbooks and in new-type reading materials. Great apprehension toward a program may be raised if "unorthodox" ideas appear in it. If some ideas are opposed to certain religious feelings or political beliefs, they may be rejected by parents. The most common cases of parents' dissatisfaction with a new program arise over stereotyped representations of religious, ethnic, vocational, and social groups. Statements that have derogatory connotations may also hurt the feelings of parents and raise opposition to a program.

Activities. Certain learning activities may seem unnecessary and a waste of time to some parents. In other cases, educational programs involve homework where students need help from their parents, or which requires the utilization of equipment that cannot be found in the home. This may impose an undue burden upon parents. If this happens, the parents, instead of supporting students in performing their work, may interfere and cause friction between the school and the home.

It is necessary to establish communication with parents and to discover what kind of student activities they disapprove of and then to work out appropriate solutions, either by changing the nature of the homework or by modifying parents' attitudes. The evaluator's role in all these cases is to collect systematic information through questionnaires or interviews about reactions to the program, and to summarize the data in a way that will help program developers improve the program.

Community Acceptance

An educational program may be of concern to the whole community and not only to parents whose children are in school. "Community," in this context, is defined as a group of persons living in an area served by a particular school or by a network of schools. The community is a concern of the evaluator from two points of view: (1) To what extent does it accept the new program? (2) To what extent is it affected by the new program?

The community's acceptance of the new program is similar to parental acceptance. The community should accept the program's aims, contents, and activities. This is also necessary to motivate the community to provide the necessary support and assistance for program implementation. Frequently educational programs rely on the utilization of community resources. A social studies program may propose learning activities that require examination of some community records. A science program may require access to industrial plants operating in the community. Without community approval of the program, these resources may be cut off from the users of the program.

Another community concern may be the reflection of particular political or social issues in the program. Frequently remarks have been made, for example, about the unbalanced presentation of female characters in textbooks. Book illustrations have been criticized for not representing different ethnic groups living in the community. It is the evaluator's role to ascertain where the community may perceive points of concern in a particular educational program, and to advise program developers on how to cope with them.

Effect

The community may be affected by a new program both economically and culturally. Clearly each educational program has an economic component in terms of cost, which, in many cases, the community has to agree to cover. But beyond the issue of expense, a new program may have an effect on the economic affairs of the community insofar as it facilitates the provision of skilled laborers and experts to meet the demand of the local labor market.

Communities may also be affected by school activities in the cultural domain. This applies mainly to small rural communities, where the school may constitute the cultural center. Students' activities in the fields of music, drama, sport, and other hobby activities may affect the community's cultural life. To assess the effects of a program of this type is one of the evaluator's tasks.

EVIDENCE ON STUDENT LEARNING

Teachers and parents may provide data concerning the students' interest in, and attitude toward, a particular program, as well as about difficulties they may encounter in using it.

Teachers

The teacher observes students' activities during class periods, examines their homework, notes their reaction to preparatory exercises, and also hears direct comments about their interest in the program. Information obtained from teachers about students' attitudes toward the new program and the nature of their difficulties provides the curriculum team with a valuable basis for revising preliminary drafts of the program or for specifying desirable conditions of program usage.

A more detailed description of types of information the teacher may provide is presented in chapter 4.

Parents

Parents may observe students' activities after school hours and know about their children's attitudes toward a variety of activities in school. Therefore the parent should be considered as a reliable source of information about students' learning.

Some issues upon which parents may report to evaluators follow:

1. Difficulties children encounter in understanding certain parts of the program
2. Difficulties children encounter in preparing homework
3. Out-of-school time that children spend on program-related activities
4. Support material, such as reference books, that children use at home
5. Help students require in performing homework
6. Interest students reveal in the subject
7. Interest students reveal in preparing homework
8. Spontaneous reports of children on what is going on in school
9. Students' enthusiastic talk about experiences related to a program
10. Initiatives taken by students to increase their knowledge in a given field
11. Application of principles learned in school in various out-of-school situations

The issues are stated in general terms. The curriculum evaluator should formulate questions related to these areas in terms that fit the unique features of a particular program.

REFERENCES

Eden, S. "The Translation of General Aims into Functional Objectives: A Needs Assessment Study." *Studies in Educational Evaluation* 1 (1975): 5–12.

Haby, R. *Pour une modernisation du système éducatif.* Paris: La Documentation française, 1975.

12

Collecting and Analyzing Evaluation Data

This chapter deals with four major issues related to collecting and analyzing data. It is not intended to be a systematic guide for researchers; it is meant to serve those who already possess a basic knowledge of methodological problems of educational research. The chapter focuses on those unique features of data collection and data analysis that are characteristic for curriculum evaluation and are not treated satisfactorily in basic textbooks.

SAMPLING

In curriculum evaluation we are usually dealing with a grade group embracing thousands of children in hundreds of schools. It is in practice impossible, for example, to check the curriculum materials and procedures on all children, but yet we need to have some idea of how they would work on all children. We therefore select certain schools and children that resemble as closely as possible all schools and children. This small number of schools, classes, or children is known as a *sample*. What we need is evidence on how closely the sample mirrors the population, i.e., how large or small the error of sampling is.

This chapter was written by Michael Bauer, Wilhelm F. Kempf,
Arieh Lewy, and T. Neville Postlethwaite.

The "Target Population"

The first prerequisite in any sampling procedure is that the group of persons to be sampled must be precisely described. The group of persons to be sampled is known in technical language as the *target population*. Let us take an example. If we say that the target population is "all ten-year-old children in the country," we must be careful to specify what we mean. Do we mean all ten-year-old children whether they are in school or out of school, or do we mean ten-year-old children in full-time schooling? If a school system has a grade-repeating system and if most ten-year-olds are in, say, grade 5, there will still be some ten-year-old children in grades 3, 4, and 6. Do we want to identify only the ten-year-olds in grade 5? Thus, it is possible to identify a target population and at the same time to agree to exclude certain children from that target population. In this case the target population is redefined to create a "sampled population," but we are very clear as to the types of ten-year-olds who have been excluded from the target population (in order to identify some of the population). We may then proceed to sample the sampled population and collect our data, but we know from experience that not all people in the sample will respond and therefore there will be a shortfall. The information we have at the end of our sampling consists of replies from what is often termed the "achieved sample." Whatever data we present, we must be clear as to what is the nature of the population that replied.

The definition of the target population is not always as easy a matter as it might seem, and it is necessary for the curriculum developers to agree among themselves (often requiring fairly lengthy discussions) as to the exact nature of the target population—whether this be of students, teachers, or of subsections of society.

The Sampling Unit

In some evaluation exercises we need to know the achievement levels reached by *each* student, or the opinions of *individual* politicians, or the suggestions of *individual* teachers. In other studies we may wish to know the performance of *classrooms* of students, or *subsets* of politicians, or different *categories* of teachers. In the first case, the unit of sampling will be the individual student, the individual politician, or the individual teacher; in the second instance, the unit of sampling will be the class, the subgroup, or the category. Thus, in order to draw a sample we would need in the first instance a list of every *student* in the target, or sampled population, whereas in the second we would need a list of all the *classrooms* of students in the population. The unit of sampling is highly related to the objectives to be evaluated and to the unit of statistical analysis to be used.

In curriculum studies where a method of instruction or a learning unit that is highly dependent on the teachers' manual is being tested, it is clear that it is the classroom (i.e., the aggregate of pupils within a class) that should be the unit of analysis and hence the unit of sampling.

On the other hand, if one is interested in identifying different sub-groups of students mastering or not mastering particular objectives, the student will be the unit of analysis. In this case a sample of schools would be drawn, and a subsample of students in the target population within the sample schools would be drawn. Although it is often administratively advantageous to test whole classes within the sample schools since this causes little disruption in the school, there are two major disadvantages in doing this. First, it is cheaper to subsample pupils, and the sample will not be more representative if the whole class is taken than if a subsample of pupils is used. Second, if several classes in the school fall into the target population and if the classes are streamed, i.e., grouped by ability so that the level of classes differs, then a great deal of care has to be taken to ensure that the range of the "ability" classes is drawn from all the schools with more than one class where streaming takes place. This is a complex undertaking, and it is wiser to take a random subsample of students from across all the classes within the school.

Judgment Samples

One common occurrence in curriculum evaluation is to use judgment samples. This is a sample drawn by the use of judgment. In chapters 2, 3, 4, and 5 the use of judgment samples was suggested for polling the opinion of teachers, parents, industrial enterprises, and the like concerning the details of educational objectives, materials, and procedures. In the tryout of materials and methods, small judgment samples of six to eight classrooms are suggested.

As we have seen, the target population must be carefully defined. Let us assume that we wish to have a first tryout of some physics materials in seventh grade. We also know that there is considerable variance between schools in the social-class distribution of children attending the schools. From the hearsay of inspectors and teachers we know that certain schools are considered good (in that the pupils in those schools generally perform well in all subjects) and some schools are considered poor. More systematically, inspectors will be able to categorize schools into good, medium, and poor. Thus, using this categorization, the curriculum center personnel can select two or three classes from each group (good, medium, poor) for tryout purposes. As the curriculum center needs more and more schools for different tryout purposes, it should collect more detailed information

Table 12.1. **Grouping Schools According to Achievement Level**

Score Interval	Code Numbers of Schools
120–130+	617, 819, 403, 192, etc.
110–119	812, 414, 323, 216, etc.
100–109	798, 412, 375, 142, etc.
90–99	089, 917, 243, 172, etc.
80–89	014, 019, 961, 439, etc.

on the performance level of each school. The curriculum center will then be in a position to keep up-to-date lists of all schools and a finer differentiation will be possible, e.g., excellent, very good, good, medium, poor, very poor, exceptionally poor.

Where standardized tests are administered in all schools at regular intervals, for example, for national norming purposes, the overall range of performance in the country will be known, as well as the average performance of each school. This gives very detailed information and, in such cases, it is possible for the curriculum center to select the number of schools it requires in certain intervals along the range. Thus, for example, if the achievement results range from 80 to 130 (on some sort of standardized test), a table such as table 12.1 can be compiled.

The code numbers with the name and address of the corresponding schools are usually kept in a separate listing, but this makes it easy for the curriculum personnel to select their schools according to ability levels. If other criteria are associated with different levels of schooling (e.g., ethnic or religious or social grouping), it is also possible to categorize schools on this basis and use some combination of such criteria for selecting schools. However, it is judgment that is being used to select schools.

Quota Sampling

Quota sampling is a more refined form of judgment sampling. Again, this is frequently used for selecting samples of persons in the polling of opinions or attitudes. Throughout chapters 3–8 and also in chapter 11 there has been much discussion of gathering evidence of the opinions of teachers and parents on the appropriateness of certain educational objectives, certain materials, or certain teacher or pupil activities. Let us assume that we need to sample seventh-grade teachers, but that we have reason to believe that the opinions of these teachers will vary according to the sex and age of the teachers and according to the regional location of the schools. As a simple example let us assume that there are five main regions in the country. These variables characterizing the teachers are often called

Table 12.2. **Schema for Stratified Sample**

Age	Sex	Regions				
		1	2	3	4	5
20–29	M	x	x	x	x	x
	F	x	x	x	x	x
30–39	M	x	x	x	x	x
	F	x	x	x	x	x
40–49	M	x	x	x	x	x
	F	x	x	x	x	x
50–54	M	x	x	x	x	x
	F	x	x	x	x	x

"stratifiers"—a term borrowed from the world of geological strata. A grid may be set up as in table 12.2.

We have *four* major age groups, *two* sex groups, and *five* regions, giving $4 \times 2 \times 5 = 40$ cells. We may then decide to have ten teachers in each cell, giving a sample size of 400. Alternatively, if we know beforehand the number of teachers in the target population in each cell and these numbers differ from cell to cell, then we may decide to take a fraction of the number in each cell. If the cells have fairly similar numbers, we may decide to use a constant sampling fraction, but if the numbers differ considerably, we may use different sampling fractions for each cell based on the total number of teachers our resources will allow us to have in the sample. Typically, we discover teachers fulfilling the characteristics of each cell and take them as they come until each cell is completed.

Probability Sampling

The advantage of probability sampling is that from the internal evidence of our sample we can estimate the error of sampling. The main difference between probability sampling and judgment or quota sampling is that in probability sampling random selection is used, such that every pupil, or teacher, or class, or parent (or whatever our unit of sampling) in the target population has a specified nonzero chance of entering the sample. This implies that a listing of teachers or classes or parents exists. Let us take an example.

In chapter 7 emphasis was placed on the use of probability samples for the quality control of the implemented curriculum. Let us assume that a seventh-grade physics course has been implemented across all schools in the country. We need to draw a sample of students in all seventh grades. First we must draw up a sampling frame. In order to do this we again need to think of the criterion we are trying to estimate (in this case achievement in physics) and to bring wisdom and/or evidence to bear on what factors are likely to be associated with large differences in performance, in order to create the strata for the sampling frame. Typical stratifiers are type of school, sex of children in the school, and urban/ruralness of the school. Where there is a multipartite school system, the selection of students into different school types is usually on the basis of general performance and hence there is usually a considerable difference (often as much as one and a half standard deviations) between the high- and low-scoring school types. There are three sexes of schools—boys, girls and mixed; or there is one sex only, mixed but taught separately, or mixed and taught together—the difference in performance is often marked between the sexes of children in schools. There are also often large differences between urban and rural communities. However, it is up to each country to determine either from the wisdom of inspectors or the country's examination unit, or from previous surveys the important characteristics distinguishing between school performance.

Within each stratum it is necessary to know the number of schools and pupils in that stratum in the target population. Thus, a sampling frame similar to that presented in table 12.3 can be formed. This works well where there are good national statistics; but even in the best of cases the statistics are often two years out of date, and in the worst cases they either do not exist or are badly out of date or unreliable. In addition, some of the schools listed in the national statistics may have ceased to function or may have been merged with other schools or have changed their function (in terms of type of school). In this case, it is advisable to take the latest national statistics, but when making a random selection of schools within each stratum to draw three parallel random samples of schools such that three lists exist (i.e., two substitute schools for each school drawn). Hence, if a school drawn in list 1 no longer exists, it can be replaced by a school in list 2.

Table 12.3 gives an example of a sampling frame. In this example, there is only one *type of school,* but the stratifiers are size of school (large, medium, small), sex of school (boys, girls, mixed), and rural/urban. If there were two types of school (say academic and nonacademic), then strata 1–18 would be academic and these 18 strata would have to be repeated below for the nonacademic school type, forming strata 19–36.

Table 12.3. **Example of Sampling Frame**

	Population		Sample	
Stratum	Schools	Pupils	Schools	Pupils
1 Large, boys, urban	X_1	Y_1	x_1	y_1
2 Medium, boys, urban	X_2	Y_2	x_2	y_2
3 Small, boys, urban	X_3	Y_3	x_3	y_3
4 Large, boys, rural	X_4	Y_4	x_4	y_4
5 Medium, boys, rural	X_5	Y_5	x_5	y_5
6 Small, boys, rural	X_6	Y_6	x_6	y_6
7 Large, girls, urban	X_7	Y_7	x_7	y_7
8 Medium, girls, urban	X_8	Y_8	x_8	y_8
9 Small, girls, urban	X_9	Y_9	x_9	y_9
10 Large, girls, rural	X_{10}	Y_{10}	x_{10}	y_{10}
11 Medium, girls, rural	X_{11}	Y_{11}	x_{11}	y_{11}
12 Small, girls, rural	X_{12}	Y_{12}	x_{12}	y_{12}
13 Large, mixed, urban	X_{13}	Y_{13}	x_{13}	y_{13}
14 Medium, mixed, urban	X_{14}	Y_{14}	x_{14}	y_{14}
15 Small, mixed, urban	X_{15}	Y_{15}	x_{15}	y_{15}
16 Large, mixed, rural	X_{16}	Y_{16}	x_{16}	y_{16}
17 Medium, mixed, rural	X_{17}	Y_{17}	x_{17}	y_{17}
18 Small, mixed, rural	X_{18}	Y_{18}	x_{18}	y_{18}

For each stratum we need the number of schools and pupils within those schools in the target population in each stratum. The number of schools for stratum 1 is designated X_1 and the number of pupils Y_1. A rough estimate has then to be made of the number of schools and pupils to be included in the total sample. This will then determine the sampling fraction. Thus, if there are 2,000 schools in the total population and one decides to test in 200 schools, the sampling fraction for schools is 1 in 10.

It may happen that a particular stratum has very few schools and pupils. What should be done in such a case? If the stratum is considered educationally of little significance, it could be dropped or merged with another similar stratum. If, on the other hand, it is considered an important but numerically small type of school, it would be worth "oversampling" that stratum. That is to say, in order to get reliable estimates (i.e., with small sampling error) for that stratum, it might be desirable to take half or all the schools in the stratum. However, when it comes to calculating national estimates (i.e., for all strata together), the stratum must be reduced back to its size proportional to all other strata. In this case two sets of weights are required—one for looking at the stratum by itself and a second for weighting it in its proper proportion in the total sample.

The selection of schools may be done on the basis of random numbers. All schools should be ordered accordingly by strata. It is convenient to assign running serial numbers to all schools where the numbering of schools in each stratum will start by following the last number of the previous stratum. The sampling will, then, be done by selecting schools at equal intervals from the numbered lists of the schools starting with a random number within the sampling fraction. Such sampling procedures take care of unequal multiples of the sampling proportion in each cell. Thus, for example, if the sampling proportion is 1/20, it would be difficult to decide how many schools should be sampled from a stratum which contains 35 schools or from a stratum which contains 19 schools. The principle of the previous ordering of all schools from all strata and the selection at equal distances provides a solution for such a situation.

After the schools have been drawn in each stratum it is possible to use various methods of making a random selection of students within those schools. Three possibilities are:

1. Working through the list of pupils in the target population with a constant sampling interval with a random start less than the interval, i.e., if one third of the students are required and there are 30 of them in a class, a number between 1 and 3 is selected at random. If it is 3, then the third, sixth, ninth, twelfth child, etc., are selected.
2. Selecting the pupils whose surnames begin with certain letters of the alphabet.
3. Selecting the pupils whose birthdays fall on certain days, spread uniformly around the year.

In the first case, this random draw must be strictly respected, and no replacements chosen by the head teacher, who could be biased. In the second case, care must be taken that there is no association between the initial letter of surnames and ethnic or other groupings in the society.

A fourth possibility exists which is that of selecting a whole class within the school to represent the totality of students within the target population. As mentioned, this has the advantage of being administratively easy. It will work well if each class is equally heterogeneous. However, if the classes are grouped by ability, it will be difficult for one class to represent the school. Furthermore, it may prove to be more expensive to test a whole class of, say, 40 students when only 20 students need to be subsampled for that school.

A further variation in selecting pupils within schools occurs if one draws a sample where schools are drawn with a probability proportional to the size of the school. If we take our small, medium, and large schools in table 12.3, and if the medium schools were *twice* the size of the small schools and the large schools *three* times as large as the small schools, we could allocate the weights 3 to large, 2 to medium, and 1 to small, allowing large schools three times as much chance to enter as a small school, and so on. However, when it comes to drawing pupils within schools, we have to invert the number so that all pupils in the population have the same chance of entry to the sample. Thus, we might take 1/1, i.e., all the pupils in the small schools, 1/2 the pupils in the medium schools, and 1/3 pupils in the large schools. The random-selection techniques of pupils within schools could be the same as mentioned above.

The sampling frame given in table 12.3 depicts a two-stage (complex) sample, i.e., first schools and then pupils within schools. This differs from a simple random sample (s.r.s.). In a simple random sample all the students in the target population would be listed and a random sample of pupils drawn from the list. It is rare for this to be feasible, and most samples are two-stage. In large countries three-stage sampling is often necessary. The first stage may be the state, province, or administrative unit; the second stage is the schools within the selected states; and the third, the pupils within the selected schools. However, a multistage (complex) sample is bound to be larger, in terms of students, than a simple random sample where both have the same standard errors of sampling.

THE "LOGIC" OF EXPERIMENTAL DESIGN

The Need for Comparisons
Curriculum evaluation may require comparisons in three different settings. First, two or more alternative programs or curriculum packages may be compared. Most often, one of these is the program already in use in the system, and the curriculum developers wish to determine if the new program can attain certain objectives more effectively than the old program. Of course such comparisons are of interest only if all alternative programs have the same objectives. Quite often, different curricula have different objectives, and even if they have some common objectives, these often get different levels of emphasis within the program, and therefore comparison of the various curricula does not yield useful results. Comparison in such cases may be justified if one has reason to suspect that a program does not yield better results, even on those objectives that are

highly emphasized in them, than the alternative programs in which these same objectives are not included at all. These considerations limit the value of comparison of educational outcomes of two different programs.

Second, one may compare the outcomes of the same program *used in different ways*. Thus, one may compare the outcomes of a program used without running special teacher-training courses with the outcomes obtained after having such training courses. By combination of program components such as textbooks, enrichment television programs, films, complementary reading material, teacher-training programs, and so on, one may construct different sets of actual programs based on a single curriculum kit. One may be interested in comparing outcomes of these different combinations of program components.

Third, alternative approaches or components within a given program may be examined; during program development a decision must be made as to which of several alternatives, performing the same function, is most suitable. Thus, for example, during the process of program development one compares the students' reaction to two alternative sets of illustrations, or to two alternative modes of presentation of the same idea, such as by diagrams or descriptive passages.

It is likely that comparisons of the first and second type will take place at the implementation stage of a program, while comparisons of the third type will take place at the early stages of program development.

In any comparison the important point is that the criterion variable to be compared must be the same for all treatments (programs or elements). Even if educational or learning objectives are not stated explicitly in the original program description, the evaluator has to specify all objectives to be used in the comparison. This is the first step in making a comparison.

Experimental Design

The objective of an experiment is to determine if a new procedure will produce the desired outcomes for the student population for which it was designed. Since it is neither desirable nor feasible to apply the procedure to the entire population, it is necessary to experiment initially with a relatively small group of students from the population. The problem of ensuring that this small group is as representative as possible of the entire population has already been discussed.

A second problem, besides representativeness, does arise. How does one determine if any observed effects are indeed produced by the new procedure and not by some other external factor? Consider a new program that has been assigned to a group of students. At the end of the course this group obtained a certain average on a test measuring the outcomes of the program. In this case it seems likely that the test results are the consequence of using the new program, since the test was administered at the end of the course; but there is no certainty that the measured outcomes are in fact caused by the new program. Some other factors, such as the students' access to television or parents' tutoring or some unknown external factor, may well have generated the measured outcomes. Furthermore, in examining the situation one cannot fully exclude the possibility that the test results measured at the end of the program were caused by the same factors that affected the assignment of the program to that particular group of students. This may be the case in sample surveys when one comes to examine the outcomes of different innovative educational programs that are introduced in several schools. It may happen that the new program has been introduced in schools having better facilities, more adequate equipment, better trained teachers, or more able students than the comparison or control schools have. The researcher is inclined to conceive the test results as outcomes of utilizing the innovative programs whereas in reality the programs were assigned to schools where initial achievements were already very high. Tests designed to measure outcomes of the program do reflect differences that are not outcomes of the program.

Thus, in order to make valid comparisons, one needs to set up an experiment. In the simplest case, two groups are formed, the control group (existing curriculum) and the experimental group (new curriculum). Again, attention must be paid to external factors in order to ensure that they are not the real cause of any observed outcome differences. Consider, for example, the case where two classrooms are chosen and the new curriculum is used in one of them. Some external factor, such as having well-trained teachers, may have determined that certain students found themselves in each of the two classrooms, and this same factor may be important in producing the observed differences in outcome. Thus we cannot decide whether the program is the cause of the test results or if the external factor causes both the assignment of a particular class to the innovative program and the observed differences in the results. Even with the utmost care in choosing groups that seem the same, some unforeseen factor is always possible.

How then can such external factors be excluded? The best way is to choose a random sample, large enough to cover both the control and experimental groups. Then the members of this sample must be assigned randomly, using a table of random numbers (cf. Fisher and Yates 1966), to each of the two groups. When this has been done, we know that no external factor is the cause of both the students' following a given program and/or the test results, since we know the exact cause of the first: the students find themselves in one of the two groups because of their corresponding random number in the table, and nothing else. Thus overall differences between the control and experimental groups can be caused only by difference in curriculum. Of course, internal differences within each group will be caused by a variety of external factors, but the objective of the experiment has been attained and the comparison of the two groups' means will yield valid results.

Analysis of Variance

The relative efficiency of two different programs can be compared by the technique of one-way analysis of variance. In a more complicated situation evaluators may wish to compare simultaneously two curricula and two teaching methods in order to determine not only which curriculum is better for the stated goals and which teaching method is better, but also if one teaching method is better with one curriculum than with the other. The solution of such a problem is done by a two-way analysis of variance. Although much more complicated designs of experiments are not usually encountered in curriculum evaluation, many such classical designs are available from other fields of research (Cochran and Cox 1957).

One-way design. This statistical technique is used to test to what extent group differences can be attributed to chance variation. An illustration of the use of analysis of variance is given in table 12.4.

Table 12.4 contains the means and the standard deviations of three groups on an arithmetic test. Group 3 utilized a new program in arithmetic, and groups 1 and 2 utilized a particular conventional program. It can be seen that the average achievement level of group 3 is higher than the average achievement levels of the other groups. Since the three groups were randomly assigned to the three different treatment groups, one may assume that the higher scores of group 3 are the result of using the new program. In order to test whether or not differences between the groups reflect chance variation only, an analysis of variance has been performed.

Table 12.4. **Performance on an Arithmetic Test**

Group	Mean	S.D.	N
3	22.10	5.63	1015
2	18.68	6.24	263
1	16.91	5.79	703

Table 12.5. **Analysis of Variance**

Source	Sum of Squares	Degrees of Freedom	Mean Square	F	
Between	11147	2	5573.5	167.1	significant
Within	65953	1978	33.3	—	at .001 level
Total	77100	1980	—	—	

Results of this analysis are presented in table 12.5. It can be seen that the observed differences between the groups are highly significant and are not the result of chance variation.

Two-way analysis of variance. In many experiments the evaluator is interested in assessing the effects of two different factors or treatments. Thus, for example, in the previously mentioned three groups, some teachers received in-service training and another group of teachers did not. Considering both the types of the program used in school and the variation with regard to in-service training, one may identify six different groups, as presented in table 12.6.

A two-way analysis of variance tests the significance of the two-factors: type of program and in-service training. The results of this analysis are presented in table 12.7. The data reveal that both factors contribute to the improvement of the students' achievement level. It is of interest to note that beyond the significance of the two factors mentioned before, a third significant factor emerges, which is labeled "interaction." This factor means that the effect of the in-service training was not the same for all three program groups. Indeed, an inspection of the results in table 12.6 reveals that the in-service training did not have any effect in the program of group 1, but it beneficially affected the results of groups 2 and 3.

Table 12.6. **Performance of Groups According to Program and Type of Training**

Program	Training	Mean	S.D.	N
1	1	16.9	6.1	379
1	2	16.8	5.4	324
2	1	15.3	5.0	60
2	2	19.6	6.2	203
3	1	21.6	6.2	134
3	2	22.0	5.5	881

Table 12.7. **Two-Way Analysis of Variance**

Source	Sum of Squares	Degrees of Freedom	Mean Square	F
Factor 1	11148	2	5573	169.1 signif. at .001 level
Factor 2	141	1	141	4.2 signif. at .05 level
Interaction	732	2	366	11.1 signif. at .001 level
Within	64979	1975	33	—
Total	77100	1980	—	—

Nonexperimental Designs

In educational practice it might be impossible to assign a new program or a particular treatment to a randomly selected group of students. It may happen that an educational system decides to introduce a promising new program in the whole system, and therefore no control groups are available. Such a situation frequently occurs in the evaluation of literacy campaigns. Obviously, it is very difficult to justify keeping a control group illiterate. Another case might be a situation where a new program has been introduced in a small number of classes on a tryout basis and where no other groups exist with similar learning objectives. In this case a comparison would be meaningless.

In both cases mentioned above the assessment of program outcomes has to be made without comparisons with control groups. However, it may also happen that a new program has been introduced only in some schools, not on a basis of random selection but rather on the basis of the schools' willingness to participate in the new program. In this case it may be possible to identify a control group similar in many respects to the experimental group, but since the assignment to experimental and control groups has not been done on a random basis one cannot be sure that the differences appearing between the two groups are caused by the utilization of the experimental program.

To summarize, it may be necessary to examine the effect of a program without using control groups or to utilize control groups that were not selected on the basis of random assignment. Evaluation studies of these types represent weaker designs than real experiments, and the user of such weak designs should be aware of their pitfalls.

The following section discusses problems related to program evaluation without using control groups or using nonrandomly assigned control groups.

Preexperimental Designs: The One-group Case

The one-shot case study. As indicated, in the context of curriculum evaluation it may be necessary to evaluate the effect of a program without being able to utilize a control group as a basis for comparison. Thus, for example, in a group of classes, a new program of biology has been introduced in which new types of educational objectives and learning activities appear. It may be inappropriate to compare at the end of the course the cognitive achievements of a student who participated in the program with the achievements of students who did not. It is very likely that those who learned a certain type of new materials will know these materials better than those who did not follow that particular course. Comparison of the two groups in this case is irrelevant for assessing the value of the program. Evaluators should here limit their interest to the performance of students who participated in the new program, and should satisfy themselves by examining whether these students attained the learning objectives of the program. Study designs that do not utilize control groups as the basis for comparison are termed *preexperimental designs*. Frequently, only results at the end of a study period are examined, using a single achievement test. Such designs are called *one-shot case-study designs* (Campbell and Stanley 1963). If the assessment of program results is performed on the basis of an end of course examination, it may be necessary to conduct a thorough observation of classroom activities in order to determine which classes implemented the program properly and to restrict the examination of end of course results to those classes where the program has been properly implemented.

A one-shot case-study design may be justified if the evaluator knows that at the beginning of the course students did not have mastery of program objectives, and if he is quite confident that the mastery of the skills demonstrated at the end of the course is the result of the program tested. This may be the case, for example, if the new program deals with teaching a foreign language that the students have not had the opportunity to study before.

The one-group pre- and posttest design. In some cases an educational program deals with skills in a domain that is not entirely new for the students. Thus, for example, a new reading program may strive to improve the reading comprehension skills of students.

In such a case the end-of-course examinations cannot by themselves reveal how much the student learned through participating in the program. It may be necessary to administer a pretest, i.e., to test the students' mastery of reading skills at the beginning of the course and then at the end of the course to administer the same test or a parallel test again. The difference in the achievement levels of the pre- and posttest should provide evidence that the students did indeed improve their skills in reading comprehension. The significance of pre- and posttest differences should be tested through a "test of correlated observations." It should be noted, however, that a significant difference between pretest and posttest results does not necessarily prove the success of the program. It is possible that a small increment in a certain skill attained by the overwhelming majority of the students yields statistically significant differences, but the intellectual gain is so small that the program's contribution is negligible.

Quasi-experimental Design

Quite frequently, educational innovations or experimental curricula are introduced in a small number of classes volunteering to use the new program. The evaluator who wishes to assess the efficiency of the program may identify a control group that has not received the innovative treatment and may compare the achievements of the two groups. However, since the students were not assigned to the experimental or the control groups on a random basis, such a design of comparison is not considered a real experiment. Campbell and Stanley (1963) term such comparison "quasi-experimental design."

In quasi-experimental designs there is less certainty than in a real experiment that differences appearing at the end of the course between the two groups are actually caused by the experimental treatment. There are at least two contaminating effects that threaten the validity of conclusions based on the comparison. First, it may well be that there were initial differences between the two groups with regard to mastery of relevant skills or the aptitude to learn certain skills. Second, it may well be that the group that participated in the experiment was better equipped, had better teachers, and so forth, which contributed to their progress more than the experimental program itself.

It is important to consider the possible impact of such contamination effects. There are no formal ways to control the second contamination effect. All that the evaluator can do is examine the situation thoroughly and try to draw a control group that operates in a setting similar to that of the experimental group. As to the control of the first contaminating effect, the evaluator may administer some kind of relevant aptitude or achievement test before the start of the program and compare the two groups in terms of initial performances. If the two groups were found equal on the initial measures, one may attribute the end-of-course differences to the differential treatments the groups received. If, on the other hand, initial differences appeared between the two groups, no meaningful comparison

Table 12.8. **Aptitude and Achievement Statistics of the Three Groups**

| Group | Aptitude | | Achievement | | N |
	Mean	S.D.	Mean	S.D.	
3	20.17	4.99	22.10	5.63	1015
2	20.53	5.04	18.68	6.24	263
1	19.21	4.75	16.91	5.79	703

of end-of-course scores can be made unless one eliminates the effect of initial aptitude differences. Fortunately this can be done through the method of analysis of covariance.

In order to perform an analysis of covariance to test the effect of a particular treatment, one needs to obtain data about the initial perform-ance of each person in the two groups and a measure of their performance after the treatment has been given to the experimental group. Schemat-ically such a design can be represented in the following way:

experimental group—observation 1　treatment　observation 2
control group—observation 1　　　　　　　　　observation 2

The numerical example given in tables 12.3 and 12.4 to illustrate the technique of analysis of variance is extended here for the sake of demonstrating analysis of covariance (table 12.8). The same three groups are compared. Group 1 received the experimental treatment, and groups 2 and 3 are two different control groups. To the data presented above, measures of aptitudes were added. It can be seen that on the aptitude measure no considerable differences between the three groups were observed. Nevertheless, group 2 had slightly better average scores on the aptitude measure than the other two groups.

In order to control these initial differences, an analysis of covariance was performed, the results of which are reported in table 12.9. It can be seen that even after eliminating the effect of the slight initial differences, the experimental group did significantly better on the end-of-course test

Table 12.9. **Analysis of Covariance**

Source	Sum of Squares	Degrees of Freedom	Mean Square	F
Between	9253	2	4626.7	176.7 signif. at .001 level
Regression	14193	1	14193	542.1 signif. at .001 level
Within	51760	1977	26	—

than did the control groups. These results provide evidence about the effectiveness of the experimental treatment.

It should be added, however, that in quasi-experimental design one can never be sure that one has succeeded in controlling all relevant initial differences between the groups being compared.

Even if one controlled initial differences in a certain aptitude, it might well be that groups differed also on other unidentified variables and therefore some initial differences remained uncontrolled. Thus it may well be that groups differed from the point of view of motivation and that the end-of-course differences were caused mainly by differences in motivation and not by differences in treatment. This is the major shortcoming of quasi-experimental designs in comparison to real experiments, where individuals are assigned to a particular treatment on a random basis. For this reason one should use quasi-experimental design only if there is no possibility of assigning individuals randomly to different treatments.

The Classroom as a Unit of Analysis

Almost invariably, new programs are introduced in entire classrooms and not to particular individuals. The performance of students studying in the same class are not independent of each other. They are exposed to the same teacher and to the same positive and negative experiences. The presence of highly aggressive children or the lengthy absence of a particular teacher equally affect all students studying in the same class.

It has therefore been emphasized frequently that in curriculum experiments one should consider the class as a unit of observation (see Wiley 1970). What does this mean in practice? Let us take an example of a new program that has been introduced in several classes. The experimental design contained treatment classes and control classes. If we take the class as the unit of observation, then the comparison of the groups will be based on the comparison of the class means only. In such a case all intra-class differences will be disregarded.

An example of such analysis is presented in table 12.10. For the sake of comparison, the analysis of the same set of data performed on the basis of class means is also presented (table 12.11).

Such an approach is justified only if the variances within the classrooms are not significantly different one from the other. If there are significant differences between the variances of the classes, the proper solution is to use a nested or a two-folded hierarchical classification analysis of variance (Kempthorne 1952). In this analysis the variation among students within classrooms within treatments provides the measure of error for the subsequent F tests of significance of effects of treatment.

Table 12.10. **Means of Class Means**

Group	Mean	S.D.	Number of Classes
3	21.33	4.07	45
2	20.27	2.82	13
1	17.53	3.31	38

Table 12.11. **Analysis of Variance of Class Means**

Source	Sum of Squares	Degrees of Freedom	Mean Square	F
Between	303.0	2	151.5	11.45 signif. at .01 level
Within	1231.2	93	13.2	—
Total	1534.2	95	—	—

With the use of classroom means only, this is not possible since variation among such means will not be a good estimate of the error variance. The set of data analyzed above serves as input for an example of such analysis as presented in table 12.12.

It can be seen that by using the class average as a unit of analysis, one may observe significant differences, and that the F ratio has a value of 11.45. Applying the nested approach one should use as error term the mean square between classrooms. The F ratio obtained in this analysis is slightly larger and has the value of 29.92. It should be noted, however, that this value is considerably lower than the F ratio obtained in the case of

Table 12.12. **Analysis of Variance, Nested Design**

Source	Sum of Squares	Degrees of Freedom	Mean Square	F
Between groups	11147	2	5573.5	29.92 signif. at .001 level
Between classes	17885	96	186.3	—
Within classes	48068	1882	25.5	—
Total	77100	1980	—	—

individual comparison. Thus results obtained on the basis of the analysis of individual scores and on the basis of the analysis of classroom averages may differ considerably.

Summary

Three types of designs were described above: preexperimental, quasi-experimental, and experimental designs. A schematic representation of these designs is given in table 12.13.

Preexperimental designs are used when no control groups are available. In such cases a posttest only, or pre- and posttests, will be used to determine the outcomes of a program.

Quasi-experimental designs are used in cases where control groups are available but where students cannot be assigned to groups on the basis of random selection. In such cases the utilization of analysis of covariance

Table 12.13. **Study Designs and Conditions for Their Use**

Type of Design		When to Use	Type of Statistics
Preexperimental	One-shot	No control group available	Posttest scores— mean percent of correct responses
		Assumed students have no preliminary mastery in domain of program objectives	
Preexperimental	Pre- and post-	Students have some preliminary mastery of objectives	Significance of difference between correlated observations
Quasi-experimental	Experimental and control groups No random assignment	No random assignment possible	Analysis of covariance
Experimental	Randomly assigned experimental and control groups	Random assignment possible	Analysis of variance and covariance

is recommended as the most appropriate technique for comparing group results.

The most powerful technique for group comparison is the utilization of experimental design. It implies random assignment of students to various groups. Although experimental design is the most valid among the different designs mentioned here, in actual educational settings it is often the case that no random assignment of students is possible and the evaluator has to employ weaker models, such as quasi-experimental and preexperimental ones.

SUMMARIZING EVALUATION DATA

One major task of the curriculum evaluator is to analyze the data at the various stages of program development and summarize them for the curriculum team. Once the data have been collected, the analysis and data summary should be very rapid so that the developers may have the results within days after the data collection. This section deals with the analysis of data from typical evaluation instruments, namely, tests, scales, observation schedules, and questionnaires. The amount of analysis will depend on the types of technical aid available for data processing. Depending on the resources of a curriculum center, there may be either no equipment, or only a sorter, or a computer. Some centers have good desk calculators that allow quite an amount of computation. Also, the type of computer owned by the center or available to it will vary in size and quality. Calculation by hand is very time-consuming, and computational errors frequently remain undetected. The use of sorters, desk calculators, and computers not only speeds up work considerably, but it also ensures the accuracy of computational results. What follows are tasks that are typically performed at centers on data from various types of instruments.

Tests
Hand-scoring of Small-scale Data Sets
At the small-scale trial stage it is typical to produce summaries of formative data. Where the pupils do not number more than about 200, the analysis can be done by hand. In this case the developers will require the percentage of correct responses by all students for each item, or also by specified subgroups of students, e.g., boys vs. girls, urban vs. rural, or children from privileged homes vs. children from underprivileged homes.

Typically the students record their responses in a test booklet or on a special answer sheet. If the students' answer sheets are manually scored, it is useful to prepare a summary sheet in which the correct responses are marked 1 and the wrong ones are marked 0.

Table 12.14. **Summary Sheet of Responses**

Items	A	B	C	D	E	F	G	H	I	J	Total
					Pupils						
1	1	1	1	0	1	0	1	1	0	1	7
2	0	1	1	1	0	0	1	1	0	1	6
3	1	0	1	1	1	0	1	1	1	0	7
4	1	1	1	0	1	0	1	1	0	1	7
5	1	1	1	1	0	0	0	0	1	1	6
6	0	1	1	0	1	0	0	1	0	1	5
Total	4	5	6	3	4	0	4	5	2	5	

An example of such a record sheet is presented in table 12.14.

In this example the items are on the horizontal axis and the pupils on the vertical axis. It can be seen that out of 10 students, 7 got item 1 correct, 6 got item 2 correct, and so on, whereas out of 6 items pupil A got 4 correct, pupil C got all items correct, and pupil F got none of them correct.

A similar summary can be prepared for each subgroup separately. Table 12.15 is an example of summary data typically supplied to the curriculum developers.

Another type of data summary that can be easily prepared without the use of mechanical equipment is the frequency distribution of test scores, and univariate statistics such as group means and standard deviations.

Table 12.15. **An Item and Results Obtained on It**

Item 1
The sun is the only body in our solar system that gives off large amounts of light and heat. We see the moon because it is:

Objective
The student should know basic facts about our solar system.

A. reflecting light from the sun
B. without an atmosphere
C. a star
D. the biggest object in the solar system
E. nearer to the earth than the sun

	Total	Boys	Girls	Urban	Rural	Privileged	Under-privileged
Percentage correct	65	72	59	73	49	75	47

The Use of Data Summary Equipment

The summary of large-scale data sets may be very tedious without the use of appropriate mechanical equipment. Centers that do not possess such equipment or do not have access to it will hardly be able to summarize such data or extract all types of information that can be used by the program developers.

The utilization of a sorting machine can be of great help for summarizing test-response sheets. The sorter can easily separate the cards of different groups of respondents, such as boys, girls, or those who had a given minimum level of achievement on a test, and this enables one to produce separate statistics for all subgroups.

But a high level of flexibility in data analysis and summary can be obtained only through the use of electronic computers. If such equipment is available, it is typical to group test items into subtests and to produce statistics for a variety of subsets of items related to the total sample and to particular subgroups of the sample.

Subtest Scores

A test may contain items that represent various subcategories of a phenomenon. For instance, it may contain some items that measure knowledge of facts, while other items are concerned with the application of principles. In addition, the same items may be classified along a second dimension related to content. Within the framework of curriculum evaluation it is useful to obtain scores separately for each subcategory so that partial scores possess important diagnostic value.

In table 12.16 the two-dimensional classification of a 12-item test is shown. For this particular test it is advantageous to calculate, in addition

Table 12.16. **Two-dimensional Classification of Test Items**

Item Number	Content Areas	Mental Functions
1	respiration	facts
2	"	"
3	"	"
4	"	application
5	"	"
6	"	"
7	nutrition	facts
8	"	"
9	"	"
10	"	application
11	"	"
12	"	"

to the total score, the partial scores for the two content areas (respiration and nutrition) and partial scores for factual knowledge and application of principles.

Statistics for Special Subgroups

Quite often in curriculum evaluation, it is of interest to obtain statistics not only for the entire sample of respondents but also for various subgroups within the sample. For example, one may find it desirable to obtain separate statistics for each school or each class; or for subgroups based on age, sex, area of residence. Depending upon the interests of the researcher, a sample of individuals may be classified along a variety of different dimensions and statistics generated accordingly.

Table 12.17 presents an example of this process. The sample has been divided into classes, sexes, and groups based on place of residence. The presentation of test results in such a manner helps in identifying students

Table 12.17. **Test Results for Special Subgroups**[a]

Group of Respondents	Total Test: No. of Items = 12		Nutrition: No. of Items = 6		Respiration: No. of Items = 6		Facts: No. of Items = 6		Application: No. of Items = 6	
	M	S.D.	M	S.D.	M	S.D.	M	S.D.	M	S.D.
All: N = 165	7.09 (59)	2.47	2.95 (49)	1.55	4.13 (69)	1.22	3.78 (63)	1.48	3.30 (55)	1.31
Class 1: N = 24	7.25 (60)	2.11	3.00 (56)	1.58	4.25 (70)	1.03	3.75 (62)	1.18	3.50 (58)	1.38
Class 2: N = 25	9.36 (78)	2.19	4.40 (73)	1.38	4.96 (83)	.97	4.96 (83)	1.17	4.40 (73)	1.25
. . .	.		.		.	.	.		.	
Boys: N = 83	7.11 (59)	2.35	2.90 (48)	1.54	4.20 (70)	1.11	3.81 (63)	1.51	3.28 (55)	1.23
Girls: N = 82	7.07 (59)	2.60	3.00 (50)	1.57	4.07 (67)	1.33	3.74 (62)	1.46	3.32 (55)	1.38
Urban: N = 71	7.80 (65)	2.61	3.42 (57)	1.64	4.38 (73)	1.25	4.11 (68)	1.45	3.69 (61)	1.43
Rural: N = 94	6.55 (55)	2.22	2.59 (43)	1.38	3.95 (66)	1.17	3.53 (59)	1.47	3.02 (50)	1.13

[a]The percentage of correct responses is shown in parentheses.

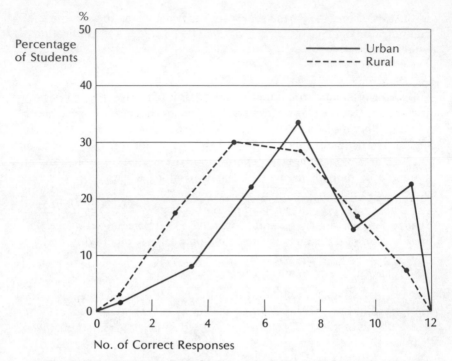

Figure 12.1. *Frequency Distribution of the Scores of Urban and
Rural Students*

who did not perform satisfactorily in particular areas of study and in the
utilization of specific skills. Looking at the table one notices that in this
case, class 2 results were better than those for class 1, and also that scores in
"Respiration" were higher than those in "Nutrition."

Another useful way of presenting differences between subgroups is by
using graphs of frequency distributions. Arranging test results in this way
can help determine the percentage of students reaching various levels of
achievement within a particular domain. A graphic representation of the
frequency distributions of test results for both urban and rural school
children is given in figure 12.1. One notices from the graphs that in the
urban group 36 percent of the students could answer correctly on more
than two-thirds of all questions, while in the rural group only 21 percent
were able to do so. The test results are rather poor for both populations,
but it can easily be seen that urban pupils performed better than rural
ones.

Table 12.18. **Item Analysis Data**

	A	B	C	D	E
Percentage of students selecting the response	65	24	3	1	7
Discrimination index	.32	.20	−.06	−.12	−.19

Item Statistics

As indicated, the percentage of correct answers to each item is a basic statistic that is of great interest for the curriculum developer. Even if the data are summarized manually, these statistics will be calculated. If a computer is available, more information will be produced concerning each item. Table 12.18 presents such data about the item presented in table 12.15.

The item analysis indicated that 65 percent marked the correct response A, while 24 percent chose the wrong answer B. The second line of the table contains the discrimination index of the responses. A positive discrimination index means that students who attained high scores on the total test tended to mark that particular response more than students who attained low scores on the total test. Looking at the discrimination indices in table 12.18, one can see that not only the correct response but also response B has a positive discrimination index, that is, high-achieving students tended also to mark answer B. This is an important piece of information for the curriculum developer, since assuming that answer B is indeed wrong, it is quite likely that something is wrong in the material and misleads good students to select answer B, or alternatively that the teachers misinterpreted some portions of the program.

The Frequency Distribution of Class Averages

A typical test summary contains information about the difficulty level of the items, but for the purpose of curriculum evaluation it may be useful to report, not only the percentage of correct responses, but also the percentage of correct responses in each particular class where the new material has been taught. This would mean the preparation of a frequency distribution of class averages. For illustrative purposes, let us say that the average score on a particular multiple-choice item is .50. The calculation has been made after all answers have been categorized as either correct or incorrect. This figure tells us then that 50 percent of the students tested were able to furnish the correct response; consequently, the difficulty level of this item is 50 percent. Given that more than one class of students has

Table 12.19. **Distribution of Class Averages on Two Items for 107 Classes**

Class Averages (Percent of Correct Responses)

Item No.	1– 10	11– 20	21– 30	31– 40	41– 50	51– 60	61– 70	71– 80	81– 90	91– 100	Total	Percent correct responses in all classes	Standard deviation of class averages
1	14	13	15	10	9	7	9	17	10	3	107	45	28
2	6	6	12	18	19	17	11	9	5	4	107	48	22

answered this question, any of several alternative possibilities may aptly describe the actual situation. On the one hand, it is possible that in each class 50 percent of the students knew the correct answer. Another possibility is that in 50 percent of the classes every student answered correctly, while in the remaining 50 percent not one student could give the correct reply. In real life one rarely encounters such extreme situations; the actual distribution would more likely reflect variations in scores both within individual classes and between them. The essential points to bear in mind are that (1) the difficulty level of an item may vary from class to class, and (2) items may differ from one another as regards the distribution of their difficulty levels for various classes.

The variation in the distribution patterns of different items is of particular interest to those concerned with curriculum evaluation. To illustrate this point one should compare the distribution patterns of the two items in table 12.19.

On inspection one notices that the distribution for item 1 is bimodal, while the distribution of class averages for item 2 approaches the shape of a normal curve. For the latter item it is reasonable to suppose that the differences in class averages reflect differences in the general ability levels of the students in the various classes. On the other hand, the two-peaked distribution for item 1 indicates that either the topic tested by this item was taught improperly or not taught at all in some classes, while in others instruction was ample and the subject was mastered by the students (Lewy 1973).

Scales

In the context of curriculum evaluation scales of the Likert type are used frequently to measure students' or teachers' attitudes toward a new

Table 12.20. **Teacher's Rating of Student's Behavior**

Statements	Not at all (1)	Not much (2)	Satis-factory (3)	Much (4)	Very much (5)
The student enjoyed working with the material.				X	
The student understood the purpose of the lesson.			X		
The student understood the materials.					X

program or toward a particular issue or value. A Likert scale consists of a series of questions as illustrated in table 12.20.

The score of an individual on this scale is the sum of the numerically coded reactions to the statements. For example, the respondent whose answers are presented in table 12.20 received a score of 12 on the three-item Likert scale, this figure having been arrived at by summing the numerical values attributed to each of his answers. In short, an individual score consists of the total number of points an individual receives for his answers on each test item.

The information needed for the curriculum evaluator contains the statistics of the items. Table 12.21 illustrates information of this type.

From table 12.21 one learns that 66 percent of the students marked the highest possible response for item 1, while no respondent marked similar answers for item 2. At the same time, however, item 2 distinguishes between the high and low scores on the entire test better than item 1.

The availability of a computer allows one to produce statistics of the following types:

Table 12.21. **Statistics of Three Likert Scale Items**

No. of Item	Percentage of Students Selecting Each Response (1) (2) (3) (4) (5)					Mean	S.D.	Correlation with Score
1		7	4	23	66	4.52	.62	.48
2	6	24	48	22		2.86	.69	.59
3	5	25	40	20	10	3.05	1.03	.53

1. The correlation coefficients between the scores on each particular item and the score on the total test, and also between the items themselves for determining the reliability of the scale.
2. Combining responses of a selected set of items into subscores as described above in the section on tests.
3. Correlation coefficients between the scale score and other variables such as scores on cognitive tests, biographical and demographical data, etc. (Such information is useful for program developers to identify whether a positive attitude toward a new educational program is associated with high scores on cognitive tests, with the sex of the student, with his socioeconomic status, and so forth.)
4. Where attitudes are measured repeatedly over time, it is possible to examine patterns of shift in attitudes for various groups and mainly for those who used a particular program under certain conditions and of those who did not use the same program or used it under differing conditions.

Observations, Judgments, and Questionnaires

In curriculum evaluation observational and judgmental data do not usually require laborious statistical computations. Frequently the program developer will be interested in the qualitative analysis of such data, i.e., what parts of the program were properly implemented, or in what types of activities did students reveal great interest. Even if the developer is interested in a quantitative summary, it will be sufficient to calculate very simple statistics such as frequency distributions of certain occurrences. Since the amount of data of these types is generally limited, the evaluator can perform necessary data analysis by using simple computational equipment such as desk calculators, without the need to utilize high-speed electronic computers.

Nevertheless, the availability of computers enables the production of additional statistics that may be useful for the curriculum developer. Thus it may be possible to combine various events and to develop indices which will characterize lessons or instructional materials.

Complex statistical analysis of observational and questionnaire data which requires the utilization of computers is described by Flanders (1970), Medley and Mitzel (1963), and Yoloye (1971).

Summary

A schematic representation of a variety of data summary types appears in table 12.22. It can be seen that if computation is done by hand, only a few basic statistics can be produced. The evaluator will mostly

Table 12.22. Data Analysis According to Availability of Equipment

Type of Data	Equipment Available			
	No Equipment	Card Sorter		Computer
Tests	Percentage of correct responses	Discrimination index of items		Correlation between items themselves
	Individual scores	Correct responses by various subgroups		Correlation between items and biographical or demographical variables
	Frequency distribution of scores	Cross-tabulation of item response with biographical, demographical, or psychological variables		Subscores and relationship among them
				Comparisons of groups (experimental designs)
Scales	Mean and standard deviation of items (small sample)	Discrimination index of items		Comparisons of groups (experimental designs)
	Individual scores	Means and standard deviation of subgroups		Development of scales
	Frequency distribution	Cross-tabulation		
Observation schedules	Frequency of signs or categories	Differences between subgroups of classes		Correlation between categories
				Combination of frequencies in various categories into indices
				Relationship between categories and external variables (e.g., population traits, lesson teacher)
Judgmental data	Tabulation of responses	Differences between subgroups of judges		Correlation with other variables
	Agreement between judges			Development of scales
				Comparison of groups

content himself with computing frequency distributions, means and standard deviations. Of course, much more complicated statistics can be calculated manually if sufficient time is devoted to it. On the other hand, because of the excessive amount of time needed to perform such computations and the high and undetected error rate of computation, it is advisable to limit the extent of manual computation.

The availability of simple data processing equipment enables the preparation of cross-tabulations, comparisons of different groups, and so forth without an undue amount of tedious labor. Nevertheless, the existence of a computer allows for a high level of flexibility in using a wide variety of complex statistical models for analyzing and summarizing data.

EQUATING TEST SCORES

At various occasions during the process of curriculum evaluation one may wish to equate scores obtained on different tests. Thus, for example, in a "pretest/posttest" design it may be undesirable to use the same test repeatedly because of the possibility that at the time of the posttest the students will remember some items from the pretest, or that teachers will coach the students on the items of the pretest. For this reason the evaluator may prefer to use a posttest different from that used as a pretest. In this case he will face the problem of equating the scores obtained in the different tests.

Theories of achievement tests offer various approaches for doing this. Three of them presented here are: parallel tests, anchor items in nonparallel tests, and sample-free calibration of tests.

Parallel Tests

Two tests are considered to be parallel if they fulfill the following conditions: they correlate highly; their means are not significantly different; their variances are not significantly different; their reliability coefficients are not significantly different; and their items represent the same objectives, skills, or tasks. Parallel tests are usually constructed by selecting pairs of items from a pool such that both items in a single pair represent the same objective or skill and have the same level of difficulty. Then one of them is randomly assigned to one version of the test, and the other one to the second version. Parallel tests constructed in this way may deal with the evaluation of a single skill, or may relate to a series of objectives or skills equally represented in the two parallel versions.

By administering one version of the parallel instrument as a pretest and the second version as a posttest to the same group of students, it is possible to examine the significance of the differences between the mean scores by using the *Students' Test* for correlated observations. The details of this procedure are described in most books of basic statistics.

The utilization of parallel tests is very convenient in that scores obtained on various occasions are easily comparable. It is assumed that equal raw scores on two parallel tests represent the same level of achievement. The disadvantage here is that due to the similarity of the two tests, posttest scores may be affected if pupils remember similar items in the pretest, or are coached for test taking. The most serious problem that emerges in using the same test repeatedly is that such a test may either be very difficult at the pretest occasion, and thus frustrate a large group of students, or alternatively, it may be very easy as a posttest, and therefore fail to measure the high achievement of the advanced students. To cope with this problem it seems appropriate to use nonparallel tests having a series of common anchor items.

Nonparallel Tests with Common Anchor Items

A different solution for comparing scores obtained on two different occasions may be the utilization of two different tests that contain a subset of common items, frequently referred to as "anchor" items. Typically, tests containing 30–40 items will have a series of 10–12 common anchor items. This arrangement allows the use of a series of items that fit the needs of the particular situation in which the test is given. The set of anchor items will enable the evaluator to develop a common scale for comparing tests differing one from the other as regards content and level of difficulty.

Of course, it is also possible to perform comparisons on the basis of the common anchor items appearing in both tests. Thus, for example, if a 30-item test was administered at the beginning of a course and a different 30-item test containing 10 anchor items at the end of the course, one may compare scores obtained on the same set of anchor items on two different occasions, and one can use the difference between these scores as a measure of growth. In this case, however, one disregards the information value contained in the noncommon items.

Regression analysis may be applied in order to utilize the information value of the tests as a whole. The two different tests should be regressed on the same set of anchor items. On the basis of the results one may equate the scores in that scores on the two tests corresponding to a particular score on the anchor set may be considered equivalent. If, for example, the estimated score on the first test corresponding to a score of, say, 6 in the anchor set is 23, and on the second test is 18, then these two scores are considered equivalent.

There is considerable advantage in using anchor items for equating test scores in longitudinal studies where one needs to introduce increasingly more difficult tests. This method may also be useful when tests are administered to groups differing greatly from one another. The utilization of different tests enables one to administer tests that fit each group's ability or achievement level. The disadvantage of this approach is the need to operate on the basis of assumptions which are not always fully substantiated. Such assumptions are the normality of the distribution of scores associated with each particular value of the predictor variable and the equality of the variance for each group of such scores. Very frequently the data do not correspond to these requirements.

Sample-free Analysis of Tests

A new and powerful method for comparing scores obtained on various tests has been developed by Rasch and his followers, which became known as the *sample-free model for test analysis* (Rasch 1960). This model introduces a series of new concepts for dealing with items and scores in general and the statistics used for comparing test scores constitutes only one of its innovative features. Rasch felt that conventionally used statistics were not satisfactory for characterizing tests. Thus, for example, the value of the item difficulty index that comes frequently to characterize test items is fully dependent on the nature of the sample. The percentage of correct responses to a particular item will be higher in an able group of students than in a low-achieving group. Rasch suggested analyzing item responses in a way that yielded parameters independent from the ability of students taking the test. To illustrate his approach, the responses of twelve students to two selected items of a test are presented in table 12.23.

Conventionally one would say that the first item has a difficulty level of 75 percent and the second item one of 42 percent. These statistics seem to present some information about two items of the test, but if one looks at the response pattern of another group of students one may find data as presented in table 12.24. In this table, the corresponding item statistics are 33 and 17.

Table 12.23. **Responses to Two Items**

Item	A	B	C	D	E	F	G	H	I	J	K	L	All	Percentage of Correct Responses
1	1	1	0	1	1	0	1	1	1	0	1	1	9	75
2	1	0	1	1	1	0	0	0	0	1	0	0	5	42

Table 12.24. **Responses of a Low-achieving Group**

Item	A	B	C	D	E	F	G	H	I	J	K	L	All	Percentage of Correct Responses
1	0	1	0	1	0	0	1	0	0	0	1	0	4	33
2	0	0	0	1	0	0	0	1	0	0	0	0	2	17

Table 12.25. **Relation between Item Responses to Two Items**

(a)

Item 2 \ Item 1	Incorrect	Correct
Correct	6	3
Incorrect	1	2

(b)

Item 2 \ Item 1	Incorrect	Correct
Correct	3	1
Incorrect	7	1

In his search for sample-free parameters, Rasch suggested a method of analysis according to which the responses of those persons who answered correctly or incorrectly, both items of a pair being compared, should be disregarded, and the computations should focus on the responses of those persons who answered only one of the items correctly. In summarizing the data of tables 12.23 and 12.24 in this way, one may get results shown in table 12.25.

Looking at the information contained in table 12.25 one may see that while the percentage of correct responses to a particular item varies from sample to sample, the proportion of those who answered item 2 correctly and item 1 incorrectly and those who inversely answered item 2 incorrectly and item 1 correctly is the same in both samples, and in the examples presented here has a value of 1/3.

In a test having k items one may construct $\dfrac{k(k-1)}{2}$ pairs of items, and on the basis of the above mentioned proportions one may compute a series of parameter estimates to characterize all items of the test. These statistics can substitute the conventionally used difficulty indices; the advantage is that their value does not depend on the ability level of the sample of respondents.

No computational algorithms are presented here. The reader interested in using this method is referred to papers that give full details of the procedures involved (Wright and Panchepakesan 1969, Choppin 1968). It should be noted, however, that the use of pairwise comparisons of item parameters yields rough approximations only, when the number of test items is greater than 2. For a more sophisticated approach to parameter estimation in this case, see the monographs by Andersen (1973) and Fischer (1974).

The original Rasch model was developed to handle a homogeneous set of items only, all measuring one single characteristic of the respondents. The homogeneity of items is determined not only on the basis of content analysis, but also on the basis of the statistical features of the results. Thus, for example, if in one sample the proportion between those who answered item (i) correctly but not item (j) on the one hand, and the group with an inverse pattern of responses on the other is, say, 1/3, and at the same time in another sample the same proportion is entirely different, say 5/1, then one may suspect that these items do not pertain to a homogeneous universe. Recently the model was further developed to allow for the measurement of growth by use of inhomogeneous item sets (Fischer 1976) and for handling sets of items that are not homogeneous in the strict sense mentioned above but measure various characteristics of the respondents with different weights (Hilke, Kempf, and Scandura 1976). Another restriction of the original Rasch model is that an examinee's response to an item is assumed to be uninfluenced by his prior responses. Weakening this assumption yields a class of dynamic test models that allow for taking learning effects into account and thus are of special interest for the micro-evaluation of training materials (Kempf 1976).

The parameter estimated can be used for equating a series of different tests provided they have some common items, or at least pairs of test have some common or bridging items. Thus, for example, it is possible to equate tests A, B, and C, if A and B on one hand, and B and C on the other hand, have some bridging items, even if A and C do not have items in common. Despite the fact that two tests differ one from the other as regards level of difficulty, the common or bridging items will have the same parameter in the difficult test and in the easy test. On the basis of the parameters of the bridging items, it is possible to develop a common scale for scoring different tests.

Again, no computational algorithm is presented here as the reader will find several examples elsewhere where it has been successfully used. For example, Choppin has used this technique to create a common scoring scale for two science tests given to fourteen- and eighteen-year-old pupils in secondary schools in England (Choppin 1976). For further examples see Spada (1976).

In the context of curriculum development one may use this technique to examine change in mastery of certain skills. Thus, for example, at the beginning of a course one may wish to administer an easy test and at the end of the course a more complex or difficult one. A set of common items in both tests will enable one to establish a common scoring scale for the two tests and thus to measure growth.

Advantages and Disadvantages of Using Different Methods

Three methods of equating test scores have been described. The advantages and disadvantages of using these different methods are presented in table 12.26. As a basis for comparison the table also contains some information about using the same test on different occasions.

As discussed, each method has its advantages and disadvantages; no single method of equating test scores can be recommended for use on all occasions. The evaluator must apply whichever method is appropriate in each particular case.

Table 12.26. **Methods of Equating Test Scores**

Type of Tests	Methods of Comparison	Advantage	Disadvantage
Same test	t test of correlated scores	easy to use	training effect boring "leaking out"
Parallel tests	t test of correlated scores	easy to interpret	laborious work to develop ambiguity of definition some training
Nonparallel tests with anchor items	regression	easy to develop applicable to groups of different ability level	not well-founded assumptions
Nonparallel tests with anchor items and sample-free calibration	common scale on the basis of item parameters	applicable to groups of different ability level	complex computational work

If only one test is available, he will be compelled to use it on a variety of occasions; but he may also split it into two different tests, which can then be treated as parallel tests. If the evaluator can select items from a large pool, he will probably use parallel tests or nonparallel tests with anchor items. If there is good reason to believe that the ability or achievement level of the students taking the test will differ greatly in the different settings of test taking, it is advisable to use nonparallel tests. Finally, if the appropriate computer facilities and necessary expertise are available, one may prefer to use the Rasch model for sample-free calibration of test items.

REFERENCES

Andersen, E. B. *Conditional Inference and Models for Measuring.* Copenhagen: Mentalhygienisk Forlag, 1973.

Campbell, D. T., and Stanley, J. C. "Experimental and Quasi-experimental Designs for Research on Teaching." In *Handbook of Research on Teaching,* edited by N. K. Gage. Chicago: Rand McNally, 1963. Pp. 171–246.

Choppin, B. H. "An Item Bank Using Sample-free Calibration." *Nature* 219, no. 5156 (1968): 870–72.

Choppin, B. H. "Recent Developments in Item Banking: A Review." In *Advances in Educational and Psychological Measurement,* edited by D. N. M. Gruijter. New York: Wiley, 1977.

Cochran, W. G., and Cox, G. M. *Experimental Designs.* 2nd ed. New York: Wiley, 1957.

Fischer, G. H. *Einführung in die Theorie Psychologischer Tests.* Bern: Huber, 1974.

Fisher, R. A., and Yates, A. *Statistical Tables for Biological, Agricultural and Medical Research.* Edinburgh: Oliver & Boyd, 1966.

Flanders, N. *Analysing Teaching Behavior.* Reading, Mass.: Addison-Wesley, 1970.

Hilke, R.; Kempf, W. F.; and Scandura, J. M. "Probabilistic and Deterministic Theorizing in Structural Learning." In *Structural Models of Thinking and Learning,* edited by H. Spada and W. F. Kempf. Bern: Huber, 1976.

Kempf, W. F. "A Dynamic Test Model and Its Use in the Microevaluation of Instructional Materials." In *Structural Models of Thinking and Learning,* edited by H. Spada and W. F. Kempf. Bern: Huber, 1976.

Kempthorne, O. *The Design and Analysis of Experiments.* New York: Wiley, 1952.

Lewy, A. "Discrimination among Individuals Versus Discrimination among Groups." *Journal of Educational Measurement* 10 (1973): 19–24.

Medley, D. M., and Mitzel, H. E. "Measuring Classroom Behavior by Systematic Observation." In *Handbook of Research on Teaching,* edited by N. L. Gage. Chicago: Rand McNally, 1963. Pp. 247–328.

Rasch, G. *Probabilistic Models for Some Intelligence and Attainment Tests.* Copenhagen: Danish Institute for Educational Research, 1960.

Spada, H. *Modelle des Denkens und Lernens.* Bern: Huber, 1976.

Wiley, D. E., "Design and Analysis of Evaluation Studies." In *The Evaluation of Instruction,* edited by M. C. Wittrock and D. E. Wiley. New York: Holt, Rinehart & Winston, 1970.

Wright, D. B., and Panchepakesan, N. "A Procedure for Sample-free Item Analysis." *Educational and Psychological Measurement* 29 (1969): 23–37.

Yoloye, E. A. "Evaluation and Innovation: African Primary Science Programme Evaluation Report." Educational Development Center, Newton, Mass., 1971. Mimeographed.

Biographical Notes on the Authors

ZOLTÁN BÁTHORY studied in Budapest, Hungary. For several years he taught in elementary and secondary schools. In 1967 he joined the research department of the National Institute for Education in Hungary. His field of interest is evaluation and curriculum. He has published books and articles on educational achievements in Hungary.

MICHAEL BAUER is a member of the professional staff of the Department of Education and Science of the German Foundation for International Development. In this capacity, he participated in several curriculum development activities in developing countries. He was a faculty member of the African Regional Seminar for Advanced Training in Curriculum Development and Evaluation held in 1975 in Ghana. His special interest is data processing and data analysis.

BENJAMIN S. BLOOM is Distinguished Service Professor of Education and Chairman of the Measurement, Evaluation and Statistical Program (MESA) in the Department of Education, University of Chicago. He is a founding member of the International Association for the Evaluation of Educational Achievement (IEA) and International Curriculum Association (ICO) and an educational consultant on evaluation and curriculum to nations throughout the world. He is author or co-author of numerous books including *Taxonomies of Educational Objectives, Handbook on Formative and Summative Evaluation of Student Learning, Stability and Change in Human Characteristics,* and *Human Characteristics and School Learning.*

CHEW TOW YOW is Deputy Director of the Curriculum Development Center at Kuala Lumpur (Malaysia). He served as a secondary school teacher and as principal of a high school before his appointment as Assistant Director of Primary Schools in the Ministry of Education, Malaysia. He has played a major role in the planning and setting up of the Curriculum Development Centre, Ministry of Education.

BRUCE CHOPPIN studied mathematics and psychology at the University of Cambridge and later received his Ph.D. in Education from the University of Chicago. He is a principal research officer at the National Foundation for Educational Research in England and Wales where he is in charge of a varied research program focusing on teen-agers. His special interests are measurement and evaluation. Dr. Choppin recently served as an evaluation consultant for the International Institute for Educational Planning and UNESCO in Israel, Tanzania, and Indonesia.

WYNNE HARLEN graduated in physics at Oxford. She has been involved in the evaluation of the Oxford Primary Science Project and of Science 5/13. Now Director of Progress in Learning Science, a project that aims to help teachers evaluate their work, she is the author of *Science 5/13: A Formative Evaluation* and contributor to two School Council publications on curriculum evaluation. She is on the editorial board of the *Journal of Curriculum Studies.*

WILHELM F. KEMPF received his Ph.D. from the University of Vienna (Austria). He holds the position of a *Wissenschaftlicher Rat* at the Institute for the Science Education (IPN) at the University of Kiel (Germany). His main fields of interest are psychological test theory, curriculum evaluation, social psychology, and learning theory. He is associate editor of the international journal *Studies in Educational Evaluation.*

HOGWON KIM received his degree from the University of Chicago. He specializes in school curriculum, instruction, and evaluation and is currently Associate Professor in the College of Education, Seoul National University, and Deputy Director of the Korean Educational Development Institute (KEDI).

GOREN LEIDE is a graduate of University of Lund (Sweden) and at present a lecturer in Physics Teaching at the Malmö School of Education. In 1971–75 he worked at the Kenya Institute of Education in Nairobi and developed science curricula for the national educational system. He is also a lecturer at the Swedish International Seminar for scientists from developed countries.

ARIEH LEWY is a graduate of the University of Chicago. He is Associate Professor at the Tel Aviv University and head of the evaluation unit of the Israel Curriculum Center. He is a bureau member of the International Association for the Evaluation of Educational Achievement and the editor of the international journal *Studies in Educational Evaluation*.

T. NEVILLE POSTLETHWAITE is a graduate of University of Stockholm. He was Executive Director of the International Association for the Evaluation of Educational Achievement (IEA) and a program officer at the International Institute for Educational Planning in Paris. At present he is Professor of Comparative Education at University of Hamburg (Federal Republic of Germany). He is the author of *School Organization and Educational Achievement*.

MARIO LEYTON SOTO is a Chilean citizen graduated from the Faculty of Education of the University of Chile in social sciences. He specialized in curriculum planning and evaluation at the School of Education of the University of Chicago. He has been a professor at the University of Chile and Catholic University of Santiago and contributed to modernizing the educational systems throughout Latin America over the last fifteen years. He has been counselor and adviser to several international agencies, such as Organization of American States (OAS), German Foundation for Development, and different ministries of education. At present he has a UNESCO assignment in Peru.

EMMANUEL AYOTUNDE YOLOYE received his Ph.D. from Columbia University, New York. He is Professor and Education Director of the International Centre for Educational Evaluation (ICEE) in the Institute of Education, University of Ibadan, Nigeria. He directed the evaluation of the African Primary Science Programme from 1967 to 1971. With the ICEE team, he has also carried out evaluations of the Pilot Rural Education Project in Namutamba, Uganda, the Primary Science Programme in the Bendel State of Nigeria, the University of Ife, Nigeria Six-Year Primary Project, and the Primary School Mathematics Programme in Mauritius.

General Index

Ability, 103, 141, 158, 211, 260
Ability level, 261
Acceptance of program, 23, 249-50, 252, 253, 255
Action research, 146
Activity school project, 190
Achievement, 10, 11, 28, 59, 64, 102, 137, 140, 156, 158, 162, 170, 211, 217, 259, 272, 289
Achievement test, 210-45
  criterion-referenced, 27, 99, 102, 215-16, 217, 218
  norm-referenced, 27, 214-15, 217
Adversary model, 9, 186
Affective objectives. *See* Educational objectives
African Primary Science Program. *See* APSP

Aggregate units. *See* Sample
Aims, 16, 38, 39, 40-41, 51, 56, 254
American Educational Research Association, 5
Analysis of covariance, 274
Analysis of curricular material, 119, 237
Analysis of variance, 269-70
Anchor items, 157, 289, 290
Anecdotal records, 205, 206
APSP (African Primary Science Program), 123, 125, 136, 139, 141, 196, 201, 202-3
Attention, student's, 97, 201
Attitudes, 48, 55, 96, 103, 107, 138, 143, 146, 159, 211, 228, 229, 257
Australia, 49

Background information, 134, 148
Balance, 51, 65, 69

299

Index of Names

304